A thar
Gende

GW00362068

Other books by the same author

Cotton Everywhere
Thanatology of the Child
A Northern Thanatology

A thanatology of war:
Gender, war, bereavement and loss

by
Christine Kenny

Quay
Books

Quay Books Division, Mark Allen Publishing Group
Jesses Farm, Snow Hill, Dinton, Wiltshire, SP3 5HN

British Library Cataloguing-in-Publication Data
A catalogue record is available for this book

© Christine Kenny 1998
ISBN 1 85642 098 1

All rights reserved. No part of this publication may be reproduced, stored
in a retrieval system or transmitted in any form or by any means,
electronic, mechanical, photocopying, recording or otherwise, without
prior permission from the publishers.

Printed in the UK by Cromwell Press, Trowbridge, Wiltshire

Contents

Acknowledgments

I would like to thank my family, and my children especially for the support they have given me during the time I have spent writing and researching this book. Thanks to my dad, Ben Miller, for patiently helping throughout the process, a daughter with less then perfect IT skills. Thirty-two participants took part in this study, and although none wished to be named, my thanks also to them. For additional support, thanks to Eric Calderbank, John Rothwell, Jack Richardson, Joyce Thompson, to my mother, Joan Miller, and to Lynne Bailey. To my colleagues in academia, a special thanks to Jeremy Weinstein and Pittu Laungani and Derek Baldwinson of South Bank University, Len Barton of the University of Sheffield, Colin Barnes from the University of Leeds and Bill Flynn of Bolton Institute. Finally, sincere and heartfelt thanks to Valery Marston for all her patience and encouragement.

To my children, Lisa, Mark, Leonard and Philip:

in the hope that you never have to experience a war

And to Algassim Jah — wherever you are

Foreword

Thankfully, I have not been a party or a witness to the 'action' which is implicit in the term, 'killed in action'. However, while reading this book, I repeatedly felt a lump in my throat, an incipient tear — although not shed (I am, after all, a man). The expectations of society are a powerful force. We feel compelled to behave in ways which (we perceive) are 'demanded' by 'them'. There is really no 'them' at all. Our actions are ultimately orchestrated by that something within ourselves which rooted itself at a time when we had no discretion, no experience to speak of. Later observations are often negated, blitzed by preconceptions which we would be hard put to rationalise. We do not trust our experience, if it happens to contradict these earliest impressions. We think that we are at fault — 'difficult' observations are stumbling blocks to be avoided. Wordsworth was right in saying: 'The child is the father of the man'.

From infancy, we are subjected to impressions and conversations which are decidedly contradictory. Yet we lack the maturity and experience to ask the right questions, so we accept. This acceptance is great for society and our parents — we fit into society. But do we fit into ourselves? To my mind this book is about people who were forced into a situation where they did not fit easily into themselves, ie. they could not be truly comfortable.

This state applies not only to soldiers at the head of the 'action' but also to those who supposedly survived. Survival is not the same thing as holding onto life. One is a purely physical state — one breathes, one eats; the other is a qualitatively valid existence which, from the evidence of this book, was denied to many 'survivors' of the two wars.

The saying goes, 'as you make your bed, so must you lie in it'. In the light of the harrowing testimonies contained in this book, I would alter this to, 'As we make your bed, so must you die in it'.

Who'd have kids?

William Kenny

Introduction

A story published in the Bolton Evening News on Saturday, July 19th, 1997 reported that:

> 'A harrowing 53 year search for Burma war hero Harry Entwistle has finally ended for his still-grieving Bolton widow Ellen. The childhood sweethearts, who were married at the outbreak of the Second World War, were cruelly separated when Harry was declared missing in action in May 1944. Brave Ellen, now 76, never gave up hope of seeing her beloved husband — but was unable to find out whether he was alive or dead. In her struggle to find evidence of his death, she appealed to war offices across the world and even went on a trip to Burma last November, funded by the Royal British Legion.'

The story continues with an account of how Ellen's search came to an end when her niece sent her news of a grave-yard called the Forgotten Army, which was situated near Rangoon. Ellen contacted the British Legion who, following enquiries, confirmed that her late husband rested there. This story, although reported only recently, provides a very good example of the long-lasting effects a war can have on the bereaved. 'Missing in action' or 'missing, presumed dead' must surely be one of the cruellest experiences of loss in any war. When there is no body to confirm that a death has occurred, then the grieving process can be seriously complicated, often leading to an inability to accept the death or to resolve the grieving process (Cruise, 1992). Paying one's last respects, as it is often referred to, can be a great source of comfort to the bereaved (Kubler-Ross, 1983; Wright, 1988). Wright, an experienced accident and emergency nurse, argues that it is therapeutic for the bereaved to view the deceased, even in cases where the body has been badly traumatised.[1] This is because in the case

---

1   Wright points out, however, that it is important in such cases to prepare the bereaved first.

of traumatic death, the bereaved are inclined to think that things are far worse than they actually are (Wright, 1988).

Wright has also observed that traumatic deaths can be even more difficult to bear if the death occurred a long way from home. Especially acute is the feeling that the deceased may have known what was happening prior to death, and the fear that he/she might have died alone:

> *'No person around will have known him, and this underlies a recurring theme, that he was someone special, a big part of their lives. Away he was anonymous, alone. His real identity, the person that he was, was not apparent.'*
>
> (Wright, 1989)

During and following World Wars I and II, thousands of bereaved people were never given official notification of death; they were never sure about what had happen to those relatives who went missing. Even now bodies are found; some are soldiers of families who have died out. On January 10th 1998, the Daily Mail reported the discovery of 27 soldiers' bodies in a shallow grave at Monchy near Arras, more 'fallen heroes' from the Battle of the Somme. Only two could be identified, and only one of these had a surviving family. The families of the remaining 26 went to their graves wondering what had happened to their men.[2] And the 'missing' experience of loss, is not confined to the two great wars, it continues in all wars, wars that are still being fought. 'Missing persons' is a very dramatic and profound type of loss which is typified by war, but there are many other forms of loss. This book explores such losses.

This text focuses mainly on the First and Second World Wars, but the issues raised are typical of the type of impact any war has on individuals and communities. Wars may change in terms of the cause, politics, values defended, and in relation to the military strategy and complexity of the weaponry used. In relation to human experience, separation, hopelessness, grief and loss, the strength of the human spirit and its vulnerability, the effects are very much the same.

---

2   Daily Mail, Saturday 10th January, 1998, article entitled '80 years on, family can salute their lost fusilier'.

The irony of wars is that they are fought in order to resolve differences. Yet if they achieve anything at all, it is the realisation and acknowledgement of human similarity. During the research and writing of this book, I have been employed as senior lecturer at South Bank University in London. I have enjoyed my experience here for many reasons. But the most important, and what I believe to be South Bank's main strength, is its diverse mix of staff and students. This enables us to develop an understanding and tolerance of difference. Celebration of difference is a good thing, no sensible person would deny that. But care must be taken not to allow this celebration of difference to distract us from the thing that we all share, ie. our shared humanity. We may be aware of this at an unconscious level. But it is not something that we consider often in our daily lives; unless the unexpected happens and we find ourselves aligned with others in this common shared humanity.

One such incident happened to me recently. I may have been more sensitive because of this project. At the time, I did not think so.

At one point when writing this book, I went through a phase where the whole concept became very high-minded and theoretical, far from its original intentions.[3] One day, at the university, one of my mature, male students came to see me. It was apparent that he was very distressed. I was unprepared for the impact of this meeting. There was a war raging in his homeland, Sierra Leone in West Africa. His family had been scattered, some had been killed and his son was missing. He had just completed his exams and called to ask me to thank, on his behalf, those members of staff in whom he had confided so far. He was now going to Sierra Leone to embark on a search for his son. I asked if he had any idea where his son was, where he would start looking? He did not know. The whole thing seemed hopeless.

For a moment it seemed to me that this student was placing himself at great risk pursuing something that had

3   The main aim of this book has been to encourage as many people as possible to consider the human cost of war at a deeper level than they might otherwise have done. For this reason, I have tried to make it as accessible as possible, so that it will reach as wide an audience as possible.

little hope of success. I felt sympathetic, but a little uncomfortable and impatient. I liked him and disliked the prospect of
the danger to which he would be exposed. Almost as if he read
my thoughts, he said I should consider that what he did, was
for his son. He admitted that the situation was probably
hopeless, but he could not give up. As long as there remained
even the slightest hope that the boy might be alive, he felt
compelled to search for him. Should he find that his son was
dead, he still considered that it was his responsibility to search
for the body and give his son a decent burial. This father
wanted very much to feel that, during the child's life (and in
the possible event of his death), as a father he had done his
best.

I felt ashamed. Viewing the matter from a purely
objective, rational perspective, the man's quest to find his son
seemed ill advised. Viewed from his own perspective, and
putting myself in his place, as a parent, I knew that he was
right. There is a saying, 'empathy is your pain in my heart'.
Like the student, I know that as a parent, you cannot give up
on your children. No matter how hopeless the situation, you
must never lose faith. Immediately, the dynamics of the
interaction changed; my earlier pessimism dissolved and I
found myself encouraging him. This incident was very brief,
lasting less than an hour. Yet in in that time-span, he and I
entered a common ground. Occupation of this space, made me
suddenly and acutely aware that although forces, such as
gender, culture and age divided us, this man was my brother.

This book forms part of a series of thanatologies, each
book viewing death from different perspectives.[4] The theme,
common to all three, is the north west of England and, more
specifically, the town of Bolton which is my home. Although I
live there no longer, it still seems like home.

In the minds of most people, bereavement is related to
the death of a loved one. But grief is the result of many kinds of
loss, particularly during a war. Thousands of people die in
wars and it is this massive loss of life that makes war so
terrible. But there are other forms of loss. War changes people

---

4   Thanatology is the multidisciplinary study of death, dying and
     bereavement, ritual, meaning, experience and history.

and when it is over, families have difficulty returning to the way of life they experienced before the war. It changes the organisation of a society, as it did during World War I and World War II when more women than ever before, went out to work in paid employment. War changes values, and not always for the worst. Between them, the two wars led to more liberal attitudes towards sexuality, and easier access to health education about sexually-transmitted diseases and contraception. They had a devastating impact on Britain's status as a world leader in economic and industrial growth and development, but also ended some of the dull and degrading tasks which many working-class people spent the greater part of their lives doing. So, although there are devastating losses, there are also gains. This book considers, at least, some of these losses and gains

Included is empirical information about changes in patterns of labour, values etc. specific to World War I or World War II. It is included where it is deemed desirable and possible, given that access to such information is limited. As a social psychologist, I consider it necessary to place popular experiences in a social context if possible. Failure to take the social context into account, leads to misunderstanding of theories and, in some cases, to undeserved criticism. Two examples relate to concepts of motherhood.

First, take the work of John Bowlby (1965). His theory of attachment has been heavily criticised by feminists (and in its extreme reading, rightly so). However, Bowlby developed his ideas from studies of the deprivation which children had suffered when separated from their parents, sometimes by well-meaning professionals, who had placed them in overcrowded institutions. He also examined the effects of separation due to the evacuation of children during World War II. When Bowlby was developing his ideas, the dominant view was that, so long as a child's physical needs were met, the child would develop normally. Thus, children were often removed from poorer homes that were considered 'unsuitable'. By considering the social context, it is clear that Bowlby's work was invaluable. It drew attention to the following:

- the importance of fulfilling children's emotional as well as their physical needs

- the advantages of the emotional security a parent provides which can be more important than a tidy home
- when a child loses a significant care giver, appropriate emotional support should be given.

Later developments of his work, also contributed to our understanding of beareavement and loss (Bowlby, 1980).

Second, consider the issues of single mothers or lone parents which are currently the subject of so much popular and political debate. These debates often centre on discussions of the Welfare State and the assumption that it is responsible for the creation of the single parent. Yet, when the history of capitalism and the growth of the Industrial Revolution is examined more closely, it becomes clear that lone parents, regardless of marital status, have been in existence since the demise of the cottage industries. From a psychological and political perspective, current rhetoric accuses not only lone mothers, but also absent fathers. Children of lone parents lack a father figure or role model and this is considered responsible for the breakdown in 'traditional' discipline. Whether the father's absence is due to the couple not entering into a marital arrangement, or to working long hours away from home, the result is the same. Thus, it is capitalism that creates lone parents and absent fathers. Lone parenthood is only a 'problem' if it costs the taxpayer money.

Learning how social phenomena evolves can help us to learn from our mistakes. Misrepresentations of what lone parenting is, ie. to associate it with marital status, can lead to missed solutions to problems. Simplistic notions of what the father's presence means in a relationship, may have hindered the attempts of men to resettle with their families after the War(s). Families might well have benefited from having their fathers' presence, but this was not possible because of the pressure to conform to a 'traditional' family organisation.

This is not to support or devalue lone parents, but to consider the historical context of how ideas evolve. Such considerations can change our perspective and enable us to see problems and possible solutions in a different way. These considerations are important in relation to the topics discussed in this book. In *Chapter 3*, for example, we look at the death of the hero and the history of how the image of the hero evolved in modern western culture. The concepts behind the evolution of this image, lead to a terrifying recognition. The cultures who created these heroes, have startling similarities to the cultures who started the ideology and justification that were the driving force behind the holocaust.

Although interested in local history, I do not claim to be a historian. However, I am a psychologist who is interested in the evolution of ideas, especially those concerned with life and death. In order to understand how ideas evolve, some historical research is necessary, and I hope to collaborate with other historians in exploring and writing further books in this series about thanatology.

The three most important roles in my life have been those of parent, teacher and writer. The reading of all research should be about informing, inspiring and providing a springboard for ideas. I hope that you, the reader, enjoy this book. But if in addition, it encourages you to pursue your own ideas, that is even better. I have never been possessive about ideas. If we are too possessive, we cannot inspire others. The ability to inspire is one of the finest human achievements.

The discussions frequently focus more on one of the two wars. This is because of the availability, or lack, of information. In *Chapter 3*, for example, when exploring the experience of men at war, I was unable to conduct interviews with men who had served in World War I. So in that section, I used letters written by soldiers at war, and published in local papers, or in other sources.

One of the main questions explored, during the research for this book, was whether death and bereavement have different meanings during a war. The response of participants to this question was varied. Some thought that it did, others argued that death is tragic no matter what its circumstances. Of those who did consider that bereavement was different, two of the most common justifications was the uncertainty and the problem, identified by many other writers, of 'missing in action'. When someone is posted as missing during a war, their fate or whereabouts remain unknown. One respondent wrote:

'yes, many people felt that the mere possibility of death for their loved ones or themselves was always with them.

> *They thought more seriously of what happened after death. Would they see their loved ones again?*[5]

If war is so terrible, why despite all our achievements as human beings, do we still not know how to live together peacefully? As discussed previously, thanatology is as much concerned with the meaning of life as it is with meaning of death. If we consider the question of what counts as a good project in life, then surely a book on the thanatology of war should also consider the possibility of what life could be like in a world without war. Is this possible? We explore this question in *Chapter 1*.

---

5   Bolton woman aged 76 years at the time she completed the questionnaire in 1997. Religion — Spiritualist Church.

Chapter I
Is a world without violence
and war possible?

Most people would agree that war is terrible and that no sensible person would want it. But, if this is the case, why do wars happen at all. The aim of World War I and World War II was to bring about everlasting world peace. Another participant who took part in the study, wrote of her experience of World War II, 'we sometimes wondered what peace would be like — I still do'. This point is quite pertinent, when we consider that since World War II we have had the Korean War, the Vietnam War, the Falklands War, the Gulf War, etc. Even as this book is written, strife continues in many countries. It is a depressing picture.

'Is a world without violence and war possible?' is a question that many pacifists have considered worth pursuing. But to what degree is a person a pacifist? There is no straightforward answer. Some famous pacifists, such as Gandhi and Martin Luther King, remained absolutely true to the principles of non-violence all their lives. Others, such as Simone Weil considered that there were times when people had to go to war, in order to ensure the promise of eternal peace. Virginia Woolf was a pacifist all her life, but she was also acutely aware of how powerless a position this could be. Towards the end of her life, Woolf concluded in despair that a world free from violence would probably never become a reality. Oldfield (1989) recites Woolf's experience as a young girl when, fighting with her cousin, she decided not to hurt him, but to walk away instead. The cousin responded to Woolf's non-violence by cruelly beating her.

If we explore further, the question posed by Woolf in the 1930s, 'How are we to prevent war?' The situation appears increasingly hopeless. Strategies supported by pacifists, such as nuclear disarmament, could from another perspective, lead to further wars. If nations do not build up arms, how can they protect themselves against an aggressor? What of opponents such as Bismarck, who considered any nation which adopted pacifist attitudes as weak, and ripe for conquest and domination. Stoltenberg (1990) notes that to be considered pacifist by some nations, is to be perceived as feminine, weak and vulnerable to attack. Yet other pacifists have shown that passive resistance can, in itself, be very powerful. Frederick Douglass, the black American slave who fought for and eventually won his freedom, and who then became one of the foremost campaigners against slavery, demonstrated while a slave, that one can avoid a beating without resorting to violence. On one occasion, Douglass's master decided to give him a beating. Douglass decided that he would not respond with violence, but he was equally determined not to put up with his master's abuse.

Being young and quick on his feet, Douglass danced around his master's yard, neatly ducking the blows aimed at him. He was determined and he won. Hours later, tired out and exhausted, his master gave up. He had not succeeded in delivering a single blow. Despite this incredible commitment to non-violence, Douglass still supported the American Civil War, because he believed that it was the only way to end slavery (Archer, 1996).

Others, such as Gandhi (1951) and Martin Luther King (Archer, *op cit*) have demonstrated the power of non-violent resistance. Even Gandi (1955) expressed concern that it might not be possible for an individual to divorce him or herself entirely from every conflict situation. Arguments that the practice of non-violent resistance can be successfully generalised to all situations, are basically flawed. Passive resistance may be useful in cases where one group wish to dominate rather than annihilate a particular group. However, if one group's aim is genocide, a non-violent response will only make this aim easier to achieve.

If a more harmonious world is to be achieved, a too pessimistic attitude should be resisted. Research is useful and important in developing theories which counteract violence at a philosophical level. But these theories need to be supported by empiricism. Given that violence is so complex, no one approach could ever resolve the problem and a multi-disciplinary approach is needed. Peace and conflict studies have been developing at a rapid rate over the last few years. In

England some excellent work is emerging from the Centre for Conflict Studies at the University of Ulster in Colraine, Northern Ireland.

Writers such as Konrad Lorenz (1966) and Desmond Morris (1967) consider that aggression is innate, universal and, to a certain extent, unavoidable. However, social learning and experience also have roles. In psychology studies, it has been noted that children who are abused, or have violent parents, are more likely to become violent adults (Kemp, 1968; Montague, 1970). Various educational and parental strategies can be adopted to encourage non-violence and empathy in children and young people, ie. by encouraging them to take part in moral debates and self-reflection (Hersh *et al*, 1980). The biological argument is also challenged by the existence of so many world-wide, non-violent societies, such as the Australian aborigines. Yet aggressive individuals can be found in non-violent societies. The issue is even more complex when considering the evidence that some societies support violence between groups, but are against violence within the group, and in others the reverse is true. There is also limited experience of societies in which violence is non-existent (Seegley, 1986). This concept is difficult to accept, given the overall prevalence of violence.

John Nance (1975) wrote of the Tasaday (a small tribe who are completely non-violent) that 'their love was everywhere — for each other, for their forest, for each other, for us, for life.' So the ability to view all life as sacred, to care deeply for life just for its own sake, appears to be one prerequisite. Such non-violent societies are rarely Utopian, often being small-scale, non-literate, and very much at the mercy of the environment (Fabbro, 1978; Howell and Willis, 1989a; Bonta, 1993). It might be assumed that the people of such societies frequently experience feelings of powerlessness and frustration, attributed by many social scientists to outbreaks of violence. Bonta (1996), in his survey of 24 non-violent peoples, noted that many situations arose in the day-to-day lives of such groups, which could lead to violence. However, the groups he studied, all had a firm and explicit commitment to non-violence and a number of tried and tested strategies to prevent outbursts. Such strategies included third party intervention to help resolve disagreements, group meetings in which problems and possible solutions were discussed with the whole group and humour. Bonta found that humour was highly effective in breaking down barriers, lightening the mood of the group, dissolving tensions and reducing the perceived seriousness of the situation. Another common theme, observed by Bonta, was a high cultural value for emotional restraint.

The cultural prevalence and/or value, which a society places on aggressive behaviour, is clearly important when the question of war is considered. Similarly, few individuals actually feel aggressive when they are recruited to fight a war. It is usually the rulers, or those in power in a society, that decide whether to declare war and often they, too, do not feel aggressive when they do this. Generally, the larger, richer and more technologically advanced a society is, the more predisposed it will be to engage in war. Nations go to war for various reasons, the most common being, 'wars are declared for the pursuit of wealth, the pursuit of glory and the advocacy of a creed' (Huxley, 1937). War is also big business, the manufacture of weapons leading to the creation of vast wealth (Kearl, 1995).

Those who refuse to take part in a war, usually fall into two categories; the absolutes, who object to war, or serving in the armed forces under any circumstances, and those who object to war but serve in the armed forces in a non-combat role (Linn, 1996). People may refuse to join in a war if they think that their country is unjust in declaring it, or because they believe that, in the event of a war, their country may fail to maintain justice (Walzer, 1970). A parodoxical situation arises, however, when a member of the armed forces refuses to follow orders that he or she considers unjust. One of the earliest documented cases of this, occurred during the war in Lebanon. During the three years that it raged, approximately 165 reserve soldiers refused to undertake their assigned task in the war zone (Linn, 1986). All were court-martialled.

A later study by Linn (1996) focused on the personality characteristics of Israeli soldiers who had refused to take part in various military manoeuvres during the Intifada. Profiles of these conscientious objectors revealed fairly consistent traits and backgrounds. Most of the refusers were highly educated, had undergone professional as well as academic training, most were aged between 30 and 35 years of age, and expressed what many psychologists referred to as, a strong, internal locus of control; ie, they had a strong faith in their ability to make decisions and act independently. They expressed political sentiments that were predominantly left wing, and most had been involved in some form of political or pressure group activities in the past. They were all very articulate and able to clarify in words and writing, their justification of what they were doing. This very detailed study is useful in that it provides some basis for hope, for the development and promotion of, not just non-violence, but directions for training people in the skills of passive resistance. It also shows that, while individuals cannot change the world on their own, a few determined people with the correct skills and determination can seriously jeopardise any military manoeuvre. Is this good or bad?

The study also shows that, if we are to come eventually to a world without war, we need to start by looking at the violence in ourselves. Violence and aggression exists at all levels in society. If we cannot reduce its incidence in the family and local community, how can we hope to challenge it at a national/international level? These questions are beyond the scope of this book. However, given that this book is about men and women's experience of war, and of how sexuality influences or is influenced by violence, *Chapter 2* considers the commonly held assumption that violence and aggression are predominantly male traits.

Chapter 2
Mum! Its not my fault! The causes and solution to 'male' violence

The author is a committed feminist, who is aware of, and feels strongly about, gender inequalities in our society. As a woman from a working-class background, she has experienced discrimination and devaluation from people with narrow-minded perceptions of class and status. Women are often less powerful than men, in similar positions, and Kenny sympathises with writers, such as Hooks (1989) who consider 'nice' non-violent, harmless, middle-class concepts of femininity highly offensive.[1] Black women and women from working- class backgrounds frequently suffer discrimination from middle-class women and from men as a group, although many of the ideas underpinning the philosophy of the early Suffragette Movement, came from the black, predominantly male, founders of the human rights movements (Clatter-borough, 1990). Similarly, the author to her discredit, admits to discriminating against others. She believes strongly that we all share a potential for violence. However, it is how we respond to this urge that is important. We can choose to direct our emotional responses in social interactions, deciding between non-violence and violence. We have the potential to love as well as to hate. Occasionally, although we do not intend violence, we are overwhelmed by our perceptions or emotions, and do not take account of the effects our behaviour has on others.

When the author became actively involved in feminism, she believed violence to be a predominantly male trait. The statistics 'proved' it. One summer afternoon, when her children were quite young, and believing them to be playing out of the house, she telephoned a friend for a chat. During the conversation, they started talking about the 'problem' of male

1   Yes, yes I know. There are multiple masculinities, femininities, feminisms etc. But for the sake of actually *saying something*, in this discussion (no matter how basic) I'd like the indulgence of making a few generalisations, darn it!

violence. Although they talked as if they had experienced the reality of this 'male violence', it was, in essence, an abstract discussion, with no significance to the lived experience with the real, flesh and blood men in their lives. But, theory does not always relate to practice. The author's thoughts on the links between theory and practice were rather muddled. She had not even realised the contradiction between the 'convincing statistics' and her own experience. So the friends talked on, roundly condemning the male sex, until the author heard a noise upstairs. She finished the telephone call and went upstairs to find one of her older sons, who was about fifteen years old, sitting on his bed, looking very upset. Hoping he had not heard the conversation, she asked casually if he was all right.[2] He looked up at her, waited for a moment, and then said "its not my fault mum."

She was stunned and the shock brought her, suddenly, down to earth. She realised then, as she should have realised before, that her son was growing up; he was growing into a man. If she really believed that men were essentially violent creatures, what were the implications of this for her own sons. If women as feminists and pacifists really are committed to non-violence, then surely the first place to start confronting male violence, is in the home. Where it exists is important. But when we confront such issues, we should do so with caution, bearing in mind the effects that 'anti-man' discourses might have on the men in our lives. And before we become so high principled about men, we should to look at our own attitudes; at the violence we inflict. Women violate men each time they talk of male violence as if it was universal. Is this what the feminist project is about? To make men hate, possibly even loathe themselves because they are men? If this is the aim, then the author wants no part of it. Sexism must be challenged, but we must do so by opening a dialogue between the sexes, not by accusing all men for the violence of a few.

---

2   The son I refer to is grown up now and we have discussed this incident at length. It was one occasion when I learned something quite important from my children. My son agreed to my including this story (with his blessing) because he agrees with me that there are important lessons to be learned from such anecdotes.

However, it remains a fact that the dominant and persuasive view is, that violence is a predominantly male, or masculine characteristic. It was this belief, in the first wave of feminism, that led to the argument that women should have a place in public life. Many early feminists were pacifists. They hoped that, by entering the public and political arena, they could help to make society more feminine, more peaceful (Oldfield, *op cit*). It is an argument that remains powerful (Gilligan, 1982; Thompson, 1983; Ruddick, 1989). From this perspective, the main criticism is directed at the assumption that the dominance of science over religion since the Enlightenment, has led to losses as well as gains. Most important is the Enlightenment emphasis on objectivity and detachment; on reasoned, unemotional argument. This argument has much mileage, and it is well supported by empirical evidence and reasoned arguments. If you are 'objective' then it is easy to make large numbers of workers redundant for purely economic reasons. It is easier to go to war, easier to kill. Evidence from this and other studies has shown that, most people have to dehumanise their enemy in order to kill them. Killing another living, experiencing human being is much harder. Rational argument can justify anything, even genocide, if you believe that some people, or races of people, are inferior and unfit to live. Members of the Eugenics Movement that began in the early years of this century believed in population control; for 'lower-class groups' of course, not for themselves (Rose, 1994).

Many of our most revered academics were members of the Eugenics Movement, including Galton, Yeats and H G Wells. Some were happy to allow controlled breeding in the 'lower orders' so that there would always be a reliable surplus of 'lesser beings' to serve the masters in society. Others, such as H G Wells, believed that the lower classes should be prevented from having children and that (as Wells called them) the 'swarms of black and brown and dirty white and yellow people' should either serve their masters or be eliminated (Casey, 1997). Such academic arguments can have terrible consequences. Taken to its logical conclusion, eugenics leads to genocide, as it did during World War II.

Rose (1994), after reading about the holocaust, describes the shock she experienced when she realised how cold, calculating and logical were the arguments presented at the time for the whole project. We need to consider what an 'objective' education can mean. The men who designed the gas chambers and the concentration camps, who very efficiently implemented this mass killing, were very clever people. Detachment can lead to acts of violence against humanity; these acts are easier if the perpetrators are rational, objective and detached.

Although the rationality/detachment assessment carries some weight, it does not necessarily support the view that violence and aggression are mainly masculine characteristics. Women can also be objective. And are men generally more aggressive? Would a matriarchy rather than a patriarchy necessarily lead to a more peaceful loving world?

Overwhelming evidence has accumulated over the years, to support the view that men are, on average, more aggressive than women. At the most basic level of society, in the family, male violence against women is far more common than incidences of violence inflicted by women on men. However, the violence of men towards women is far outstripped by the violence men inflict on other men (Segal, 1990). This is especially so against men who are considered different, by virtue of their race or sexual orientation. Men are the predominant fighters in wars and other smaller, local, personal conflicts. Men who try to intervene in violent situations, often become the victims of male violence themselves (Connell, 1987). This is one reason why the police are reluctant to intervene in cases of domestic violence. A large number of policeman in America lose their lives at work because they try to intervene in such cases (Hall, 1991).

There are many arguments and theories which are proposed to explain and support the assumption that violence is a male trait. Most popular are the biological arguments that associate violence with male sexuality and, most notably, with the hormone, testosterone. For example, it has been noted by Stoltenberg (1990), Connell (*op cit*) and Galtung (1996) that, in war, it is predominantly older men who plan military strategy, while most of the killing is done by younger, sexually ripe males of around eighteen to twenty years of age. Much importance has been attached to the explicitly phallic appearance of war weapons; war terminology that mimics the language of rape (eg, 'we sure fucked them didn't we?') Modern military operations often consist of invading an opening with several missiles — gang rape (Galtung, *op cit*).

Across cultures and history, the torturer is typically male, the victim female. Inflicting torture often involves violation of female sex organs, most often the breasts and genitalia. Rape of the enemies' women is considered the prize of victory in many conquests[3]. Violence, death, fear and sex are all closely related. But also equated with sex is love, romance, gentleness and mutual respect. Biological explanations can and do account for this. In all cases, when arousal increases, physiological changes occur. Raised adrenaline, rapid pulse, perspiration, uncontrolled vocalisations, blurred vision, a momentary loss of a sense of conscious, unified self, all this happens in fear, violent responses and, of course, orgasm (Galtung, *op cit*). The Blitz showed that these responses occurred in women as well as men. Following World War II, many women attributed their, so called, promiscuous behaviour, to the fear and anxiety of the Blitz. Sexual attitudes and behaviour did become more liberal during World War II. This is typical of most total war situations and has been shown by subsequent research. Viewed from a purely biological perspective, theoretically, the female hormone, oestrogen, has as much potential for stimulating violence in women as testosterone does in men.

Overall, when scrutinised more closely, biological arguments fail to answer the question of whether a world without violence is possible. They are pessimistic and unhelpful. If men are violent because of their biology, then there is nothing to be done. It is an oppressive view, to men and to women. It is oppressive to victims of abuse because it provides an excuse for their abusers behaviour; it is oppressive to men because it positions them all as potential abusers. What about non-violent men? In her research, Hall (*op cit*) found that most

---

3   This does not imply that all men are rapists. On the contrary, many men who engage in combat are appalled by the sexual violence the witness in other men. This, of course leads to further questions, id. Why do some men rape in such situations, while others do not?

of her male participants felt deeply threatened by perceived pressures to conform to tough, unfeeling stereotypes of masculinity. As for the perceived reduced ability of men to care, Hall found that, generally, men care very deeply for the significant women, children and men in their lives. An increasing number of men are claiming that they too are oppressed by the pressure of having to conform to a rigid masculine role. While challenging the claim that men are oppressed in respect of professional or economic opportunity, it is reasonable to reject the perception that men are aggressors simply because they are male. Recent work has also began to challenge the idea that women are, generally, less violent.

Violent women

The first question to consider is, how reliable are statistics? Male victims may find it difficult to admit to suffering from abuse, especially if it is from women. In addition, there is growing evidence (notably presented by Segal, 1990) to show that, in some English communities, aggression in girls is as highly prized as aggression in boys (Gordon, 1988). Women's violence against children far outweighs men's violence against women. Women appear to have the same potential for violence, but they express it in more indirect ways, eg. with sarcasm, or by encouraging men to inflict violence on others, on their behalf. Women can and do oppress other women (De Bois and Ruiz, 1990). Finally and perhaps the worst kind of violence, is that of self-imposed martyrdom. It is probably the worst kind of violence, and one where the victim is the oppressor. The perpetrator maintains an attitude of humility and oppression, while inducing feelings of guilt and remorse in her/his respective family.[4]

Some of the work discussed is relatively new and poses interesting questions for the future. The research conducted for this book shows that men feel grief, vulnerability and fear in war just as much as women, and that they are just as oppressed by violence. The discussion is not intended to

4   I am speaking very generally here of course.

excuse or minimise the importance of male violence, especially when directed at women. How we move towards a more harmonious world is a question that is vital to the well-being of future generations, and we cannot just blame men. Violence is present in all people, men and women; in ourselves, and we must understand and acknowledge our own responsibility. One thing is certain, when we ask, Who stands to lose? the answer must be that war is everyone's loss.

Chapter 3
The death of the hero:
The experience of war and
its impact on war veterans

Everybody loves heroes. Those huge, muscular, fearless men of steel, who fight relentlessly to defend abstract principles, such as freedom, justice and the right to pursue happiness. But when the hero falls and his veneer disintegrates to reveal his humanity, his vulnerability, his sheer ordinariness, he becomes an outcast. When the men closest to us are lost in a war, we blame the media, the military, the powerful men in government, anyone but ourselves. Yet if we examine the cult of the hero, we find that it is women who adore them; women who romanticise them, worship them and encourage them. It was women who sent the white feathers, who cheer at the boxing ring and who throw flowers and shout endearments as the men march away. Women worship heroes. Like men, women, too, can be stimulated by the threat of extinction.

And yet it is women, as mothers, daughters, sisters, wives and sweethearts, who have the most to lose from promoting this image. Segal (1990) observes that it was in the mid nineteenth century that western ideas of 'manliness' started to evolve. But, to exist at all as a meaningful category, 'manliness' had to coexist with 'womanliness'. Thus, man defined his manliness according to her degree of 'womanliness'; woman, her womanliness against his manliness. Manliness is expressed in action, womanliness in response. He kills and eventually gets killed, she waits, and eventually grieves.

This assumption about the way things are, carries with it a comforting sentiment that the majority of women abhor violence, whereas men live by it. This sentiment fuels the underpinnings of much feminist, pacifist rhetoric. In this chapter, we trace the roots of the heroic, masculine ideal, its genesis in the realms of fiction and their widescale obliteration in the battlefields of war. Throughout this discussion, the author focuses her discussion on the experience of men at war. This does not assume that she supports the notion that the source of violence is located in the psychological make-up of men. Analysis of male violence, as expressed and given meaning by war, is helpful, and in relation to the aims of this book, essential. But if we are to develop a deeper understanding of aggression, we must also consider women's potential for violence. It may be that, in general, men express more overt aggression, but it should not automatically be assumed that there is less potential in women. In this chapter we explore how the masculine veneer evaporates in the realities of war. War is a climate in which people are forced to confront their vulnerability; to assess their humanity, the essence of what they are, that which cuts across race, culture, gender and social class. The other, negative aspect of this vulnerability could be to detach them from their humanity, so that they can survive.

This chapter is concerned mainly with the experiences of men at war. But it is not about how callous, brutish men collapse in the face of reality. It discusses how men and women create heroes and then suffer the often terrible consequences. Concepts of heroes and of appropriate masculine qualities are important in any discussion of war. Such concepts appear to influence the attitude of men to war, and their willingness to enlist. Stoltenberg (1990), for example, notes that the outbreak of the Vietnam War coincided with a revival of the Women's Liberation Movement and of many other human rights movements. This was at a time when women and men were challenging traditional gender roles, and when people of all social classes and groups were beginning to challenge white, western male authority, violence and supremacy. At this time in history, many young men were beginning to question and openly challenge the image of tough masculinity to which they were expected to conform. The 'new man' who evolved from this period in history was far less willing to enlist and take part in a war.

Segal (1990) considers that contemporary ideas about manliness, and of the hero as we understand him, can be traced back to the mid nineteenth century. She argues that there was a growing rejection of effeminate behaviour in men. This rejection of femininity was reflected in all aspects of British culture. The works of Shelley, Keats and even

Shakespeare, although praised for their literary skills, were criticised for their emotionality and morbid introspection. Segal notes the growth of the public school sector in the nineteenth century, and the growing numbers of middle-class parents who sent their children away to be educated in institutions that adopted harsh military regimes, poor food and Spartan conditions.

Kenny was reminded of many of the novels of this era by authors, such as Charles Dickins and the Brontes (David Copperfield and Jane Eyre). She suggests that, although the course of history may be written in dominant academic texts, ie. the **instruction** of history in schools, there always exist subversive texts that 'disrupt' the main flow. Such subversive texts are always there for those who **explore** history and are determined enough to search for them. It is also interesting to note how dominant values are resisted, eg. working-class resistance to the Boy Scouts Movement. The development of organisations such as the Boy Scouts were an attempt by the middle-class, to impose their notion of 'manliness' on to the working-class. The working-class had their own definitions of 'manliness', and it differed from that of the middle-class in important ways. The working-class 'hero' became the middle-class 'hooligan'. Prominent political figures of the nineteenth and early twentieth century did much to promote the middle-class 'red blooded' man. Julian Grenfell for example, argued that 'preparing to fight in time of war is the greatest game and the finest work in the world', while John Carlyle argued that 'every man is created to fight' (cited in Segal, 1990; Oldfield, 1989). Running parallel to the growing militarism, was the development of extreme racism. For example, French children were taught the supremacy of the French over the Germans, and German children were taught that the Germans were superior to the French.

In Germany, Bismark, who was one of the most influential German statesman of his time, glorified military power, authority, nationalism and, of course, masculinity. He firmly believed that a nation's level of civilisation could be measured by the killing power of its military machine. Heinrich von Tretschke, one of Bismarck's most devoted disciples, and a very distinguished German historian, argued that 'the features of history are virile, unsuited to a feminine nature. The weak and cowardly perish, and perish justly' (cited in Oldfield, 1989).

Bismark's philosophy had a practical and direct impact on the education of young German men. For example, in 1910 Kaiser Wilhelm II ordered the formation of a youth army, the Jungleuschlandkund, who were instructed that 'If your emperor orders it, you must open fire on your own mother and father'. The slogan of the Jungleuschlandkund was:

> *'war is beautiful. We must wait for it with the manly knowledge that when it strikes, it will be more beautiful and more wonderful to live forever amongst the heroes on a war memorial in a church, than to die an empty death in bed, nameless.'*   (cited in Oldfield, 1989)

Around the turn of the century, this glorification of war had infected even the very young. In France, schoolboys actually petitioned the President for an extension of compulsory military service. In England, writers such as Kipling called for 'every red blooded boy' to be prepared to die for his country. True to his principles, Kipling further, in 1907, suggested that young boys should be drilled for the army from the age of six until they became 'magnificent men marching in sunlight' (Oldfield, *op cit*).

This celebrated, archetypal hero, had a not so apparent, implicit self-distruct mechanism. Its complete expression could only be realised in total extinction, the ultimate expression of heroism became the ultimate sacrifice. Thus, by the time World War I broke out, death in combat became both feared and desired. The years around the turn of the century, saw a period of greater stability and gradual improvement in social conditions. This brought possibilities for a better quality of life and a greater longevity than people had ever known before (Illich, 1977). These changes brought with them different perceptions about life and death, creating time and opportunity for fantasy and a thirst for adventure; a thirst that might have developed greater urgency precisely because of the apparent stability and related predictability of life. It became insufficient to merely celebrate death, which instead become glorified, especially if it took place on the battlefield (Littlewood, 1993).

In 1914, thousands of young men rushed to enlist at the drill halls, to embark on an adventure that they firmly believed would be over by Christmas. Seduced by Darwinian ideas of natural selection and the revered public school image of manliness and good living, these brave young men firmly believed that they were on their way to share in the conquest; 'The war to end all wars.' Some were so enthusiastic to go into action when they enlisted, they feared that the war might be over before they arrived at the Front. The rush of volunteers at the start of World War I soon became unmanageable. Restrictions, such as increasing the height requirement, were imposed to check the flood. Bolton news reports of 'feelings of gloom in the men enlisted in the territorial army' accompanied photographs of elated recruits at Doffcocker and Edgworth. The whole atmosphere was more appropriate to that of a prize holiday rather than of troops going to war.[1] Correspondence home from soldiers at war, must have considerably increased the sense of excitement at the prospect of 'joining in.' One soldier wrote of the RAF:

> *'You would delight in some of their manoeuvres. H G Wells' imagination never pictured the feats of our aviators half as brilliantly as they are in reality. When there was a fight in the air, and perhaps 20 machines engaged, the twisting and twining of the machines made onlookers quite breathless.'*[2]

It is natural for the writer cited above to be impressed by the skills he observed. However, the tone of adventure in such letters could have led some of the men back home to feel that they were missing the action. Letters that were published from soldiers to their families, were heavily censored before they were sent to relatives, to ensure that they did not contain information which might undermine the war effort. There were, however, humanitarian principles underpinning censorship.

---

1   *Bolton Journal and Guardian*, August 14th, 1914
2   Letter cited in Richardson and Richardson, 1995, page 87

This was to ensure that bereaved relatives would not, without warning, see images of their dead in the morning paper (Dryer, 1995). But, in the absence of any contradictory information, the effects of the propaganda machine were very powerful and effective. Only compare the exultant levels of patriotism for World War I, with the anti-war campaigns of the Vietnam War. Unlike the press coverage of World War I, portrayals of the Vietnam war graphically represented the horrors. Not long after exposure to such coverage, thousands of Americans were shouting the slogan 'Hell No! We Won't Go! (Norman, 1990).

Much of the early correspondence from the men was quite accurate, in that it reflected the spirit of those early months when many of them still thought it a great adventure. The overall tone was of a general jocularity, suggesting more a holiday postcard than a letter from someone at war. The example below is an indication of the kind of message received during these early months:

> *'Detective Inspector Hall has received a communication from Plc Wtarbuck (5422) 1st Company Coldstream Guards, a detective in the Borough Police Force, now a prisoner of war in Germany, to the effect that he is doing well under the circumstances 'We have parcels of food, cigarettes, etc sent to us' he writes ' and they come free of charge. I hope that you have a very happy Christmas and a bright and prosperous New Year. I know that mine will be a poor one, but never mind, perhaps there are better days ahead of us.'*

> *'Writing to his mother at 100 Orlando St, Sapper W Westwood (20212) of the Royal Engineers (55th Field Company) says that he had enjoyed Christmas, the weather was frosty and that the enemy seemed to be singing in English. 'I received a fine present from Princess Mary' — this being a pipe and tobacco in a box with all the Allies represented on it.*

However, another letter published in the same paper on the same day is much less 'chirpy' and has about it an undercurrent of dissatisfaction:[3]

'There is not much marching done now, we are always in the trenches. It never seems to stop raining and sometimes we are up to the neck in it. Its no use grousing though, for its got to be done or the Germans might get to Bolton and put everyone on crutches, as they have done here. There is some talk of our Battalion being relieved by Kitchener's Army, and we all say, let it be soon. We are all very well looked after and have everything we need.

The letter above suggests that the enthusiasm was beginning to diminish for some soldiers, and this is hardly surprising, given that many who enlisted had been were ill prepared for what was to confront them. For implicit in the heroic culture on which assumptions of British valour had been built, was the idea that war is clean, perfect and even beautiful. It was a myth that concealed the realities of dirty, undignified death, or of the fact that few disabled veterans match the clean, athletic and fit glorification of the hero represented in art and literature. Life at the Front must have been a rude awakening for those who enlisted. The appalling conditions were a nightmare, while the smart uniforms, initially worn with such pride, soon became rags worn by demoralised men, surviving as best they could in the filth and damp of the trenches. Many of those young 'red-blooded men' who enlisted with such valour at the start of the war, were struck down within a few days. As their 'red blood' oozed into the dark earth of the trenches, they met isolated, piteous and undignified deaths. It is the author's view that the very isolation of these deaths was the cruellest irony of all.

The hero celebrated in western art and culture is a public and spectacular being. A hero, such as this, requires the presence of an audience in order to exist at all. Unlike the grand representations of the hero in art galleries and on stage, there were no spectators to witness and celebrate the final sacrifice and total extinction of these men. Those spectators who were present, were too busy worrying about their own survival to 'celebrate' the death of anyone else. But no matter how divorced from reality the myth might have been, it had to

3   The two extracts above, and the one below are taken from the *Bolton Journal and Guardian*, page 5, 8th January, 1915.

be preserved, partly because it offered the only comfort possible to those families, who had lost their 'red-blooded young men.' Only days before his death, James Mackin of Farnworth wrote home:

> 'rest yourself content that your only true loving son James has fought his way so far like a true English hero. We expect some more dirty work shortly and I hope by the time you get this letter you will hear that we are at Bagdad.'[4]

The myth of the hero was, thus, preserved throughout the war, particularly by the media. The *Bolton Journal and Guardian*, for example, devoted pages to reports of the war.[5] These stories included short biographies of 'The Mothers of England' and their son's who were serving at the front.[6] Newspaper headlines such as the following 'Another German Disaster/Austrian collapse/Due to Lack of Endurance' and reports that the British were showing 'Valour Against Amazing Odds' added further to the feeling of adventure and assumed supremacy of the British in war.[7] Amid all this 'valour' and 'endurance', the Allies, apparently, had plenty of time on their hands for a 'brew and a fag'.[8] Such headlines of the time suggested that the war 'game' was all very simple; it was a game of monopoly, which the British (of course) were winning. Reports told of trenches that had been 'brilliantly won' assured readers that 'every capture of a trench represents a loss of ground for the enemy; each will bring the war to its inevitable end.' [9] Meanwhile, the Germans (those who had not 'deserted in hundreds') were 'completely demoralised' 'losing heavily' and 'building huge funeral pyres' to cope with the 'wholesale cremation of German soldiers'.[10]

---

4   Cited in Richardson and Richardson, 1995.
5   This series, reported in the *Bolton Journal and Guardian* was entitled *The War In Picture and Story*.
6   However, by 1915 the *Role of Honour* and its accompanying biographies of *Fallen Heroes* made increasingly depressing reading.
7   *The Bolton Journal and Guardian*, 28th August, 1914.
8   As indicated by newspaper representations of 'macho' men in uniform which accompanied appeals for 'Smokes for the Lads.'
9   *Bolton Journal and Guardian*, 8th January, 1915.
10   *Bolton Journal and Guardian*, August 14th, 1914.

Presumably, there were too few allied dead at this time to be concerned about funeral arrangements.

The Bolton newspapers continued to report with the same optimism that had characterised reports from the start of the war. However, there were uneasy undercurrents, obvious to those who chose to scrutinse them more closely. For example, two women on holiday in Germany, who had been advised to leave 'quite unexpectedly', assured reporters that 'all the Germans with whom they had any association had treated them with the utmost kindness.' Nevertheless, they had been advised to leave as soon as possible. Another report, published in the same paper and on the same day, confirmed that the drill halls throughout the area were 'alive with men waiting to be told what to do'.[11] Four nurses from Bolton Royal Infirmary had volunteered for overseas service and fourteen members of the Borough's police service had also been 'called up'.[12]

The opportunity for overseas service motivated many of the young men and women who enlisted and the climate in the territorial army was reported as gloomy. Later reports confirmed that 'men are eager to begin foreign service', that 'the whole town is excited' and that there had been 'a splendid response to the call.'[13] Incentives were offered to encourage enlistment, but few were as unusual as that offered by a local mill owner, Alfred Topp, who paid for new teeth for all volunteers. Taken collectively, the reports and publications of correspondence, painted an optimistic and exciting picture. The letter quoted below conveys a very different situation: [14]

> *'The dugouts have nearly all blown in, the wire entanglements are a wreck, and in amongst the chaos of twisted iron and splintered timber and shapeless earth are the fleshless, blackened bones of simple men who poured out their red, sweet wine of youth unknowing, for nothing more tangible than Honour or their Country's*

11 *Bolton Journal and Guardian*, July, 31st, 1914.
12 *Bolton Journal and Guardian*, Friday, July 31st, 1914.
13 *Bolton Journal and Guardian*, Friday 14th August, 1914.
14 This letter was written to Vera Brittain by her fiancee Roland, during their separation during the war. The letter is published in *Chapter 3*, page 197 of her book *Testament of Youth* (Brittain, 1933)

Glory, or another's lust for power. Let him who thinks of War as a glorious golden thing, who loves to roll forth stirring words of exultation, involving Honour and Praise and Valour and love of country, as thoughtless and fervid of faith as that inspired by the priests of Baal to call on their own slumbering deity, let him but look at the little pile of sodden grey rags that cover half a skull and a shinbone and what might have been ribs, or at this skeleton lying on its side, resting half crouching as it fell, perfect but that it is headless, and with the tattered clothing still draped round it, and let him realise how grand and glorious a thing it is to have distilled all youth and joy of life into a foetid heap of hideous putrescence! Who is there who has known and seen who can say that victory is worth the death of even one of these?'

Many of the soldiers cited in Richardson and Richardson's (1995) publication, were skilled and articulate writers and even now, there is a sense of excitement in reading them. The writing below is both exciting and thought-provoking:

'They (the East Lancashire Regiment) were met by heavy rifle fire, and men fell fast, but still the other brave lads kept on. The Germans jumped out of the trench when our men were four yards away, and then the clanking of steel began. The struggle was a fierce one, and lasted four hours and the Germans cried for mercy. Opposed at such great odds, it was a hard task, but our men went tooth and nail at the Germans. It got so bad that several of the men were fighting with their fists and others were using their feet. The rifle butts were also frequently used. I was opposed to two Germans with fixed bayonets, and just as they were going to 'pin me' I swung my rifle round with the butt, knocking them down, and the rest was easy. There was one poor lad lying wounded on the ground, and the German was about to bayonet him, when I rushed in and I was just in time to thrust the bayonet through the enemy's head.'[15]

---

15   Cited in Richardson and Richardson (1995), page 83, dated 5/ 3/1915

Reading such accounts, many years after the events took place, it is easy to forget the bravery and be horrified at the violence. Despite attempts to strive for a balanced perspective, the author was unable to avoid the influence of her own motherhood and it was impossible to ignore the pain of that unknown mother, whose son became one of the thousands 'known only to God' on March 5th 1915. What were the feelings of this woman as she considered her son's body, rotting where it had fallen in the cold isolation of a filthy trench. Cruel steel tearing into her son's soft flesh is not a memory to be treasured, and perhaps it would be better to remain ignorant of such detail. The years that parents devote to their children appear meaningless, insignificant and nonsensical when we read such reports. But if he had not been killed, then he would have killed another man. This need to kill or be killed, reflects the contradictions of the hero culture. The war imperative to kill clashes with other, powerful and competing values of western society. These values emphasise the sanctity of human life and the loss of a single person is considered a tragedy. In sending people to war and demanding that they kill, we are asking them to break one of society's greatest taboos 'thou shalt not kill.' Costello (1985) cites Marshall's (1947) assertion in 'Men Under Fire':

> *'The Army cannot unmake (western) man. It must reckon with the fact that he comes from a civilisation in which aggression, connected with the taking of life, is prohibited and unacceptable. The teaching and ideals of that civilisation are against killing, against taking advantage. The fear of aggression has been expressed to him so strongly and absorbed by him so deeply and pervading, practically with his mother's milk, this is part of man's normal make up.'*

Costello refers to American research findings in World War II showing that less than one in six American soldiers said that they were able to open fire on the enemy when ordered to do so. The study also found that fear of killing rather than fear of being killed appeared to be the major contributing factor in the development of Post Traumatic Stress Disorder, and fear of failing to kill when ordered to, was next. Dealing with the contradiction between the sanctity of life and the need to kill was hard for men fighting the war. Some found release in writing of their feelings. A World War II veteran who took part in this study, reported that he and many of his comrades often wrote poetry when they were at war as a way of coping with their emotions:

> 'Some of us spent a lot of time writing poetry too, yes, that's another thing about war. You'd get these really tough men, men who in civvy street wouldn't be seen dead writing poetry, would spend hours writing it when they were away. And they would share it with their friends, yes, no one ridiculed anyone for it, because they understood. You see, poetry is somehow different, different then just writing about your experiences . . . deeper. Yes, its amazing some of the lovely, beautiful poetry I've seen written by men at war. Sometimes men wrote it just to occupy their minds, but mostly it was a way of saying things, saying them in a special way, that seemed somehow more important, then I mean.'

Men who served in World War I also used writing to express their emotions. Such evidence suggests that, even if such men aspired to live up to a masculine ideal when they went to war, once they knew what it was like, they had a deep need to express some emotionality. Parsons (1974) wrote that many of the best poems written during World War I were produced by ordinary, rank and file men, who served at the Front. These poems have not, in Parsons opinion, received the recognition they deserved, and he attributes this to that fact that they cannot be appreciated, or understood, from within a traditional academic framework. When World War I broke out, poets, educated in traditional ways, felt ill equipped to articulate the grim realities of war. They found that the language, they used before the war inadequate. It could not convey such carnage and brutality. There were some notable exceptions, such as Owen and Sassoon, but Parsons considers that some of the best poetry came from ordinary men, who had confronted the terror of having to kill other ordinary men, or risk being killed themselves. Parsons included several rank and file poems in his collection 'Men who Walked Away' because he considered that they conveyed such powerful, authentic sincerity, and this compensated for any flaws in vocabulary and grammatical style.

However, written or spoken words cannot fully express emotions that are personal and lie outside the language boundary. There are limits to the level of trauma that people can endure. They gradually become immune to the feelings of horror, sorrow or revolution, which violent death provokes (Cannandine, 1981). This immunity is reflected by a person's inability to describe what his/her experiences, ie. there is a limit to the degree that words like 'horrible' 'terrible' etc, conveys the meaning of 'terrible', 'horrible' (Dryer, 1995).

In war, the sight and stench of death is everywhere. Cloete (cited by Cannandine, 1981) describes how, during World War I, the bodies of the dead were left where they had fallen. Rotting in the sun, the corpses turned swollen and blue — 'frozen in their death position, dead bodies lay around in every conceivable condition'. Of his experience of World War II, one of the participants in this study challenged the author's claim that, as a nurse, she had seen death:

> *'Oh, so you've seen death, no disrespect love, but you think you've seen death. I mean we have a lot of death here (in the residential home) a lot of older people die, and the nurses, I mean, they are lovely, but they think that because they have laid a body out that they have seen death. Its not the same here love, not in a hospital. I mean, for a start, most people who die in a place like this, die when they are ready to die, and its a process you know, it can take days, weeks even. But the point is that when someone has, what you might call a natural death, that is, they are going no matter how tragic it is, when they are ready, it takes time, and during that time they are losing weight, and to an extent, the body is getting rid of its toxins. I mean, don't get me wrong, I know that a dying body creates toxins, I know that because of all the people here who I've seen die. But its not the same, not even remotely the same, as the kind of rot, why decay, that you get in the body of a young man caught in his prime, caught when he is healthy, maybe only a couple of hours after he's had a good meal — because that good meal*

when he is dead, that adds to the stink! And then there's the conditions. I mean, here its all clean, the body is laid out, it may be on the ward for a couple of hours at the very least, then off it goes to a nice clean fridge. That's not the same my dear, really its not, as a heap of dead bodies, all cut off in their prime, all rotting and stinking, along with whatever it was that they last ate, stinking from their gut. So you think you have seen death? Love, I'm not being awful, I'm just trying to make you see the difference. I don't care how many years you nursed, you didn't see death, you haven't smelt death, you haven't felt what its like to infect your skin, get right inside you like it does in war. And what it does to you'.

For many soldiers, humiliation at the prospect of such public decomposition can be feared more than death itself. During World War I, some men were so tormented by the thought of it, that they made desperate pacts with friends; should one or the other die, then it was agreed that the survivor would do all that he could, to ensure that the deceased would get a decent burial (Cannandine, 1981; Dryer, 1995). Those who entered such partnerships must have known that they offered a false sense of security. The living were often too concerned with their own survival to worry about burying the dead. As one young Farnworth man wrote to his family:

'There are plenty of German and English soldiers dead, and on the battlefield we are running over the dead, and in front of us we can see hundreds of dead bodies and cannot get to them to bury them. They are all piled up in heaps about 600 yards from where I am now.'[16]

In war, the priority given to the burial of the dead, depends very much on the urgency of the situation, the time available and the morale of survivors. In the early months of World War I, enormous effort was made to bury the dead in shallow, unmarked graves. However, soldiers who arrived later soon realised that such burial attempts were futile, as they came across the corpses of comrades in various states of decomposition when digging new trenches. Even after facing

16   Letter cited in Richardson and Richardson (1995), dated 2/7/1915

such terrible hopelessness, occasions still arose when the unknown and, in some instances, the enemy dead could be buried with dignity and tenderness (Dryer, 1990). Sometimes, little is left to bury in a meaningful way. Shovelling the fragmented remains of bomb victims into sacks was almost a daily routine in the trenches of World War I. In the confusion of later conflicts, these could be mistaken as sandbags; until their horrific contents spilled out! 'The bodies crawled with maggots . . . we worked with sandbags, stopping every now and then to puke' Cloete (cited by Cannandine, 1981). Sometimes, when digging fresh trenches and breaking through to meet the enemy on the other side, men could be forced defend themselves, hacking their opponents to bits with spades, shovels, pick-axes; anything that they had to hand (Dryer, 1995).

   Death was not the only concern and was sometimes the last. Life in the trenches in World War I could be so miserable, some soldiers felt that they would welcome death, disability or even the stigma of a sexually transmitted disease. Terrified by the prospect of further combat, some invented the most elaborate, and even dangerous ploys, in order to be discharged home. In Paris and London, prostitutes with venereal disease charged extra rates to men who were deliberately trying to contract the disease. If a prostitute with the infection was not available, gonorrhoea discharge would be purchased from infected men. This was generously smeared on the genitals or eyes of men so desperate, they preferred to risk blindness rather than face another day in the trenches (Davenport-Hines, 1990). A Farnworth man serving in World War I wrote of the trenches:

> 'After an hour or so we were able to sit down, but I could not get warm and I had no money to buy anything to help me. The boss of the hut gave us each a packet of cigarettes, but I kept thinking of my bed at home, and felt shut out from the world. It was an experience I can never forget. Next day it was terrible going to our dugout; there was mud everywhere and everyone seemed to be washed out. We had to dig our blankets and kits out of the mud, and to wash everything in the sea.' [17]

For the soldiers posted to Gallipoli, there were chronic water shortages or available water was often polluted, infecting thousands with typhoid, dysentery and septic poisoning. The situation became even worse during November, 1915 when, due to appalling weather, men drowned and froze to death. A World War II veteran's memories, suggest that conditions had not improved much during his time in service:

> *'I remember after a few days travel, when we had stopped for supplies, we really began to feel sick, all over really, the whole thing. The smell of petrol, the smell of the tank, the noise and fear, more than anything it was with you all the time. They gave us ear plugs to deal with the noise, but they were hopeless, when a gun was fired they would just pop out. So the whole thing was awful, the smell, it was uncomfortable, there was no home comfort, and the fear that was always with you.'*

Men's lives were at risk, not only because of the dangers of combat, but also because of poor conditions, cold and disease. While some men refused to think about their own death, others feared, not so much death itself, but the pain and indignity that suffering caused. Men did suffer long, painful deaths during the war, some in isolation. Those who died among friends had a terrible impact on the survivors, particularly if they lost limbs. Witnessing any death (even a so called 'good death') can be very traumatic. But witnessing a death in which the body of the deceased is dismembered is particularly harrowing. Speaking of his service in World War II, one veteran responded to the question, 'can you remember what was your worst experience', thus:

> *'My worst experience, well I would say, seeing my friend have his head blown off right in front of me. It was just blown clean off his shoulders. And the funny thing is, you couldn't see who did it, or even where it came from (the bullet). I mean, that was the worst thing, not just seeing where the enemy was, I mean sometimes we were facing them, but other times, like with my friend, it came from over there (points over his shoulder). But then there were*

17   Letter dated 21/12/1917 cited in Richardson and Richardson (1995).

*lots of occasions when you were seeing people blown to
bits, you just cut it out, otherwise, thinking about it
would have drove you mad.'*

Although some participants in this study said they had cut
such traumatic experiences out of their minds, others
remarked on the impossibility of doing this. One man referred
to his experience, as having been burnt on his memory:

*'There was one instance in particular, a terrible
experience I had, and do you know, I can remember it,
like it only happened yesterday. This day, we had been
out to recover some tanks, one of the Churchill tanks had
caught fire, and we had to go to recover it once the fire
had died down. Now I'd got used to opening tanks and
finding all the crew dead inside, not that I'd ever got used
to it, but you know, I'd sort of got used to what to expect.
But on this particular day, I opened the side door to the
tank, and as I opened it, there were a pair of hands
welded to the door, and as I opened the door fully, I saw
that they were attached to a full set of arms, dismembered
you know, I can't remember what happened after that, I
must have passed out, but that was a terrible experience,
burnt on my mind that is.'*

Western society discourages people from discussing 'morbid'
events in detail. This may be useful if it helps to prevent
trauma victims from dwelling too much on negative
experiences. But it can create problems for victims who have
been denied the opportunity to express their emotions. After a
war, it might prevent them adjusting to civilian life again.
Talking, or writing about unhappy experiences can help us to
overcome them. Kenny's study showed that, once reunited
with their spouse, some of the women interviewed were very
sensitive to the fact that the latter had witnessed not only
death, but in many cases, the traumatised death of friends.
Even young children had great empathy and sensed their
fathers' grief. One participant recalled: 'as a youngster I
remember my dad coming home on leave and being very upset
and very quiet. He had witnessed the death of a comrade.'[18]

18   59-year-old woman, Spiritualist.

This extract suggests that witnessing the death of a friend had an even greater impact. The men interviewed for this research spoke quite passionately about the friendships they made with other men during World War II. Nevertheless, they still spoke of their ability to avoid emotional responses, if a friend died:

Participant: 'I've seen friends of mine, real friends, blown to pieces right beside me. And I mean at war, you really have friends, friends that would give their lives for you. In civvy street, you have friends, but not necessarily friends that would give their lives for you. I mean, you loved your mates, they were your life, they could make the difference between you having a life or not. Its no easy thing to feel that kind of friendship, and then to lose a friend like that'.

Christine Kenny: 'Yes, yes I'm sure it must have been terrible. So how did you feel? I mean, how did you cope with that?'

Participant: 'Well you didn't, you cut it out! That was the funny thing also, that you could feel such deep friendship for a man, and then forget about him, cut him out of your mind completely, within a couple of hours really, of him being dead. Well, yes and no! I mean, at the same time that was all part of it as well. I mean, if your best friend was killed at the side of you, you hated the enemy, at least, for that point in time. And when you mix that hated with kill or be killed, you've got some pretty effective killers. I mean, during the fighting, I just cannot tell you the hatred you could feel towards the enemy. I mean, it really was terrible this drive to kill. Like I say, I'm no killer love, really I'm not! But I was a killer then. So you see there was a part of you that grew, that wasn't you at all really. This was why it was so difficult when you came back home. Because at war, you did not think about people, that is, people who were dying. You cut it out and you just got on with it.'

This participant refers, not just to friendship, but to his love for some of the men that he served with. He describes how the intensity of such love, came from trust, from the co-operation of men who looked out for each other. This commitment to friendship in war, that leads men to risk their lives, has been commented on by other writers. Dryer, for example, in The Missing of the Somme, writes of his father, who, during World War I, left his trench in place of his friend, who was feeling particularly fearful that day. The first task to confront him on his return, was the task of shovelling into a sack, the few pieces of his friend that remained. As the participant observed, such experiences could leave men so inflamed with hatred for the enemy, that they were eager and willing not just to kill, but to show as much disrespect for the enemy dead as they could. This lack of respect for the enemy dead could be expressed in overtly brutal ways, such as the blind hatred and drive to kill described by the participant cited earlier, who continues below:

Participant: 'I don't remember actually facing the Germans to kill them. I just remember hating them, especially when a friend had just been killed, and like I say, you didn't always know you had done it, so it was just the enemy, just them, really. I remember charging at them, and this thinking, kill or be killed, or, you know, it was just, kill! kill! kill! You did it with all your heart, you gave it everything you had. What I mean is, I don't remember killing people, actual Germans. I can't remember, if you see what I mean, any time when I killed an individual German . . . I just charged in there . . . I just did it. Like, when I told you about seeing my friend have his head blown off, well I suppose I felt mixed up if anything. I didn't know who killed him, but I knew that some bastard was responsible. I knew that it could happen to me, like, kill or be killed. I also knew that we could very rarely take prisoners. I mean, don't ever believe all this rubbish about taking prisoners, because you couldn't, you had no one to look after them, and neither had they. So you just killed! Kill or be killed and that was it.'

In the course of her interviews, the author found that many of the veterans who spoke of banishing such experiences, provided an outstanding analysis of what happened. The participant above, for example, acknowledges that when he felt that he had to kill, there was usually more than one reason for it. He identifies fear, self-preservation, anger and a need for revenge as potent ingredients in the drive to kill. The need for revenge, and to make somebody pay, leads him to stereotype and objectify the enemy. As a consequence, he perceives them, not as separate human beings, but as the clustering of a unified whole; the hated 'other!' This objectification extended to enemy living, enemy dead and enemy not quite dead, as suggested by the letter cited below:

> '*I lay against one of our buglers, and just in front of us was a dead German officer. The bugler, wondering whether he was dead, touched him with his bayonet, and then the German came to life. You see, he was not dead properly.*'[19]

The letter above is interesting for several reasons. First there is the fascination of the somewhat ghoulish interest in the dead. Poking the (dead) body in this way, the bugler shows the same interest in exploring the meaning of 'dead' that many young children demonstrate. As they become increasingly aware of the meaning of death, children also become interested in different states of consciousness. Because of this it is not unusual for young children to touch the face, or to try to open the eyes of a sleeping person. It is at this age (7–8 years) that children will poke and prod the carcass of a dead animal, if they find one. Secondly, the extract is suggestive of another dimension to the phenomena of social death, discussed in *Chapter 7*. Briefly, social life and death refers to the way in which concepts of the boundaries of death are extended or reduced. When the author read the extract above, she found herself asking 'why didn't the two soldiers get him some medical help? Why did they just leave him to die?' But then she remembered the harsh reality she had learned from some of her participants, that taking prisoners was usually avoided.

It also occurred to her that soldiers in the trenches, might have considered fetching help a waste of time. They were aware that mortally wounded men, friend or foe, rarely survived. Those who were not 'properly' dead were, in effect dead. The status of the German was similar to that of those on

19   Letter cited in Richardson and Richardson (1995), dated 2/7/1915

death row. Indeed, inmates on death row refer to each other as a 'dead man'. Further, as each 'dead man' walks to his execution, others are alerted to this event by the call 'dead man walking'. In hospitals where nursing and medical care is available and comatose patients survive on life support systems, it seems inconceivable that the dead can be dead long before biological death occurs. On battlefields, the dead can 'still be walking.'

Included are not only the wounded who are barely alive, but also those who were sent home so badly wounded, they were simply waiting to die. Examples in the Bolton and Farnworth area included John Lightbrown, who was gassed in 1918 and dead three years later, and another victim of gassing, Peter Greenhalgh from Farnworth, who was nineteen when he died in 1919. Frank Hoyle, from Farnworth, suffered multiple traumas at war, before he finally died at home of pneumonia in 1918. He was twenty-two years old. Relatives of such men may have sensed that their death was only a matter of time. In such cases, the course of anticipatory grief and social death may have been accelerated. What happened when such men did not die as anticipated. What place did they have in a family and community that had already mourned their loss?

Coping with such uncertainties was difficult enough for those at home, so how much worse for those at the Front and for the 'living dead', what must it have been like for them? In many ways, the uncertainty of a living death, can be worse than dealing with certain death. Cannandine (1981) noted that, although many British soldiers refused to risk their lives for the enemy, they would 'run the gauntlet to get their guns or watches.' Why did soldiers take from the enemy dead? Cannandine writes that the soldiers took personal possessions from the enemy dead. How is a sense of individuality expressed, ie. the 'I' who shouts from the very core of what we are? Personal possessions are one way of identifying an individual. By taking their personal possessions, the dead are stripped of their identity. Made naked in this way, the dead are truly powerless. The person who renders them powerless is, or may perceive themselves to be, powerful. It can be very reassuring to feel powerful because we are then in control. The powerful cannot become the living dead, because the living dead have no power, or life. How terrible that people can become so unsure of the validity of their humanity, they deed to affirm it by stripping others of theirs (Cannandine, 1981).

In the literature, accounts of war suggest that much of this hatred is partly generated by a sense of guilt caused by witnessing death. Those who survived had little opportunity to bury their dead friends and some were so overcome by grief, they denied the occurrence of the death. Such men would hold conversations with the dead person, mimicking the voice of the deceased, or eat a meal on his behalf. The gravity of the loss and hopelessness such men experienced, is profoundly conveyed by a soldier who wrote home, 'my poor old pal Tom Whitworth is missing, and I have felt lonely without him.'[20]

Grief and respect for the dead may need to be deferred when corpses could be put to useful purpose. A soldier who served in Vietnam saved himself by hiding from the Viet Cong under the corpses of his comrades. The nurse who relayed this story to Norman (1990) told of how the young man broke down in tears after telling his story. This suggested that people can retain their humanity despite the most horrendous experiences. It is this humanity that leads some people to feel compassion rather than contempt for the enemy. A World War II veteran recalls that:

'It could be very confusing. Like, on the one hand you could be hating the enemy, yet many a time you would meet up with them, and they were great. I mean, I had no hatred for the enemy, none of us did. We've laughed and chatted to them many a time, you hear about this and it really did happen, lots of times. The Germans were just like us, in every possible sense, same kind of humour, same way of life, that is, apart from the SS. So you liked them, and could even have a funny kind of respect for them. So you could feel real grief when you saw the enemy dead, because you knew that that was somebody's son, or whatever. So there were times when you would want to grieve, not just for the Allied dead, but for the enemy dead as well. I mean, the Germans, they were just like us, just

20 Cited in Richardson and Richardson (1995), dated 24/7/1915

34

ordinary lads, they didn't want to kill us anymore than we wanted to kill them. And for all that, I'm talking about genuine respect, there was a lot about those German soldiers that you could genuinely respect.'

This liking and respect was mentioned by another World War II veteran who remembered occasions outside of the conflicts, when he and his comrades met up with the enemy unexpectedly. On such occasions he assured me, men were more likely to share a cup of tea and a game of cards than rush into another combat. Vietnam nurse veterans interviewed by Norman, reflected on how their attitudes towards the enemy changed during the course of nursing them. In Vietnam, women and children were also terrorists and, because they had lost friends, the nurses a felt deep, initial hatred for prisoners of war, regardless of their age or sex. Gradually, they came to recognise the fear that these POWs had of them. They were so afraid that the nurses might be poisoning their blood, that some pulled out their transfusions. Viet Cong women cried themselves to sleep at night, mourning lost families and children. The nurses found it very hard to hate people who had experienced such suffering. In a similar vein, Britain recalls her first encounters with injured POWs during World War I:

'It was somewhat disconcerting to be pitch-forked all alone — since VADs went on duty half an hour before Sisters — into the midst of thirty representatives of the nation which, as I had repeatedly been told, had crucified Canadians, cut off the hands of babies, and subjected pure and stainless females to unmentionable 'atrocities.' I didn't think that I had really believed all these stories, but I wasn't quite sure. I half expected that one or two of the patients would get out of bed to try to rape me, but I soon discovered that none of them were in a position to rape anyone, or indeed do anything but cling with stupendous exertion to a life in which the scales were already weighted against them.'[21]

Such compassionate stories support the author's view that, despite the enthusiasm for war generated by propaganda,

21   Brittain V (1933, Chapter 8, page 374).

when faced with the reality few people wish to kill. Yet it is ordinary people who do kill. The following is an anecdote told by her maternal grandfather of his experience of World War I. It concerns a mechanic who had been sent to recover a truck which had broken down in No Man's Land. Fixing the truck proved to be more difficult than he had anticipated and he lost track of the time. It suddenly became very dark and the man considered it unwise to return in the dark. He concealed himself in a nearby pit, and went to sleep in his makeshift bed. In the morning, the mechanic woke startled to find himself facing a young German soldier about his own age. Transfixed and unable to speak, the two men faced each other for a few minutes, then they 'ran like hell' in opposite directions. Back with his English comrades, the mechanic told his story quite openly. He admitted that he ran because he had no wish to kill the German. His decision not to attempt to kill was partly influenced by his empathy for the German who was just as afraid to die, and just as unwilling to kill as he was. His comrades appeared to understand this, and did not think him cowardly or unpatriotic.

Dryer (*op cit*) considers that one of the most moving occasions in war occurs when people from each side in a conflict, recognise the humanity of the other. He cites as an example, the case of a German battalion commander who, at the British retreat following the Battle of Loos in 1915, ordered that 'no shot (be) fired at them from the German trenches for the rest of the day, so great was the feeling of compassion for the enemy after such a victory'. Another act of compassion, although on a smaller scale (also cited by Dryer) was of a British soldier who, as he lay wounded heard a young Saxon boy crying out for his mother. Seeing that he was dying, the Englishman took the boy in his arms saying 'all right son, all right, mother's here with you'. Sometimes, reluctance to kill led to the development of co-operation. In the early months of World War I, for example, a group of British and Saxon soldiers positioned near Yares agreed that they would not to shoot one another. To create the illusion that some fighting was taking place, soldiers from both sides shot their rifles into the air. The men became quite friendly, sometimes meeting and chattering together over the fences.

Unfortunately, the British company officer who had agreed to the truce, became ill. His replacement, a 'fire eating patriot' insisted that his men open fire on some Saxons he sighted, harmlessly fixing a fence. Thus ended the truce and 'a large number of benevolent Saxons were ignominiously wiped out.'[22] Sometimes, traditional occasions, such as Christmas, provided a more official agreement for a truce, as documented in letters from soldiers published in some of the Bolton papers.

> *'An interesting letter illustrating how our soldiers at the front spent Christmas has been received by staff at the Post Office from one for their number, Sapper W A Farrall who is serving with the signal section of the Royal Engineers. Sapper Farrall thanks his colleagues for a pipe and tobacco forwarded to him and adds: "Things are very quiet in our part of the line. On Christmas day there wasn't a shot fired in the whole Division. There was a kind of truce declared. By means of a megaphone one of our officers wished the Germans on the opposite trenches a 'Merry Christmas.' They returned the compliment and added that any of our troops who wished to visit them in their trenches were at liberty to do so. Several of our chaps accepted the invitation and were well received. "*

Sapper Farrall also wrote that 'in the afternoon there was a football match played between the trenches in full view of the enemy. They kept the truce honourably.'

Depressingly, another letter published in the same paper on the same day reported that:

> *'We were watching the Germans and our fellows play football all day. The following day we were firing at each other as before.'*

There is a touch of sadness and regret in this letter that the co-operation of one day can be followed so quickly by killing the next. In this letter, there is a sense of questioning the purpose of the war in which the writer was engaged. Despite personal questioning of the validity of war and the horrors they encountered, most men continued to endure the

22   This account is given in Brittain's Testament of Youth on page, 168.

situation. This was not always due to valour, but because
failure to do so carried the death penalty. Officers had the
power to inflict this instantly, on any men who failed to fight,
who ran away, or who displayed any signs of fear. Stories of
the war which the writer heard when growing up, suggest that
many so-called deserters were brave men who had endured too
much.

Another of her grandfather's anecdotes told of a young
soldier, who had for the most part, fought very bravely, until
one day he 'lost his bottle'. Terrified of another battle, the
young man ran into a nearby field, where he fell to the ground,
covering his face. His officer followed and shot him in the
head. To what degree such stories have been added to and
elaborated over the years, it is difficult to say. But the writer
has been told other such stories by several of older men she
knew, who served in World War I. The relatives of executed
deserters were told that the deceased had died of wounds. In
recent years, there have been campaigns to gain a pardon for
these executed men (Dryer, 1995).

It is natural to sympathise with such men, but given that
their comrades were also experiencing the same discomfort
and danger, it is understandable that indignation would be felt
towards those who escaped (or tried to escape) the dangers.
During World War I and World War II, there was also bitter
resentment against the men who failed to remain loyal. A
World War II veteran recalled the intense hatred that men
could feel towards women who sent 'dear John' letters:

> *'The 'dear John' letters were terrible, because for many of
> the men, the young ones especially, thoughts of their girls
> back home, was the only thing that kept them going. I
> mean people don't understand. I've heard a lot of
> criticism of how men in the Forces treat the women, if
> they come across them, who send 'dear John's'. And
> that's all very well. But people don't understand the
> effects those letters had on the men, they have never seen
> the effects that letters like that could have. I mean to say, I
> lost three of my mates because of those dammed things.
> You see, one of the things that kept the men going was the
> thoughts of their families and girls, some had got
> married before the war, and others, like me, decided to*

wait, but whatever arrangement they came to, there was a general understanding that they had a loved one to come back to, a home, a life to build when they got back. And added to that there was the terrible things they were seeing, the terrible conditions that they had to put up with. You know my dear, somehow, thoughts of a normal happy life after, become even more important. You can't judge the effects that something like a 'dear John' would have in peacetime, or if a woman finishing with a man just straight to his face, its just not the same. I mean, these people who have bad things to say about how we treated women who sent those letters, they have no idea. I Lost three of my mates because of those. They shot themselves. I was actually with one of them when he did it. We were all sat around one day, and well we all had revolvers. And my friend was just quietly reading this letter from his girlfriend. He never said anything, never told us what it was about, he just went quietly behind the tank and we heard this shot. We went to the back of the tank and there he was, blood all over the place, he was just there, lying on the ground. And I suppose that she must have felt terrible, but the thing is, they had no idea when they put pen to paper, the state of mind that their men would be in when they read that letter. It was irresponsible, just irresponsible. Well, the men had no time for women like that, they felt very strongly about that. And there could be real hatred for women who sent 'dear Johns' and people who criticise them for that, well they just have no idea, no idea.'

The author has no data on 'dear John' letters of World War I, but has assumed that the effects would be similar. As World War I continued, men were increasingly reluctant to enlist. Those at war considered that every available man should be made to do his 'bit' to ease the situation. Despite general expressions of disapproval and indignation, many men invested considerable effort to avoid enlisting. In some cases, this could be achieved by using the system. An Edgeworth farmer claimed exemption on the grounds that his work as a greengrocer was of national importance. His tribunal was unimpressed. He was fined £2 and handed over to the military services, at which he proclaimed 'if I am not entitled to exemption I may as well be hung, drawn and quartered where I am.' The words of the farmer accurately captured the attitude of many English people to the war.[23]

Gradually, it became clear that the war would not be won with the quick victory expected. Scepticism grew and recruitment slackened off. Letters from soldiers at war lost their initial optimism and were replaced by accounts, such as the one cited below:

> *'In the casualty lists you will find the name of Lft Dixon, of our regiment, who was killed. I was one who helped to carry him away from the trenches. We have only been here four days and have had five killed and 11 wounded. Joe Lomax, who slept in the same tent as I did in camp, got killed on Monday. We are in a hot shop. I could write a month about what I have seen, and if I told you everything you would never give over crying.'*[24]

Other soldiers expressed loneliness and misery. More than anything else, they wanted to be back with their families. Nostalgia for home was expressed, together with sadness for the dead who would never return:

> *'On Christmas day we could hardly hear a thing only the birds, and when I got to the bottom of the gully on my way to the beach for battery rations, I could hear the band playing 'Christians Awake.' I had a feeling I cannot describe; I felt so lonely and so much in need of those dear to me at home, and I could easily have cried. I passed a lot of graves, and thought those poor fellows will be absent, for the first time perhaps, at their table at Christmas'.*[25]

Other men wrote of events they had seen which caused considerable distress to the civilian population. Many at home must have been aware of the suffering caused by the war to the people in Europe from the very beginning, but most preferred to ignore such realities. It was only when personal stories evoked images of human suffering that these realities were

23 *Bolton Journal and Guardian*, October 6th, 1996.
24 Letter cited in Richardson and Richardson (1995), dated 2/7/1915.
25 Richardson and Richardson (1995), dated 21/12/1915.

accepted. The letter quoted below strikes a cord in any human being, especially in mothers:

> *'There is not a house standing in the district, the Germans have blown them all down and smashed everything in front. I went into some of the houses this morning about four o'clock, and in one came across a woman with her baby across her arms and both dead, lying across the bed. They must have been there a long time. In one of the villages we came across, we saw some weird sights. The first house we came to had the roof taken off, and in the lower room I think it was, I saw a man and a woman sitting at a table, as though they had just finished a meal, and were leaning on the table for a rest. On getting inside to speak to them we saw that they were both dead, and had been for weeks. A little further on we came to another house in which was an old man and woman, and a young woman, whom we took to be their daughter, and a bonny little boy, who seemed to be about 4 years old, all gassed.'* [26]

Considering the effect such letters must have had on the families who received them, it seems quite reasonable that enthusiasm for the war diminished. The Battle of the Somme finally brought home the severity of the war. On the first day, in July 1916, there were 57,000 casualties, of whom 19,000 died (Richardson and Richardson, 1995). The enthusiasm to enlist was failing before this battle was fought. By October 1915, instead of recruitment being limited by regulations such as those of height, the system was changed from voluntary to compulsory military service. Information about all eligible men per household was collected and those previously rejected on medical grounds were called up. The age for military service was extended, for younger men from nineteen to eighteen years and for older men, it was extended to the age of fifty. At home and at the front, resentment was felt against those who managed to escape military service (Richardson and Richardson, 1995). As one Farnworth man wrote to his family:

---

26   Richardson and Richardson (1995), dated 2/7/1975.

'The single young men who are doing nothing but talking and drinking in the pubs, who are fit for service, ought to be sent to prison if they don't join and do a little duty for their country. They mustn't have any English blood in their veins.'[27]

At this point in the war, a link was still made with 'red blood' and 'real men' — real English men. The talk of how easily the Germans would be defeated and how they were begging for mercy had stopped. On the contrary, the writer continued by acknowledging that the enemy were a force to be reckoned with:

'They (that is, they who have not yet joined up) would join if they could only realise what this place looks like after the Germans have done their dirty work.'

Freud argued that those who fought in World War I never forgot their experiences. Some swore never to share these with their family because they believed no one could ever understand. To suppress all memory of traumatic experiences can prevent people from coming to terms with them. Given the problems encountered by many families after the wars, it appears that such memories, repressed in the unconscious, had long-lasting effects. Cannandine wrote of World War I:

'Those six millions who had served at the front had seen more death in their relatively brief span of armed service than they might reasonably have expected to encounter in a lifetime. And the deaths that they saw were violent, horrible, bloody, degrading and brutal, when if they had been civilians all their lives they would probably have limited their repertoire of death to old age and natural causes. At the same time, the soldiers themselves had been the agents of death, killing, maiming and wounding in a manner that would be unthinkable in civvy street. Shock, guilt, anguish, grief, remorse: these were only some of the emotions which such an experience left behind. Above all, a desire to forget, and yet also a recognition that such experiences could not, must not be forgotten.' (Cannandine, 1981).

27   Richardson and Richardson (1995), letter dated 2/7/1915.

People were more cautious about declaring war when indications of a second outbreak appeared in the middle thirties. In 1939, reports of events in Europe that threatened peace had none of the patriotism that had characterised the buildup to World War I. Reports leading up to World War II expressed the public dread of another war. On September 1st, 1939, *The Bolton Evening News* topic of the week declared 'We Do Not Want War, Yet: Dangerous Powers of the Dictators' and that:

> *'It might have been. Yet now, a bare 21 years after the end of the Great War, the children born at the dawn of peace, are being conscripted in readiness for a new war, and those who served in, and survived the last are wondering how soon they will be in uniform again.'*

Although pessimistic, the article expresses the belief prevailing at the start of World War I that war, should it breakout, would be over in a matter of weeks. The promotion of tough endurance and macho masculinity is also very strong, and suggests that Darwin's Theory of Evolution still captured the public imagination. Theory could be used manipulatively by the media to promote propaganda messages. The English may have lost their naive patriotism, but there was still a need to persuade people to enlist willingly in the event of war.

> *'Shorter it (the war) may be, it is only because of our increased powers of destruction; but even that is not certain, for there seems to be no limit to man's power of endurance. Civilised man's very refinements of mind enable him to command endurance. If his nervous system is more sensitive, he has in comparison greater control over his behaviour than his earlier ancestors or primitive contemporaries. He is too extraordinarily adaptive, well accustomed himself, almost as though he was insensitive, to living under the terror of air raids or hurrying underground. And he can accustom himself to the horror — both the endurance and perception of them.'*[28]

28   *Bolton Evening News*, September 1st, 1939 — an article titled '21 Years After'.

Oldfield (1989) asserts that 'every war brings the next war a little nearer.' The Boer War, for example, contributed to the development of World War I. Likewise, World War I contributed to the outbreak of World War II. Oldfield argues that this happens because once nations experience a war, they become less inhibited about using war as a method of solving disputes. In 1939 there was little enthusiasm for another war. The motives for enlisting had changed. Willingness to fight appears to have reflected, more generally, in an increased political awareness. Much of the anger expressed was, according to some respondents, mainly directed at the pacifists and those politicians who had failed to protect Britain's military might. The author is a pacifist but acknowledges that research has shown nations are considered weak by other nations, if they are perceived to lack military power. Stoltenberg (1990) attributes this to the devaluation of femininity, because to be disarmed is to be made feminine, like a woman. To be like a woman is to be soft, passive, easily dominated. Indeed, this contempt for the perceived weakness of femininity was part of the glorification of the hero, as discussed earlier in this chapter.

The rise of the Nazi party which glorified military power and expressed contempt for femininity dominated German policies. Many prominent pacifists of the time acknowledged the danger. Virginia Woolfe, the feminist pacifist, could not be persuaded that war could ever be a solution, but was very pessimistic about what a victory for Hitler would mean for human rights, and especially women's rights. The role of women within in Germany at this time, was to bring 'forth those great men of war' (Oldfield, *op cit*). In her scrapbook, Woolfe expressed the ambivalence caused by her commitment to non-violence and her fears of what defeat might mean. Her scrapbook contained a record of newspaper cuttings of German women who had been imprisoned because of their refusal to conform to the German feminine ideal of that era.

In 1939 Europe faced yet another war. Those who went to fight this second time were exposed to the same discomforts, the violence and death that characterises not only World War I, but any war. Those who become POWs, and separated from direct combat, had horrors of a different kind to endure, as the following writer, recalling his experience of a Japanese POW camp, recalls:

> 'The conditions were horrible, latrines were dug on the square and were full up soon after completion. Lads worked day and night in shifts digging these, and the cook houses were almost on top of the latrines. No one had to walk over this given area and the machine guns saw to that. There were men down with dysentery and diphtheria and others liable to catch it. Their average diet consisted of: a scoop of vegetable stew or fish (dried salt fish) and rice. On the Siam-Burma railway we lost about 17,000 men (British) who mostly died, when they hadn't more than a couple of months to go before the end of the war.'[29]

The data collected for this book suggests that, at an experiential level, there was little difference between World War I and World War II. In both wars, those who went to fight had to endure terrible conditions, violence, fear and death. In both wars, those exposed to such experiences developed their own psychological coping strategies. Some objectified the dead, while on other occasions they were unable to escape some recognition of the loss to humanity. Sometimes they would bottle up emotions; on other occasions they would grieve openly, or express grief in writing. Sometimes they liked the enemy; sometimes they hated them. Sometimes they made light of it; one man, for example, speaking of his World War II experiences, said that, following one of the skirmishes in which he and his comrades had been involved, 'there wasn't a clean or dry pair of pants in the troop'. Fear of having to kill was as great the thought of being killed. The ability to kill is necessary for survival in a war, yet it is killing that caused the greatest trauma, and indeed, loss of self to those who killed. Experiences of World War II differed most significantly because of the Blitz. Those who went away to fight knew that, in many respects, those back home were in greater danger than those at war. One of the participants admitted that this

---

29   POW diaries and memories, by Frank Round. Source — *Living Around Here: Stories From the Area Around The New Bury Community Centre*, No 5, Autumn 1996, published by the New Bury Community Centre

was hardest to deal with, because you cannot cut out those who you love — you cannot objectify them:

> *'But when you came on leave, you wasn't that person (who had objectified the dead) you couldn't be that person with your family. First of all you loved them, or at least cared for them, and secondly, you were a civvy again, while you were on leave that is, so you were out of that mode of thinking. When you were home on leave, say you were in the pictures with your girlfriend and an air raid started, you were more afraid, more afraid, because you couldn't sort of cut them out. They were the people that you lived with, so if they got killed in a raid, they were your people, it wasn't the same as when you were away at war. When you were away, you only had yourself to worry about, but at home, you worried about the safety of everyone else.'*

There were also important political differences that did effect the attitude of those who went to war. Plans for the new Welfare State following the Beverage Report, nourished the belief of people who served in World War II that they were fighting for a better world for themselves and their families. The training and education that they received in the military services increased their quality of life. Finally, most of the World War II war veterans who took part in this study, reported some very positive experiences. But despite the gains, those who experienced the two wars were never free of the long-term effects. For some, the trauma was so great that it led to severe mental health problems (see *Chapter 10*). The author's initial interest in the experiences of war began with a former study that had nothing to do with death or war at all. The study was intended to research older women's experiences of the textile industry, but so many of the older participants gave spontaneous accounts of the war and that roused the author's interest.

Having listened to some of her participants' stories of war, she began, for the first time, to consider its impact. Finding words to describe the indescribable seemed impossible and the chapter on war in her first book to emerge from the research, was the most difficult to write.[30] A year after the publication of the book 'Cotton Everywhere', the author gave a presentation about her research to a group of older Bolton men. After the presentation, which included some discussion of the chapter written about the war, Kenny asked the men whether or not they would like to comment on some of the issues discussed. Many did, and spoke with anger, with passion and with regret, of their experiences of war. In particular, they spoke of the friends they had lost. The atmosphere in the room became very emotionally charged during the discussion, and it was clear to the author that many of the men had been carrying unhealed, mental wounds for many years. In any war then, it seems that no matter who 'surrenders' there really are no winners, only losers!

30   Kenny C (1994) *Cotton Everywhere*, Aurora Press, Bolton

Chapter 4
Life on the Home Front

In May 1939, the peace of early summer was shattered by the declaration of war broadcast by Neville Chamberlain. The sense of despair, was tempered by an almost hushed sense of relief, although most people did not want to believe that the 'War to End all Wars' had been exposed for the myth that Winston Churchill and others had proclaimed it to be. There was a feeling of urgency. The need to prepare for enemy attack was paramount. Many parents tried to adopt a 'matter-of-fact approach' to cover their sense of dread. But children are too perceptive to be deceived, and, as one 75-year-old participant recalled:

> *'I was only five when war broke out, and in those days parents did not discuss matters of importance with children. We had to be seen and not heard. But I do remember my family always listening to the radio for the news.'*

Instruction on the use of gas masks was given in schools and recruits to the armed services began to enlist at an average rate of 25 a day.[1] In the months between May to August, 1939 Anderson Air Raid Shelters were hurriedly erected. People regularly checked the local newspapers, to make sure that they were up-to-date with the latest war news and technologies. Some of these technologies would appear very strange to the technocrats of the 1990s. Few were as bizarre as a 'baby safe' gas mask, developed for children under twelve months of age. This contraption provided 'Mum' with matching headgear, and a 'snappy' hand pump attachment to make the use of the appliance (supposedly) easy.[2,3] News of the German invasion of seven Polish towns, increased the urgency to install first aid depots and provide trenches and shelters throughout the town. Schools, theatres and cinemas closed

1   May 2nd, 1939 *The Bolton Evening News*
2   *Bolton Evening News*, August 14th, 1939
3   September 1st, 1939, *Bolton Evening News*

and coffee bars were packed with people discussing the outbreak of war, all eager to discover the latest news.[4] The reality of war advanced with alarming speed.

> '*I remember rumours of rumblings of war and gas masks were issued to every man, woman and child. Corrugated iron shelters were erected in the gardens or brick shelters were put up in back yards. Windows had strips of sticky paper cut into patterns on them to cut down the danger of splintering. Everyone had matching curtains, black ones, very well fitted, so that no chinks of light were visible to enemy bombers. Street lights were a thing of the past, and food, cloths and petrol were all rationed*'. [5]

When asked of her immediate memories of the Blitz, one 59-year-old woman wrote:

> '*The coupons, pat hot water bottles, gas lights in the house, tin bath in front of the fire. Very bad winters, six feet of snow, but lovely summers, open fields, May Queens, trips to the seaside once a year to see relatives. The trams from Bolton to Horwich, the darkness at night. Everywhere was blackout, there were more conversations, the radio*'.

The sketch above suggests a determination to remember bright, traditional, safe and sensual things. But the attempt fails, and the story comes to a foreboding conclusion. The narrative concludes with, 'The darkness at night. Everything was blackout'. Many of the stories suggested an apparent need to remember the good, to emphasise tradition, stability and the binding elements of the community. This suggests that in times of chaos, people may be more inclined to cling to anything that suggests stability. One women recalled:

> '*I also remember very little transport, 'Shanks Pony' was the norm. In other words, we walked most places. I used to love May Day when everyone that owned Shire horses would dress the horses up in all their finery, eg. vivid coloured ribbons in their pleated manes, with polished*

4   *Bolton Evening News*, September 3rd 1939.
5   73-year-old woman, interviewed 1997.

brasses adorning their magnificent bodies — a sight to behold. I also remember the 'Rag Bone man' who pulled handcarts and shouted 'Rag Bone, Rag Bone' as they walked the streets. Our mums would send us with any old clothing to give him and in return he would give us what we called a 'Donkey stone' which you rubbed on the edge of your doorstep, when mopping. It made the edge of the doorstep white, like chalk. Also, everyone would sweep outside their own house daily, making everywhere look a lot tidier than today. I suppose, yes, we did call them the good old days, but they were not greedy days; they were hard yes, but there was a sincerity about people and life that you don't see today'.

The Ministry of Health announced at the close of August of 1939, the intention to evacuate schoolchildren and other priority groups from the inner cities.[6] This was swiftly followed by news of the arrival at Turton Station of three hundred and thirty four 'happy little exiles'. A thousand more followed within the next few days. Appeals for essentials, such as cots and blankets had been warmly met. Evacuee hosts expressed sentiments such as, 'I shall treat them like my own' and 'I have had the house decorated in a cream colour in honour of them'.[7] Ten days later an exodus of evacuees departed the town.[8] Evening papers reported 'happy little exiles' — 'not so welcome now'. [9] A published catalogue of grief compiled by Bolton evacuee hosts outlined some of the problems.[10]

The evacuation reflected a concern for the safety of children in inner cities areas. Once settled in their new homes, evacuation proved a very positive experience for many of those involved. Problems arose when poorer children were placed in the rural, relatively middle-class communities. Foster parents in Turton were shocked at the (reported) dirty, bedraggled and lice-infested state of the children who came into their homes. They had little understanding of the lifestyle in an

6   September 1st., 1939, *Bolton Evening News*
7   September 12th, *Bolton Evening News*
8   September 11th, 1939, *Bolton Evening News*
9   73-year-old woman, interviewed 1997.
10   We discuss the experience of the evacuees

inner city slum. One foster mother was so shocked by the poorly clad little waif who arrived at her door, she immediately began stitching a new frock, and the evacuees had little knowledge or understanding of the social graces considered normal in these rural communities.

The calm of these peaceful, suburban homes was shattered by the invasion of noisy, energetic, messy children. Prized and polished furniture was scratched and ruined. Outraged residents complained of evacuee mothers who stank of drink and made little effort to control their dirty, lice-infested offspring. However, the evacuation must have been an alienating experience for those who had been uprooted from their own communities. Some of the evacuated mothers may not have presented themselves in a very good light, simply because they felt depressed and socially isolated.

Unexpected visits from families of evacuees, expecting tea and scones were a further source of embarrassment for horrified hosts.[11] Customs such as popping in unexpectedly for tea, were considered quite normal by evacuees from poorer, working-class areas. Criticism of the dirty state of the children on arrival might not have allowed for the effects of travelling miles in an overcrowded steam train, gushing out clouds of black smoke. Reports of these events suggest culture shock, rather than blame in both parties. In the haste of evacuation, people were ill-prepared to meet the differences they encountered. Those who made the evacuees welcome had done so in a true spirit of generosity. It is not surprising that they felt aggrieved when things went wrong.

Despite the original good intentions of the evacuation, a culmination of complaints dampened enthusiasm. People from the inner cities began to resist pressures to send their children away. Legislation was implemented when it became increasingly difficult to find willing hosts.[12] Some people found the stress too much. A retired school teacher with a history of mental health problems, could not tolerate the prospect of five evacuees moving into his home. Following an unsuccessful appeal to officials, the man gassed himself. A woman from

11   September 11th, 1939, *Bolton Evening News.*
12   *Bolton Evening News* September 4th, 1939.

Caernarfon was fined £5 for refusing to allow an evacuated mother with two children into her home. Reports of similar acts of civil disobedience began to crop up with increasing frequency over the days that followed (*Bolton Evening News*, 1939).[13]

The Engineering Society of London issued calls for women to enlist in the munitions factories and related industries.[14] Women from rural areas were asked to become foster mothers. Within a matter of weeks, women were moving away from their traditional domain of the family, into the public world of work. In the north, these changes had long-term consequences for industry, patterns of work and employment prospects. Munitions work attracted younger workers from the textile industry. Single women also enlisted for service in the armed services and the St John's Ambulance Brigade. These changes depleted the reserve of younger workers in the mills, a downward trend that followed the course of their demise. There were local as well as national trends of course. Men working in industries, such as coal, steel and engineering, were exempt from military service, and family life in areas, such as Wigan, was relatively unaffected (Marshall, 1974). Bolton was one of the northern areas that took a large number of evacuees. The women who fostered these children adopted a role that did not challenge traditional divisions of labour within the family. Opportunities for women in other spheres of the caring professions also opened up.

The Ministry of Health made urgent appeals for midwives and nurses to return to (or remain in) the professions. Strong official denials were issued about reported plans to call up young women without children for service. [15,16] However, given that women worked in just about every other area, it would be interesting to consider what might have happened if World War II had continued for many more years. Opportunities were also availabe for women to work in professional areas, such as banks. However, it should not be

13   *Bolton Evening News*, September 5th, 1939.
14   September 1st, *Bolton Evening News*.
15   *Bolton Evening News* July 3rd 1942
16   *Bolton Evening News*, July 3rd 1942, Minister of Health, *op cit*.

assumed that working women were always accepted on an equal footing with men. Many encountered sexism, ridicule and harassment from male colleagues, especially in the heavier industries. In these contexts, some men may have felt threatened by the presence of women and responded by refusing to take women workers seriously. Some men could be dismissive, others were deliberately unhelpful. A minority expressed their hostility openly and aggressively, while others adopted a more insidious approach, deliberately making the work harder for the women than it needed to be (Costello, 1985).

This latter form of oppression is very difficult to deal with. First, it is difficult to prove. Victims risk becoming branded as 'paranoid' if they try to articulate, let alone challenge what is happening. The struggle against such prejudice is debilitating and provides 'proof' that the workers concerned are less capable. If they insist on drawing attention to the discrimination, then it can be argued that they are simply making excuses for their (supposed) inadequacies.

Second, it acts as a defence mechanism. No one likes to feel that they might be an oppressor. Such self-knowledge can be very damaging to a person's self-image. Appeals for fair play are not helpful. People have a vested interest in clinging to their beliefs, especially positive beliefs about themselves that they are anxious to protect. Such confrontations are not helped by the fact that the fears, which cause such behaviour, tend to be irrational. Unfortunately, the sorry face of humanity often proves that the nicest people are responsible for some of its nastiest behaviour. This kind of hidden discrimination also allows the perpetrators to 'forget' what they have done. 'Amnesia' of this type occurs almost as soon as the mechanisms for failure have been set in place.[17]

Assertiveness may not always helpful to less powerful groups. Behaviour can be interpreted in different ways. Using gender as an example: if a man is angry, he is angry; if a woman is angry, she is 'hysterical'. Many studies show that, in

17 It is for reasons such as those discussed above that the author supports the view of Finkelstein (personal discussion, 1998) that attitudes are very difficult to change. The more powerful groups in society define the less powerful in ways that allow the former to keep intact a positive self-image.

the workplace, men frequently 'butt in' when women are talking (Lakoff, 1975). It is rare for such behaviour to be attributed to bad manners in the men concerned. It is the woman who is at fault. She lacks assertiveness. She has a problem making people listen. Where men and women had traditionally worked together as equally respected skilled workers, such as in the weaving sheds, there were fewer problems (Walton, 1987).

Women did far more than replace men in traditional male occupations. In addition to full time employment, they had to cope with running a home and bringing up children, while coping with the inconvenience of shortages of food and other resources. They also experienced the daily stress of fear that the telegraph boy might call and, during World War II, the dangers of the Blitz. These demands stretched women's pat- ience and tolerance, sometimes to their limits. Most women met the challenge well. However, no individual could be expected to cope alone with such overwhelming responsibil-ities, and a complex system of interdependency developed. Traditional, patriarchal principles were replaced by a more matriarchal approach. Again, regional differences are important. Bolton working-class communities have always had a strong matriarchal tradition and a long history of married women working outside the home. In such areas, it might be more appropriate to state that patterns of labour, rather than family organisation and dynamics, changed during the two wars, 'Families in general were closer in those days, both geographically and emotionally and I believe that the members were able to help each other more positively than is the case today'.[18]

Working women are rarely able to 'clock off' at the end of the day. At work they were under pressure to present themselves in a feminine way, even during the war.[19] This concern that women maintain a 'feminine' image, even in the most difficult situations, can lead to a neglect for their basic needs. Indeed, it can put their lives and safety at risk. Nurses

18 75-year-old woman interviewed in 1996.
19 Goodman P (1993) *Her — Stories of the Second World War* unpublished paper presented at Manchester University.

interviewed by Norman (1990), for example, spoke of American supply stores in Vietnam that sold makeup and stockings, but not tampons or sanitary towels. Nurses had to wear their starched and uncomfortable nurses uniforms, even in the most unbearable heat. During night bombing raids, officers and soldiers were instructed to take cover under the beds. Having been designed with men in mind, the beds were low. Any woman with the hint of a bust could not fit under them.

During the two wars, women adopted androgynous rather than masculine traits. Such behaviour patterns did little to encourage, or maintain their hold in traditional male-dominated occupations. Within a hard, tough, working-class, masculine subculture, androgynous traits, because of their equal balance between expressions of masculinity and femininity, may have led to women workers being granted the status of effeminate (much despised) honorary men.

Most participants in the study remembered the rationing and the shortages. They also had fond memories of the community spirit that prevailed. The government had a strong commitment to ensuring that everyone had enough to eat. They sponsored meals-on-wheels and mobile canteens that sold cheap soup and sandwiches for those who were unable to provide a meal at home. Some families fared better during World War II than they had ever done before. Rationing limited the amount of household items available for each family but was popular because it was fair. Rationing (at least in theory) affected everyone, regardless of social status. Coffee, cheese, butter, canned goods and meat were all rationed. People improvised with foods, such as spam, rabbit, macaroni cheese and tuna. Housewives had to develop new cooking skills. Making food cooked from a base of rubbery dried eggs and milk appear appetising presented quite a challenge. For those who liked to eat out, restaurants offered, lovely juicy (horse-meat) steaks. People were also encouraged to use cheaper cuts of meat, such as pigs brains and cows udders.

Newspapers and magazines frequently featured recipes and advice on nutrition. Mothers from all social classes learned how to feed their families well and cheaply. Popular recipes included, 'war and peace pudding', made from flour, suet, mixed fruit and grated raw carrot. Carrot croquettes, made from a mixture of potato, flour and grated carrot were also popular. Householders were encouraged to 'dig for victory' growing their own vegetables. The cartoon figures 'Doc Carrot' and 'Potato Pete' promoted greater use of available vegetables. Recipes consisted of very basic foods, but were given a touch of fun and spirit with names like 'carrot fudge', 'patriotic pudding', and 'all clear sandwiches'. Other household products were in short supply. People used soap to the last, grated sliver. A chronic toilet paper shortage was generously relieved when enemy aircraft dropped a shower of propaganda leaflets. Printed on quality paper, softer and 'kinder' than the coarse home grown varieties, this donation was greatly appreciated (Reader's Digest, 1995b).

As we have noted, women were encouraged to maintain a feminine image throughout. This took inventive genius in such hard times. Tan lotion and gravy browning were spread on to bare legs and eyebrow pencils drew false seams. Beetroot served as a substitute for lipstick and rouge. Despite the emphasis on femininity, women were keen to be comfortable and practical at work. Sales of slacks, jeans (sometimes decorated with patches) and 'sloppy Joe' jumpers began to soar. The result; a tomboyish feminine style that has remained popular to the present day.

> *'I remember the blackout, excessive work hours and restrictions in social life. Involvement by women in tasks which were traditionally men's work were readily and eagerly undertaken. I also remember the rationing.'* [20]

Although these activities may have increased women's confidence and independence, there were problems when the declaration of peace led to calls for a return to traditional family values. The problem had an impact on children as well as adults. One of the respondents who took part in Turner and Rennell's study, reported a history of stormy relationships with men. She attributed this to having been influenced by strong, independent female role models during the war. She

---

20   76-year-old male, CE interviewed in 1996

added that, in her view, men are inclined to find such women very threatening.[21] Despite women's involvement in paid employment, representations of the good homemaker and mother continued to be very powerful throughout the war. Women had to contend with a host of contradictions. The 'goodly' woman has great capacity for martyrdom. She is selfish if she is unwilling to make sacrifices. If she sacrifices too much, she is then perceived as ignorant and in need of help and advice. The following reinforces this contradiction:[22]

> *'Only too often mothers risked endangerment of their health and the growth of their babies by giving part of their rations to other members of the family, Mr Ernest Brown, Minister for Health, told the conference of the National Association of Maternity and Child Welfare Centres of London today. Expectant and nursing mothers* ***should see that*** *they obtained their extra rations.'[23] (author's emphasis)*

The statement above reflects little appreciation for the problems encountered by working mothers. There is no acknowledgement of the conditions and multiple responsibilities that make an appropriate response difficult, if not impossible. Such limited understanding did little to enhance the Welfare State's potential to provide effective support for those who needed it most. Recruitment and training of predominantly middle-class professionals may have added to the problems. In some cases, advice given by health visitors on nutrition could be bitterly resented by poorer mothers, who did not have adequate finances to give their children 'good' food, such as chicken. Other cheap nutritious meals enthusiastically recommended, such as porridge, were time consuming and messy to prepare for busy, working mothers. The porridge might have been cheap but the fuel required to cook it was not (Holdsworth, 1988; Payne, 1991).

The growing independence of women, and perhaps in part because of it, encouraged an increasing scrutiny of

---

21   Cited in Taylor and Rennell, 1995, page 137.
22   *Bolton Evening News* July 3rd, 1942
23   *Bolton Evening News*, July 3rd, 1942 — article entitled *Mothers who take risks: Rations for other members of the family.*

motherhood. Professions concerned with child health and development evolved and become increasingly specialised. Despite possible long-term benefits, mothers must have been confused by the continual changes, contradictions and conflicting advice these professions suggested. For example, during World War II, child care experts such as Trudy King (cited by Holdsworth, *op cit*) encouraged mothers to adopt very strict, four-hourly feeding regimes and to restrict children to the minimum of handling.

After the war and following the publication of Bowlby's work (1965) mothers were given advice that completely contradicted this approach. Although this caused resentment, women did little to resist conforming to the constantly changing, professional definitions of what constituted good mothering. The author has no desire to deny the value of good, well-informed professional childcare guidance. But events in World War II provided examples of what can happen, when there is little understanding or appreciation of class or cultural differences. During World War II it was the professions who, perhaps unwittingly, provided the major source of moral policing.

For mothers who failed to 'measure up', punishment was severe. This is illustrated by a case reported in 1942 of a mother sentenced to three months in prison for child neglect. Dr V T Blackburns, present throughout her trial, alleged that 'during twenty years of slum clearance at Bedford and Blackburn I have never been in such a filthy and disgusting house'. Social workers concluded that the woman's home was unfit for animals to live in, let alone children. The only mitigating circumstance to excuse this woman's lack of enthusiasm for scrubbing and cleaning, was her restricted mobility. The woman was disabled. She had a meagre income of £2 per week with which to maintain herself and her four children. Such a small allowance would allow little to spare for the purchase of cleaning materials. This report suggests that the main concern was the woman's perceived inadequacies as a housewife. Great emphasis was placed on the dirty state of the house and on the fact that the children had been subjected to the unspeakable horror of having to sleep under rags. No mention was made of the quality of the relationship this mother may have had with her children.

It may be that the report records a genuine case of child neglect. But before we come to any conclusions, there are several points to consider. Rags, for example (and what counts as a rag anyway is open to debate), might be all a person can afford if they are poor. Providing rags to cover a sleeping child may not fit the glossy image of the ideal home. But any attempt to provide something to keep out the cold suggests effort, rather than neglect. As for the dirty state of the house, and contrary to popular myth, soap and warm water (try cleaning with cold) do cost money. Three months in prison seems a very harsh and, indeed, unreasonable price to pay for a dislike of housework. The children's separation from their mother during this time may have been more damaging to them than living in a dirty house. Placing them in (possibly inadequate) foster care may well have proved detrimental to their well-being.

Closer examination of the case suggests, it was not motherhood, but rather housewifery that was the issue. The woman's four children were illegitimate. She was poor and disabled. This appears to be a case of an unconventional woman (considered 'unfit' to be a mother) suffering discrimination. There is nothing new about the discrimination single mothers experience, or indeed, of the criticism to which mothers in general are exposed. The good things that mothers do are too often ignored, but when they make mistakes, the morally righteous are all too quick to criticise. Prior to the introduction of the Welfare State, high infant mortalities were attributed to the perceived ignorance of poor, 'incompetent' mothers (Holdsworth, 1988). Conditions such as poor housing, sanitation and diet were largely ignored. This strict policing of working-class mothers continued for some considerable time after the war. Penalties for women considered 'unfit' remained severe.

On August 18th, 1945, a mother from Bath was imprisoned for three months — without hard labour because of her health — for child neglect. The prosecution alleged that the mother's bedroom was a 'palace' compared to the children's bedroom which was a 'tip'. The mattresses were alleged to be filthy. A cupboard in one of the downstairs rooms was filled with damp cloths. This cupboard was apparently full of spiders, moths and beetles. Old coats had been used to keep the children warm in bed. Even today most children's bedrooms are a 'tip' — ask any mother. Again, the women was on a low income. The author again argues that it is surely better to sleep under old coats than under nothing at all. She also observes that any kind of linen, left in a damp cupboard, will tend to attract creepy crawlers. Did the woman have an alternative place to store the linen? Many homes were damp at this time.

Again the author would argue that this case illustrates a lack of understanding for the poverty that was still widespread at that time. It was some years after the war before people experienced any real benefit from the Welfare State. There used to be a saying in the working-class communities of Bolton, 'Bedrooms are private'. During her research into women's experiences of the textile industry, the author discovered the origins of this saying. Apparently, it was quite common in some households into the mid fifties for people to use old coats as blankets. Poorer families had a strong desire to preserve their self-respect and dignity, and priority was given to rooms into which visitors would be invited, such as living rooms, and to outside clothes rather than under garments or nightwear. Very poor people tended to discourage visitors.

One women spoke of a friend of hers who came from one of the poorest families in the street. The parents forbade their children to bring anyone into the house. One day the woman stood waiting outside for her friend to come out. Suddenly, the wind blew open the front door. The family were sitting around the living room table drinking tea from empty marmalade jars.[24] When considering such cases, the author found herself much in sympathy with the work of John Bowlby (1965). Bowlby was one of the most eminent child psychologists of the post-war years. Basing his argument on observations of children in crowded institutions and juvenile centres, he argued that a mother's love was one of the most important

---

24   This woman was aged 86 years at the time of her interview in 1991.

needs for a child during the first five years of life. Critics have pointed to weaknesses in Bowlby's early theory. Depending on interpretion, his theories could lead to working mothers suffering unnecessary guilt. However, long-term his work benefited children by reducing the power of over-zealous social workers to remove children from poorer homes, without first giving sufficient consideration to whether this would be in the best interests of the child.

World War II brought improvements for all mothers, regardless of marital status because they all received financial help and child support from the State, and subsidised school meals, vitamin supplements and nursery care. Women also become more sexually liberated due to the two wars. Information about sexuality and birth control was more readily available and this helped to improve the quality of life for working-class people.

What were the causes of the freer, and some maintained, more promiscuous attitude to sex prevalent during the two wars? Was it a need for security, love and romance? Or did sex provide an outlet for stress, particularly during the Blitz? These questions are explored in the next chapter.

Chapter 5
Love, sex and war

Costello (1985) argues that sex and war have always been inextricably linked.[1] His view is shared by many other writers who observe that in the military, fear of death contributes to more liberal sexual attitudes.[2] In any total war situation, sex can provide a means to release tension. This applies to men and women. In the face of death sexual activity affirms the validity of a person's existence. If it can be blended with at least some suggestion of romantic love, sex becomes a touching reminder of one's humanity. Many prominent military men have observed and commented on the way sexual conduct becomes more liberal during a war. Rouse for example (quoted by Costello, *op cit*) asserted that 'there is a wide-ranging association of war with sexuality, complex, intricate, intimate and at every level'.

The observation (most notably by Freud in his 1917 *Reflections on War and Death)* that war, death and sexuality are closely linked, has been supported by statistics and anecdotal accounts of war.[3] Freud argued that the urge to procreate, to kill and to die lie at the extremes of human experience. These drives become confused during a war, or indeed, any other conflict situation. Other workers, such as Kastenbaum (1986) note that the physiological changes induced by fear and sexual arousal are identical. Baldwinson (1995) has shown how connections between sex, war and violence are represented in literature. Drawing on two examples, Herr's (1978) *Dispatches* and Heller's (1955) *Catch 22*, he shows how the authors draw parallels between a sexual 'score' and the anticipation of a kill.[4,5]

1   For further reading, see biography, in particular the work of Costello, 1985; Wicks, 1991 and Davenport-Hines, 1990.
2   That is, for themselves, not for their women.
3   This refers to the increased birth rates and incidence of STD during World War I and World War II.
4   'Snowden' — extract from *Catch 22*, Heller J, 1955, Jonathan Cape.
5   'Hell Sucks' — extract from *Dispatches*, Herr M, 1978, Pan Books.

War aphrodisia is the technical term given to this phenomena. It is traditionally used when referring to military personnel. In a total war situation, such as the Blitz, it appears to have an influence on civilians as well. War aphrodisia can amount to little more than increased sexual arousal. Many feminists have strongly criticised the tendency to make violence appear sexually exciting. They challenge assumptions that there exists a natural connection between the two, arguing that such associations are socially created. Circulation and exposure to pornographic material encourages such associations. However, controlled studies that have sought to establish a correlation between exposure to pornography and male attitudes to women, do not support the feminist argument (McClelland, 1997). Longino (cited by Cavalier, 1996) defines pornography as 'verbal or pictorial material which represents or describes sexual behaviour that is degrading or abusive to one or more of the participants in such a way as to endorse the degradation'.

Pornography theorists such as Dworkin and MacKinnon (1992) argue strongly that representations linking sex and violence, and which portray women in forced acts of rape, perpetuate the rape myth. They consider that the ways people are forced to view pornography without their consent, constitutes a violation of human rights. The rape myth encompasses a variety of beliefs about sexuality, rape and violence. Such notions include: the belief that victims of rape 'ask for it', perpetrators are predominantly from minority groups (in America, 90% of rapes occur between people of the same ethnic background) and that attacks are committed by strangers (80% of sexual attacks are committed by someone the survivor knows).

The myth also assumes that only women are victims of rape. Around one in ten men have experienced rape and, in recent years, more male victims have come forward to speak of their experiences. This admission can be very difficult because 'a man who openly acknowledges that he has been raped is violating everything we are taught to expect a man to be' (Rape Fact Sheet, 1998)[6]. So what *do* we expect a man to be? What do we expect a woman to be? Relating this question to war produces some disturbing answers. Consider for example, rape of the enemy's women.

Sex crimes increased after World War II. These crimes were often committed by younger men, who joined the forces before they had developed the necessary skills to relate to women. Of such offenders, Turner and Rennell (1995) write:

> '*Amongst unmarried serviceman, contacts with women of their own kind, friendship, affection and marriage may have been a deferred delight, a fantasy elaborated during service life whenever the unsatisfied needs of tender relationships were felt. Now, sheer ignorance of womankind may make for awkwardness, shyness and fear of the very people who were worshipped from afar. Violent feelings may be noted — a belief that women should conform to his fantasies of perfection.*'

Although brief, the above analysis is quite complex, attributing several factors to the causes of sexual violence. To what extent do biological or social explanations help us understand sex and violence, particularly in war? During World War II many women, as well as men, attributed their liberal sexual conduct to the stress of the Blitz. And yet data gathered for this book, contained stories of romantic love, of lonely, anxious people seeking hope and comfort in someone else. There was nothing to suggest that this should be reduced to a mere sex drive. Yet the biological arguments, particularly the parallels drawn between physiological changes common in fear *and* sexual arousal, are convincing. Even if such parallels do exist we need to ask, 'Are they natural, or are they a learned responses?' An academic text must take a balanced view and these issues are explored further in this chapter.

Among the military authorities, opinion is divided as to whether or not sexual desire is best expressed within a traditional institution, such as marriage. Married men have an understandable concern for their families. Becoming a parent can lead to a greater appreciation of the value of human

6   The author emphasises that her comments do not atempt to dismiss or
     trivialise male survivors of rape.
     Rape Fact Sheet (1998) Myths and Facts about Sexual Violence (Internet
     Publication, Rape Information Home Page).

life. This makes killing even more difficult. During World War I and World War II, marriage rates increased rapidly. Seeking a traditional context, such as marriage, may have given people a respectable outlet for sexual feelings. This view once again seems 'base' and reductionist. Diaries, poems and love letters written during World War II suggest much more.

Having read many of these, the author has been struck by their emotional intensity. In the 1990s such literature might be considered embarrassing. Romances that developed in the space of a few months were affirmed in letters that promised lifelong love — 'you are the only women that I have ever loved,' 'I will love you always.'[7] Such passionate statements seem to suggest their writer's need for love (any kind of love, no matter how transient or superficial) rather than a simplistic urge to relieve 'pent up' sexual emotions. By the same token, much of the work did not suggest any authentic commitment to a lifelong partnership. The subtext suggests 'if I die, at least I have known love'. This need for love and affection led ordinary men and women to write poetry, probably for the first and only times in their lives.

In such cases, the view that 'the light that burns brightest, burns out soonest', may have rung true. The haste to marry may have caused some of the problems couples encountered after the war. Equally, the problems could have been due to the strain of separation, rather than reunion. The author notes that there were several reports of couples who had changed their minds about divorce *after* the war.[8] It is difficult to know for sure whether the cause can be attributed to romance, a need for love, or for a release of 'base' sexual instinct. But it does appear that attitudes towards sexuality become more liberal during a war, and it is this phenomena that is explored here.

The Marriage Guidance Counsel was established in 1933. Its work was interrupted during the war years, but it

7   For examples, see some of the autobiographic material cited by writers such as Wicks (1991), Costello (1985), Turner and Rennell (1995), and Ryle's publication of her mother's diary, *Missing in Action,* all listed in the bibliography (1979).
8   The author noted three such cases in the *Bolton Evening News* reported between May and August of 1945.

was quickly re-established in 1943, at a time when divorce rates began to soar (Turner and Rennell, *op cit*). This suggests that couples were suffering relationship breakdowns before the war had ended. This may have been partly due to number of couples who rushed into a hasty marriage. Driven by strong emotions, a desperate need for love and security and the threat of death and separation, couples who had known each other only a few months hurried to get married. Couples were marrying at an average rate of 1,000 a day in America following Pearl Harbour (Costello, *op cit*). Many of these young people might never have considered marriage in peacetime. Sometimes people felt a need to give some legitimacy to a sexual liaison, especially if the woman was pregnant.

The increasing divorce rate did not lessened the popularity of marriage. In Bolton, in the weeks immediately following the declaration of peace, there was a spate of 'peace time brides'. A number of weddings were reported in the local papers. Although many had married in haste just before or during the war, others decided to wait until it was over. The motives for postponing their marriage were very similar to those that led others to rush into marriage, ie. uncertainty and lack of security:

> *'That didn't seem like a very good idea (getting married before peace had been declared) because you see, you had no real idea of what might happen. There was if you like, no clear vision of what might happen in the future like. So we decided we'd get married as soon as the war finished.'* [9]

The two wars saw a higher incidence of illegitimate births and venereal disease. Despite these negative developments, there were long-term gains. Health and sex education become more widespread, prevention and treatment more accessible and available. This was a liberating alternative to the suspicions and fears suffered by previous generations. Most nations had avoided the responsibility of introducing sex education as a method of controlling and reducing the spread of sexually transmitted diseases (STD), such as syphilis. Instead, they

9   World War II veteran interviewed in 1997.

blamed other nationalities for any rise in its occurrence. Thus, throughout history there are records of pseudo names, ie. the French Disease, the Neapolitan and German Disease and so on.

The situation was exacerbated by moralists in high places. Such people used their influence to deny the public access to information. Lack of accurate information caused a dangerous proliferation and circulation of myths, often with serious consequences. There was a common belief that sex with a virgin could cure syphilis. Believing this myth, a soldier infected with the disease raped a fourteen-year-old girl during World War I.[10] The Royal Commission on Venereal Disease was founded in 1913. Most of its members had biased, moralistic sexual attitudes. They were particularly suspicious and fearful of working-class sexuality. In 1914, one of the commissioners, a Mrs Burgwin, expressed deep concern for the 'terrible crime' of contraception. Women who used it she insisted became 'physical wrecks' and they produced inferior offspring. The prevailing belief held by Commission members was that having some level of STD in the population was a good thing. It served as a deterrent against premarital sex and with this in mind, they preached celibacy rather than safe sex. Hostility to condom use was expressed most venomously. The Bishop of London published widely on the topic. His claimed that his main ambition in life was to build a bonfire of condoms that he could dance all around. Attitudes were very slow to change. Reports attributing the spread of STD to the conduct of unclean people capable of the vilest crimes, remained persistent well into the 1940s (Davenport-Hines, 1990).

The sharp increase in STD during World War I meant that steps aimed at controlling the spread of the disease, could no longer be avoided. But there were tensions between military opinion and civilian officials. *Chapter 3* explored how the celebration of the hero in British culture had led to the emergence of rigid ideas about appropriate gender roles, especially in the military. The emphasis on tough 'manliness'

10   This incident occurred during World War I and is recorded in
     Davenport-Hines (1990).

had contributed to more liberal heterosexual attitudes. One military judge had argued strongly that a man must love well if he is to fight well. Such polarity of values between military and civilian street moralists, did not make for a co-operative state of affairs. Recognition of the importance of the issue did lead to a more ready availability of condoms, at least in the armed forces. This alone had implications for the quality of working-class family life. Following World War I there was a gradual fall in birth rates among blue collar workers.

During World War II, the commitment to check the spread of STD grew. The War Office, backed by the Ministry of Health, launched an impressive sex education campaign. Condoms were distributed freely. The health education approach implemented was extremely sexist. Responsibility and blame was placed squarely on women's shoulders. Prostitutes were presented as particularly dangerous sources of infection. At least, the problem was out in the open and talked about, but with greater frankness in the working-class rather than in middle-class populations (Davenport-Hines, *op cit*). Sexual liberation was one of the positive things to emerge from the two wars.

World War I marked the beginning. But more traditional attitudes returned with the Depression. Nevertheless, knowledge and a greater tolerance had become firmly established by the end of World War II. This reached a peak in the swinging sixties, and had a 'knock on' effect on sexual attitudes more generally. Women had already proved that they could cope in the former masculine world of work. Gradually, they began to liberate themselves sexually as well. World War II introduced a total war situation and women were adopting more masculine traits. On the one hand they had to control their feelings in the face of chaos and fear. On the other, they needed comfort and affection. During the Blitz, women began to express their sexual feelings (like men at war) in more overt ways. It would seem that during the Blitz sex provided an outlet for stress and tension. This was true for men and women. The following extract indicates links that may exist between violence, stress and the need to relieve it, sometimes on to a 'sex object.'

Participant   *But then we had to calm down as well, things that you would never have seen before, I mean the French Foreign Legion, well it was shocking what they got up to. I saw my first strip show when we met up with them, oh, (laughs). One of those strip shows, well it was the talk of the camp for days, unbelievable, really unbelievable.*

Christine: *Why, had there not been strip shows in civvy street?*

Participant: *Oh yes, but, well these were very different, I daren't tell you what they were like, and I think, well the men were more likely to go, to need that kind of thing, what I mean was, it was another way of coping, you could get all carried away at one of those strip shows, it sort of released . . . you know . . . some of the tension, that's what I mean. And then there was those women, well they would come selling their wares, if you see what I mean? The French Foreign Legion had these women who followed them, and they were very generous like, they didn't mind sharing. Well, there wasn't a fella I knew that didn't take advantage of what was on offer. I mean, some of those women were huge apart from anything else. I mean, in peace time many of us young chaps would have ran a mile to have a big sexy women coming at you like that, really, they'd have been frightened out of their wits, but not in war, oh no not in war, oh boy we really took advantage of what was on offer.'[11]*

The participant explained that this was a light-hearted way to relieve stress. As with all sex shows, however, this could have done little to promote positive attitudes to women. Servicemen were encouraged to develop a romantic picture of their wives while they were away. If the wife did not live up to this ideal, there could be problems. It is clear that

11   World War II war veteran interviewed in 1997.

double-standards existed. In extreme situations such objectification can have violent consequences, such as rape. [12]

The trench warfare of World War I presented less of a
threat to those at home, although not in every case. One of the
most impressive World War I stories uncovered by the author,
concerned the sighting of a Zeppelin that had bombed some
areas of the town of Bolton. Participants who had witnessed
this, recalled not initial fear, but rather awe and astonish-
ment. In the days that followed, when the extent of the
bombings became clear, this changed to anger. Newspaper
archive material verified the oral accounts given. This air raid
appeared quite tame in comparison to the Blitz. But the
Zeppelins passing on September 24th 1916, presented a forbid-
ding promise of things to come. It claimed fifteen lives. The
report of its passage presents as good a testimony of how
human curiosity overcomes fear, as it does a factual account:

> *'In the streets leading to that unfortunate south-central
> area, there were literally thousands of people. It was
> apparent that no matter how scanty their attire, they had
> not forgotten their clogs. The dash and clatter of those
> clogs on the pavement was a defiance of the Zeppelin, for
> there was seemingly no fear that the German raiders
> could hear that penetrating sound. It was risky, it was
> true, but the music which rang from the footwear was
> wonderfully reassuring.'[13]*

Eye witness accounts likened the Zeppelin to a glowing red
cigar, or a pencil sharpened at both ends. Others said that it
looked like a plank in the sky, with little circles of light
sweeping out. Hysteria at the attack reached its peak on
October 6th, 1916, when the burial of victims caused
'remarkable funeral scenes'.[14] It may be that the Blitz had a
greater *quantifiable* impact on civilian life. But personal loss
in its human terms, cannot be measured in this quantifiable
way. It would be little comfort for those bereaved in 1916, to
know that air raids during World War II proved even more

12   See Costello, 1985.
13   *Bolton Journal and Guardian*, Friday September 29th, 1916.
14   *Bolton Journal and Guardian*, October 6th, 1916 — report of the burial of
      victims.

destructive. Improved war technology in World War II meant that no one was safe. Some of the most lucid memories of participants were of gas masks and bombings. Gas masks may have been comforting in the early months of the war. At this time people were new to the Blitz and had no notion of what little protection these offered. An 80-year-old male ex serviceman wrote:

> *'My own experience was of complete and utter bewilderment, eg. I was stationed in Wales (in the country) and yet other city inhabitants — civilians — were living in dreadful conditions in which bombs were dropped nightly on their homes by the enemy.'*

People got used to the sirens and the bombings. But to do so, they suppressed their fears and appeared immune to the danger. Within a year of the outbreak of war, people had stopped carrying gas masks around.[15] This apparent indifference to the danger evolved gradually. A 77-year-old male participant recalls:

> *'In the early days of the war when we were weak, the German's would send over bombers full of 'blast bombs.' These were small bombs that did little damage, but made a loud bang and kept people awake. Working all day and being kept awake all night can make life a bit difficult. But people soon got used to it and slept on. It just shows, you can get used to anything.'*

People are heedless to danger when they live with it day after day.

> *'My recollections are still very clear of the sirens sounding. We used to go to the air raid shelter in nighty/pyjamas, etc, with our gas masks. It was always flooded with water and we would sit on slatted wooden benches. My mother decided that if we were going to be killed, we might as well stay at home, and so we had a mattress under the stairs.*

15   This information from the study is supported by a report in the *Bolton Evening News* on February 10th, 1943, that after three and a half years of war, most people in Bolton no longer carried their gas masks, and this applied to both service men and women.

This indifference was more common in Bolton then any where else. It may be because the town fared well in comparison to larger cities, such a Liverpool and Manchester. Children especially appeared to have had little appreciation for the dangerousness of the air raids. As one woman put it:

> 'The war was casually talked about but it seemed unreal and far away. Kids thought the Germans and Japanese were the bad group, there seemed little realisation or fear that the country might be occupied'. [16]

But children must have been affected. The same participant continues by writing of bereavement:

> 'The real significance of it wasn't apparent because the fathers that were killed were so far away; each day a different child would be reporting a father's death'.

What sense did children make of all this? Accounts by respondents suggest that they were far more sensitive to the dangers, and to the severity of the situation, than adults thought. A 71-year-old woman wrote:

> 'The large numbers of people afflicted by casualties and the sadness and difficulties generated, eg, neighbours of mine, one brother killed — bomb disposal, another side, youngest brother lost on submarine, elder brother killed in the Army, in North Africa. My cousin, KIA Sicily. Another friend WOP/AG RAF, lost over Germany. What a tragedy — what a waste!'

Lucilla Andrews (1977) nursed in London during the Blitz. Below she provides a graphic account of the chaos, confusion and fear that prevailed in the Capital following an air raid:

> 'Immediate ward treatment of air raid victims had been altered. Instead of, as earlier in the war, instantly removing the patients clothes, washing and putting them into clean night clothes, it had been found less shocking — where individual injuries made this possible, to leave them in their own cloths until the shock wore off. The

16   Female participant who was about nine years of age during the war. Age at the time she completed the questionnaire, and information related to religious affiliation, not provided.

> *filthy dust hung in the ward air and mingled with the*
> *smells of fresh and dried blood, of sweat, and the ugly,*
> *unmistakable smell of human fear. To be buried alive,*
> *whether injured or not, can and usually does cause acute*
> *clinical shock. Once that shock began to wear off, memory*
> *and fear of repetition made beads of black sweat glisten*
> *on the still grey faces that, whatever the individual age,*
> *looked old'.*

Andrews continues, 'even when victims escaped physical trauma (and possibly live burial) there was always the fear that a loved one may have been killed'. This immunity to long-term stress, has been theorised from several perspectives. **General Adaptation Syndrome** (GAS) refers to a person's diminished ability to recognise that they are stressed. Stress prompts the release of natural substances and these lead to a reaction known as the 'fight or flight' mechanism. This is a mechanism for survival and the physiological changes are similar to those induced by sexual arousal. The body experiences a surge of energy that enables it to run from danger, fight back, or as some biologists argue, indulge in passionate sex. In cases of ongoing stress, the substances continue to be released, but the person no longer recognises the stress signals and a massive burden is placed on the heart. This is very serious as it can lead to collapse. In severe cases it causes death.

Responses to bereavement and trauma are very similar. Denial is a very effective defence mechanism. Distraction is also helpful. This may not change the situation, but it can change a person's perception of it. The participants appeared anxious to remember the good times as well as the bad. Recollections of happy events were extremely vivid and they had a tendency to romanticise the past. Images, sketched by such memories, are bright, colourful and sensual. The stories seem to indicate to an increased yearning for life. Could such a yearning for life lead to a heightened sexual awareness?

Recognition of the stress people endured during the war, may have persuaded authorities to adopt a relatively lenient attitude to sexual promiscuity. This attitude quickly changed with the advent of peace. In the months following May, 1945, there was an official clamp down on 'immoral' behaviour that might pose a threat to the institute of marriage. In Bolton a twenty-year-old 'girl' was described by the authorities as 'a menace and a danger to the public'. This 'little menace' was sentenced to three months hard labour for 'teasing' and 'charming' army officers out of money.[17]

During the two wars, there were many single women who feared that they might never experience sex. They observed that virginity, although valued in the young, tends to be ridiculed in older women. They resolved that they would not become old maids. The consequences of an unwanted pregnancy could be severe during World War I. Attitudes were more rigid. If an unmarried mother could not depend on others for support, she would have to resort to a home for unmarried mothers. Even worse were the hospital lock wards. These were harsh establishments where women had their freedom and dignity stripped away from them. Lock wards had been established for the treatment of venereal disease and conditions there were appalling. Mothers admitted free from any symptoms, often developed them soon after discharge (Davenport-Hines, 1990).

Conditions improved during World War II. The dangers of the Blitz may have been the cause of some cases of war aphrodisia. 'Yanks' presented further attractions. Innocent friendships quickly became intimate. The pursuit of happiness found its full and complete expression in World War II Britain, as hundreds of women lost their virginity to an American dream. A chaplain was perplexed to observe a strange American partiality for wearing heavy trench coats, even in the sweltering heat of June. He was outraged by his subsequent discovery that these doubled up as 'tents' when no hotel place could be booked.

Black GIs received their fair share of flattery and attention. English women were impressed by their gentlemanly manners. But they knew that racism can be very contagious, so they took steps to secure success. A rumour circulated. Black GIs were *really* White GIs. Undercover

17 *Bolton Evening News*, July 27th, 1945 — the report was not clear whether the source of offense here was the 'service' offered, or the young woman's failure to provide it.

agents you see? They had been injected with a special skin darkening fluid, to make them more effective during night patrols. It worked like a charm. But it gave rise to a lot of confusion. Many an English maid after the war, waited patiently (and endlessly) for her Black lover to turn White (Costello, *op cit*).

Knowledge of an infidelity did not necessarily lead to a breakdown in a marriage when the husband came home. A lot depended on the wife's rationale for having entered into it, and the husband's ability to understand. Again we need to consider what needs a relationship serves. Some women did not have extra marital affairs because they had lost interest in their husbands. Nor had they fallen in love with someone else. Quite the contrary, some women felt so lonely for their men, that they would sleep with anyone, imagining that as they did, they were making love to their absent husbands. Men who became involved in such relationships often understood what was happening. But few seemed to care.[18] However, no matter what prompted their wife into having an affair, some husbands felt unable to forgive and walked out. Such rejections were a deep source of shame and remorse for many women. The veteran below recalls:

'My second wife always said that it takes a very special man to accept another man's child. I never really knew what she meant by that until after she died. I was a widower when I met her, and I did know that she had been divorced from her first husband years ago. She'd never discussed the ins and outs of it, and I never asked. Anyway, I found out at her funeral, of all places, yes. Her son told me, her first husband wasn't his father, the son that is. Apparently, she'd had an affair while her first husband was away, and when he came home and saw the child, he just walked out . . . she never saw him again. My stepson said she'd always feared me finding out, and that really hurt me. I mean, surely after all those years we'd been together, she could have trusted me. And another thing that hurt, it was knowing that she had carried that

---

18   Costello, *op cit*. Some servicemen attributed their infidelities to wives and sweethearts back home, ie. to the same causes.

secret, you know, that fear of what I might do if I found out. I wouldn't have held it against her, honestly I wouldn't. But how could I tell her that... she was dead'.

Sometimes it was not so much the availability of sex but rather, the lack of it, that caused concern. Improved communications led to a perceived threat from black (sex) propaganda. However, Tokyo Rose proved such a sexy, uplifting tonic to Allied troops that steps were quickly taken to promote her broadcasts. One American, commenting on her husky voice, praised her inspiration to the men. She reminded them of what they were fighting for. The enemy provided bountiful supplies of porn material. These crude (supposed) images of service men's wives, engaged in some highly erotic acts of sexual depravity, somehow lacked the power to demoralise. Disappointingly poor, their titillation score rested at minus ten. But, on the bright side, they were a good basis for writing comic strips and, being entirely 'green', provided a reliable and continuous flow of paper for the men's room.

Espionage was practised by both sides. There was a prolific circulation of leaflets warning people of (bedroom) walls with ears and dangers posed by idle tongues. Sexpionage posed a more sinister threat, although Germany's World War II heiress to Mata Hari, proved something of a disappointment. Late one night on an English beach, a gorgeous blond appeared. Like Venus from the ocean she emerged, having sailed up to the shore in a dinghy paddled by her lover. Her demeanour suggested little appreciation of the suspicion that sea-drenched, high heel shoes might arouse in a rural, seaside town. At the station, an observant train-master rang the police. A quick search of her handbag found her in possession of a brand name German sausage. Thus, an otherwise promising career, was brought to a swift conclusion. (Costello, *op cit*).

Sexuality had a high profile during the two wars. But the author feels that biological explanations, although helpful to a point, offer little basis for understanding. The argument that in times of crisis people are inclined to confuse the biological signs, that fear can become 'sexy' may have some relevance. It may also suggest that, in a society which has long associated sex with violence in pornography, war provides an excuse.

In this chapter the author has adopted a relaxed approach to exploring the issues. She would stress, however, that, although in this context she has felt free to do so, this is only because her discussion has centred on sex between consenting adults. It is necessary to acknowledge that too casual an association of sex with violence can have terrible consequences. Feminists have for many years argued that assumptions about the sex drive often excuse or encourage sexual violence. The author adds that, despite all the arguments acknowledged in this book that add support to the biological view, she remains unconvinced. Her research suggests that sexual conduct during the two wars was driven by a variety of issues. These were based on entirely human motives which separated the emotional needs of men and women from the basic biological instincts of the sex drive. Below a participant recalls how he felt about his reunion with his wife:

> '*Paralysed, my dear, paralysed with fear. Frightened in a funny kind of way, of my girlfriend. I wondered how we would get along together after being apart for so long; whether we could accept each other because we had been apart for so long. I'll never forget that first day when I came back home and I was off to see my wife. I'd let them know that I was coming home ten days before I arrived. I'd sent word that I wanted to get married immediately and asked that they start organising the church and do, and all this. When I arrived at her door, I was filled with real terror. I was so terror-struck that I couldn't think straight. I knocked on the door and no one came. I stood there, I was unable to think. And I thought, 'well do I knock again, or do I go around the back. Well I stood there pondering for a minute, then I decided to walk around the back. Anyway, I knocked on the back door, and my mother-in-law-to-be answered. Oh, she was overcome to see me. She shouted my girl, my wife, and she came running down stairs, and it was wonderful. We had the first kiss we had shared in four years, yes, it was wonderful.*'

The extract above is like so many stories gathered for this book. There is no wild and lustful sex drive here. There is only love, tenderness and a desire to get on with ordinary life. On the basis of this, the author argues that sexual conduct during the two wars, although more liberal, was not motivated by people's need to 'empty' themselves. A need for love, for comfort, for security. A need to feel that someone, somewhere cares. A need to have a child. A child who will continue to live after you have gone. All of these explanations (and many more) offer greater insight into the issue of sex in war, than any biological explanations.

Chapter 6
Clogs to clogs:
How the two wars contributed to the decline of traditional northern life and culture

The conclusion of both World War I and World War II was understandably celebrated throughout the land. But such gay, optimistic reports diverted attention away from the fact that industrial growth in Lancashire was starting to decline at an alarming rate. The two wars had disastrous consequences for the county as a whole. Nationally, however, the impact was patchy and variable. The middle-classes were the long-term beneficiaries of Lancashire's industrial success. In comparison, during the periods of rapid growth and expansion, which were then followed by decline, the working-classes had existed in overcrowded, badly planned and socially deprived inner towns and cities. During the nineteenth century, men, women and children worked long hours. They had done so for a pittance and in appalling conditions. As a result, working-class people had became relatively skilled at dealing with the economic instabilities caused by successive and unpredictable spells of boom and strife. In this context, a strong and distinctively northern culture evolved. Ironically, it seems that this deep entrenchment in family concerns may have contributed to the present culture's reduced ability to deal with industrial demise and a need for change. This chapter traces how the two wars, and the economic instability of the inter-war years, may have contributed in the long-term, to this demise.

People, and indeed the groups with whom they interact, do not develop in isolation, but rather as part of a dynamic, interactive process between themselves and the environment. The two wars brought about many different kinds of loss, and for the most part we have explored these from a more personal, relational perspective in this book. However, wars change the social, structural and economic aspects of communities. Such changes shape, and are at the same time shaped by, the responses of those who are effected by them.

This chapter is a relatively brief one. It acknowledges the broader changes that came about because of the two wars. These changes are important because they added to the sense of grief, loss and uncertainty that people were experiencing at a more personal level. The chapter serves as a reminder. The message it conveys is, 'Don't forget that in addition to all the personal losses, people were having to cope with this little lot as well'.

The stability of the Edwardian period benefited all sectors of British society, including the population of the industrial north. But the brief influence of this prosperity may have eroded the working-class solidarity that had existed previously. It saw the birth of new generations of working-class people, who had largely forgotten, or indeed, knew little of, the harsh social conditions endured by their forebears (Dale, 1995). Working-class solidarity diminished. Divisions based on race and religious differences began to emerge. At best this was expressed in neighbourhood 'tittle tattle', at its worst, it caused minor outbreaks of violence. Such divisions are always regrettable, but proved disastrous in a situation where the bubble of prosperity was about to burst.

By 1913 Lancashire was facing growing competition from abroad. At the outbreak of war, high priority and wages were paid to those working in the munitions industry. This attracted thousands of skilled workers away from the more traditional industries. Some never returned, preferring to try their luck and fortunes in other areas. There followed a rapid decline in population, which created a 'knock on effect' for industrial development. Disruptions to the delivery of raw materials, coupled with a reduction in the availability of overseas markets, contributed even further to an economic slump. This accelerated as the war advanced. Social conditions rapidly deteriorated, but the crisis of war can divert attention away from wider issues. People expect to struggle, although this knowledge did not always prepare them for the reality.

Family life does not come to a grinding halt when war breaks out. Members have to be fed, clothed and cared for, and all this at a time when resources become increasingly scarce. Reports as early as 1914 conveyed mounting concerns about food scarcities. Many Bolton women were very distressed because they could not get flour. This was a crisis for poor families, because flour provided a base for cheap and filling recipes. Women were instructed on the one hand to 'be calm ladies'. On the other to 'waste not, want not' because 'this is no time for selfish buying in of great buy-ins of flour and ham for those who have money to lay out.'[1] People gained little comfort from appeals to 'look upon the crisis as a member of the community and not a private consumer of ordinary victuals and drink,' because, 'we must conserve all available food supplies to the best of our abilities, regarding the provision of the home as a sacred trust'. Too many at this time, had started to feel the pinch.

Many of the Bolton men who had enlisted came from poorer families. These found it difficult enough to provide food, even in peace time. Deep concern was expressed for 'women, children and babes in arms' who were experiencing extreme poverty, even in the early stages of war because many of the recruits did not have large wages to begin with.[2] However, despite these hardships, and in some cases because of them, people appear to have worked very hard to bind their communities together. This community spirit was commented on by almost all the older people who took part in this study, as were the food scarcities:

> *'People just did what everyone did. The only option that is open to every man* (person) *is to live through one day at a time, and make use of whatever they had to the best they could. I also remember that people helped each other a great deal. Then, as society became more affluent, and better commodities became available, we saved up hard for whatever we wanted. Food was scarce, and as there were seven in my family, I only had half an egg on Sunday. I suppose mum and dad had a full one. We could not afford fruit, but I make up for it now. But in our generation of war years the damage had been done to our health, via stodgy foods that would fill you up, hence a generation of arthritic joints, etc, that does not show until*

1   Report in the *Bolton Journal and Guardian*, War and the Housewife: A
     Practical Way in Which Everyone Can Help published on July 31, 1914.
2   The *Bolton Journal and Guardian*, August, 14, 1914.

you reach the more mature years. But some of us keep young at heart.' [3]

There is a powerful sense of survival. The story has a strong sense of immediacy and appears to ignore long-term planning for the future. Although set in the context of war, such short-term planning was a characteristic of Bolton life owing to the economic instabilities of the past. After the war, a short boom followed the declaration of peace in 1918. This was deceptive, and reflected more the optimism of employers than any real improvement in the market. Many believed that things would improve after the war. Migration of skilled workers and lack of investment in new machinery left Lancashire industry poorly equipped to compete with imports from abroad. Poorer families were hit very hard, and this could not be attributed solely to the difficulties some of the war veterans had when trying to obtain their war pensions. In Bolton's Nelson Square in 1920, the scale of the problem was publicly (and ironically) acknowledged, at the unveiling of the Cenotaph. The Duke of York had visited for the occasion. A Mr McQuire, who was then president for the local branch of the Discharged Soldiers and Soldiers Association, appealed to the Duke of York to:

> *"permit us, on behalf of the ex servicemen, widows and dependents of Bolton, to extend to your Royal Highness a few important grievances which are existing at the present time, and sincerely trust that you will exert your influence to have them remedied. We strongly protest against the Select Committee's decision on the 27th just, which will result in about 60,000 ex-servicemen being deprived of their out of work donations on July 31st and consider also that all pensions should be increased in proportion to the increased cost of living."* [4]

Many single women who had worked during the war found themselves unemployed. Those who had worked in more professional, prestigious areas were particularly angered by this situation. Determined to remain in the labour market,

3   62-year-old man, interviewed 1997, Christian Spiritualist.
4   'Ex Service Men Petition the Prince: Out of Work Pay, Pensions and Help for Comrades: Reported in the *Bolton Journal and Guardian*, July 30th, 1920.

they continued looking for work. The problem was discussed at length in one of the Bolton newspaper in 1919.[5] This article has been reproduced (see *Appendix I*). The reader is referred to it because it reflects the problems and prejudices that post war women had to endure. The tone of the article is humorous and 'chatty', but reflects unease for the 'modern' girl; for her freedom and financial independence. The article refers to her as 'a new breed of woman', meaning women who have 'forgotten their place'. It ridicules those who wished to stay in the more professional occupations, with its implication of 'having ideas above your station', and refers to the women as 'girls', thus playing down their adult status.

Despite the ridicule, the article also appears sympathetic. There is an acknowledgement of the women's intelligence and education. But overall, the women are presented as naughty, tiresome little girls. The housewives of post War I and II were significant because they were the role models for generations of women who followed them. Many women, having been given opportunities for greater responsibility, autonomy and respect, find it very difficult to fit back into traditional gender roles. This finding has been reported in other studies. Many of the nurses involved in the Vietnam War, for example, found returning home to work in civilian hospitals very difficult. They could not endure being subordinate to doctors after Vietnam, where they had taken far greater responsibility.

The close of World War I brought wide-scale unemployment for men and women. In a previous study, older women interviewed by the author remembered clearly the post World War I years. They gave vivid accounts of the poverty, the mass unemployment and the financial and emotional hardships suffered. Writers such as Orwell and Greenhalgh, have also captured in literature, the savage poverty and indignities endured. The first signs of serious economic decline emerged in 1920. After this depression, hopelessness and despair set in. Strikes broke out all over the country, some leading to outbursts of violence. During the General Strike of 1926, workers attacked a bus driven by undergraduate 'scabs.'

5   Article published in the *Bolton Journal and Guardian* in 1919.

Fearful that this might indicate the start of a complete breakdown in social order, possibly even anarchy, the government called in the Armed Forces, who began patrolling streets in armoured trucks.[6]

The Wall Street Crash of 1929 delivered a crushing blow world-wide. In the winter of 1932–1933, there were three million unemployed (a quarter of the work force at the time) in this country alone. Ten percent of the population were living below the poverty line and any incidental expense led to a shortage of food to eat. The dole provided barely enough to keep people alive. Access to any fund of help was limited and checked by the means test. To an extent, the middle-classes remained ignorant of what life was like for the poor, their misery being concealed in the dense jungle of the inner cities. In terms of quality of life, the middle-classes also had their standard of living eroded during the depression. Indeed, George Orwell suggested in *Keep the Aspidistra Flying* that the stress of having to keep up appearances could be just as demoralising as having to struggle without the 'essentials' of life.

However, despite these hardships, people were also enjoying some improvements in the quality of life. Technology had advanced. Most homes in the 1930s had electricity and gas cookers instead of coal or coke ranges. Housing also improved, even in poor areas. Indoor water supplies had become fairly commonplace. Gradual improvements in sanitation introduced a cleaner, pleasanter environment. Radio, newspapers and occasional visits to the cinema would be enjoyed, at least some of the time, by everyone. But even such improvements did little to ease the hopelessness of the Depression. This was summarised brilliantly by Ruby Valle in *Buddy Can You Spare a Dime* (Readers Digest, 1995a).

Back in the north, mining continued to prosper relatively well after World War I compared to the textile industry,

6   George Orwell (1933) The road to Wigan Pier. In: *The Conditions of the Working Class*, Hutt A, ed. Chapter 4. See also discussion in Constantine S (1981) *Love on the Dole and its reception in the 1930s* Literature and History of how *Love on the Dole* was modified to make it more acceptable to 1930s middle-class readers. Both sources discussed and cited by Walton, 1987.

which was the worst hit. The engineering and chemical industries were just beginning to feel the bite of recession. In the 1930s, however, developments in Japan delivered severe blows, significantly reducing Lancashire's ability to cope with the rapidly growing competition. During the harsh years of the Depression, hundreds of war widows struggled to support their families alone. At the same time, the war had given birth to another kind of 'widow'. The women who effectively lost their husbands due to mental health problems, the most serious of which led to a condition now known as Post Traumatic Stress Disorder. But a strong social spirit still prevailed. One woman recalls how:

> *'families supported one another more, an attitude to help as much as they could, a comradeship, a caring, ie. clothes passed down, someone would bake and share with someone who had only a little income. They would mind one another's children after school while the mothers worked.'*[7]

On the darker side; and in a culture where the 'bookie', the pub and the street brawl always added interest and spice to hopeless, dreary lives, crime and violence became rife. Rising unemployment in particular, increased the divisions in working-class communities. Different racial and religious groups blamed each other for the problems.

Participants in the author's 1994 study remembered areas of Bolton that were considered unsafe in the 1930s, where no sensible person would ever wonder alone at night. Such areas were covered by police patrols no less then four men strong. Some of these areas are known, even today by born and bred Boltonians, as 'spake azzi.' Some concerns about the 'spake azzi' were caused by acts of actual, documented violence. Other sources of fear were more imagined than real.[8] People 'spake azzi', inside, outside and about the 'spake azzi'. 'Tha needed ta spake azzi (speak easy) tha sia, lest tha cor overerd bi one o them.' Anyone and everyone 'spake azzi' (police included) because of the lack of

7   59-year-old woman, interviewed 1997; Methodist.
8   Translation of the original spake azzi (speak easy) goes something like this — watch out, there's a bobby about!

trust that developed for anyone considered different or as an outsider, during the Depression.

Because of 'scapegoating', religious affiliation began to take priority over class position. Once established, its accompanying bigotry, sectarianism and narrow-minded morality eroded working-class solidarity and the potential for powerful, political action. This highly judgmental tone of the time was reflected in cases such as the sacking of Bolton's union leader Albert Law in 1923. His alleged 'crime' was the somewhat vague accusation of engaging in 'immoral' conversations with his piecer.[9] The power of the Trade Unions was also eroded by the fact that fewer people had sufficient money to keep up their contributions. In the years between 1920 and 1930, workers in the mining and textile industries in particular, lost most of their bargaining power as a series of incidents, such as the failure of the General Strike, eroded their power even further.

The above discussion suggests only a partial impression of what life was like in Lancashire during the Depression. It is important to remember that many working-class people were law abiding, opposed to violence of any kind and did their best to survive with dignity. Large sections of the community strongly disapproved of drink and gambling. The Temperance Movement remained active throughout the years of the Depression.[10] Unfortunately, it is shocking and deviant behaviour, particularly of the so-called under-classes, that attracts the biggest headlines. During the Depression, these less attractive aspects of working-class life fuelled the conviction of some middle-class people, that the poor deserved to be poor.

Memories of these post World War I troubles made the British government anxious to avoid a repetition after World War II. Long before its conclusion, strategies had been implimented to prevent a second post war depression. During

9   See Walton, 1987.
10   This information was provided by informants who took part in the author's 1994 study. However, photographs taken by Humphry Spender, who took part in the Mass Observation Study of the 1930s, provide images of committed Temperance Workers conducting their affairs in various parts of the town.

the course of World War II, foundations for the Welfare State were set in place. Families were provided with food and vitamin allowances and increased access to health provision and education. A number of schemes were introduced to help demobbed men into the kind of jobs they wanted. Despite disappointments, on the whole these measures were invaluable. Millions of booklets were distributed to ex service personnel, giving advice on how to cope with their re-entry into civilian life. Each received clothing coupons to the value of £12.00 and a demob suit.[11] So there was a real commitment to helping people resettle after World War II. Unfortunately many of the problems were of a personal nature, not easily 'fixed' by public policies.

In the services, men and women enjoyed the benefits of further education and training, opportunities for those from poorer backgrounds which would never have arisen in normal circumstance. They were able to look for professional and skilled work that would not have been available before World War II. Many ex service personnel continued their education after the war, some graduating with university degrees. The Beverage Report heightened public morale. Now people really could believe that they were fighting for themselves and their families: for a 'Brave New World' in which poverty and inequalities would be eliminated, allocated to the past. Bevin, a committed socialist, placed housing at the top of his political agenda (Turner and Rennell, *op cit*).

Reports in the Bolton Evening News throughout 1945, reflect this commitment locally. On 29th August, 1945, Bolton Corporation announced its aim to build over 1 900 new homes over the coming two years. The next day, Mr S Townnoes of the Central Housing Advisory Committee announced a coming delivery to the town of temporary prefabricated homes.[12] Bevin and Buchanan, the two ministers for housing, did not need to start from scratch because the coalition had already erected 2 000 temporary homes, and there were 15 000 in storehouses waiting erection. Thirty thousand temporary homes were also coming from the USA with a further 5 000

11   Wicks, 1991.
12   August 28th, 1945, *Bolton Evening News*

from Sweden. One of these prefabricated homes featured in the *Bolton Evening News* on August 23rd. Situated in Bury, it stood in its own garden and it was full of the latest 'mod cons'. The proud occupants, who had been living in the house for six weeks at the time, spoke of how lovely it was to have their own home. The wife 'took me (the reporter) into the kitchen to show how she just had to put on an electric switch for hot water'.

For families who had lived in rooms, or overcrowded cottages, these prefabs must have seemed like a dream come true. They had fully fitted kitchens, gas cookers, spacious fitted store cupboards, a fitted sink and a gas boiler. They also had indoor toilets and baths; this at a time when most working-class households had to make do with a tin bath and an outdoor toilet. There were concerns expressed at soaring house prices. Prices for a pre war house had been around £250. Post war prices rose to around £1,000. A scheme was introduced to control prices.[13] Town planning improvements were not limited to providing homes. Throughout 1945, there was news of other health and environmental improvements, such as improved sanitation, drainage and drinking water. In the few months following the declaration of peace, families begin feeling very optimistic about post war Britain. Families were to be reunited, and there was the promise of a brighter future for everyone. Or so it seemed.

World War II had delivered another financial blow to the nation, costing Britain an estimated £120 billion. The cost in terms of human life, in Britain and the Commonwealth, came to an estimated loss of around 452 000 lives in the services, and a further loss of 60 000 civilians (Ziemke, 1994). In Lancashire, competition from abroad continued to undermine attempts to re-establish some of the older industries. Lack of finance and a motivation to invest in more up-to-date technology, further weakened the north. The country, as a whole, benefited from the brief economic boom of the 1950s, but by the late 1970s, the coal and textile industries were practically obsolete, and the engineering and chemical industries were rapidly suffering from a similar inertia.

---

13   August 21st, 1945, *Bolton Evening News* report on increased house prices.

Bolton has been badly affected, with a growing recession and unemployment that has soared from the 1970s onwards. The close knit family communities with their accompanying loyalties have had a mixed effect on the town's ability to cope. On the one hand, support from extended families has been invaluable for many people, particularly women. Part-time work with unsociable hours has greatly increased with the demise of the textile and clothing industries. However, family loyalties make it hard for younger people to break away, explore new options or learn new attitudes and skills. Greenhalgh stated in 1987 that the proverb 'clogs to clogs', has finally come to pass in the north.[14] As for the new Welfare State, we should be careful not to belittle or dismiss the overall, long-term *social* benefits that have evolved. But it did little to address, or indeed resolve, the problems of a more personal nature that developed within families after the war.

---

14   Clogs to clogs is a saying, and a rather moralistic one at that, that things
     go full circle in terms of success and failure. It is a saying that the author
     dislikes and does not favour, stemming as it does from the moralistic view
     that people who have ideas 'above their station', get their come-uppance.
     Sadly however, in relation to this discussion, the saying seems appropriate,
     which is why it was used as the main title.

Chapter 7
Coming home: A cause for celebration?

This and the following chapters discuss some of the difficulties encountered by World War II veterans when reunited with their families after the war. This concludes with a discussion of Post Traumatic Stress Disorder (PTSD) in *Chapter 10*. In 1980 PTSD was added to the American Psychiatric Association Diagnostic and Statistical Manual of Mental Disorders (DSM-111) (Friedman, 1998). Since then it has become the most common diagnostic terms used to describe the cluster of symptoms commonly observed in victims of trauma (Balwin, 1997). The accurate classification of this condition, and the development of appropriate diagnostic criteria, has done much to enhance our understanding of the short- and long-term impact of trauma. This has obvious implications for the development of appropriate support systems.

The evolution of our understanding and an acceptance of the existence of PTSD has been uneven. Not all victims of trauma develop 'full blown' PTSD, although most express symptoms to varying degrees. An established consensus of the types of catastrophic trauma that most frequently lead to its development include; witnessing or experience events, such as rape, torture, war, genocide and disasters (Friedman, *op cit*). However, its development in specific individuals is dependent on other issues that are complex and dynamic. The symptoms of PTSD are not always immediately apparent; they evolve gradually over time. Traumatic experiences filter through personal, emotional and cognitive processes that are entirely subjective. As with pain, people's trauma thresholds vary. These thresholds are multifaceted and shaped by variables, such as personality, past experience, gender and culture.

At this stage in the discussion, it is sufficient to comment that one of the variables that has led to the delay in a more sophisticated understanding of PTSD, is the time-lag between the trauma experienced and expression of the first symptoms. These time-lags may be delayed for years after the occurrence of the original traumatic event. Noting the complexity of this 'time circuit mechanism', it is useful to begin this section with an account of the sources of stress to which reunited families were exposed following World War II. It is hoped that the reader will gain a deeper understanding of PTSD, by the following the progression of events recorded in the intervening chapters.

After World War II, it was assumed that resettlement would be a relatively smooth process for most reunited families. The political climate was optimistic. Implementation of the policies that underpinned the new Welfare State started before the war ended. But the anticipated safety nets that were expected as the scaffolding for a more egalitarian society were put in place, were a bitter disappointment to many people. Official declarations of peace at the close of World War II were something of an anticlimax. This may have been due to the inconsistent information leaked from various sources prior to the declaration.

Hitler's death was announced on the 1st May 1944 and this was followed the next day with news of the fall of Berlin (VE day). Over the following days, fragments of information filtered through of celebrations and festivities throughout Europe. A German radio leak revealed 'the gravest hour of the Reich' (that is a complete surrender) and continued 'in this gravest hour of the German nation, we bow in deep reverence before the dead of this war. Their sacrifice places the highest obligations on us. Our sympathy goes out above all, to the wounded and bereaved, and to all on whom this struggle has inflicted blows'. Hearing this news, a head of the Gestapo stationed in Denmark reportedly 'went white, sat down trembling and began to weep'.

Despite the humiliation of defeat, many Germans were as relieved as the Allies that the war had ended. In Holland and Denmark, German soldiers wholeheartedly rejoiced in the festivities as people 'lit rolled newspapers for torches, flew the flags of the Allies and danced and embraced in the streets.' Stockholm to Copenhagen telephone lines were jammed by calls from thousands of Scandinavians as they rushed to contact relatives and friends back home for the first time since the occupation.[1] Reports on May 4th of VE day celebrations

---

1   *Bolton Evening News*, May 5th, 1945.

declared:

> '*Forty flood lights are today ranged in the Palace Yard
> waiting to turn Big Ben on victory night into a fiery
> pillar, symbolising a triumph for freedom. When these
> lights are switched on in a golden blaze, it will be a fitting
> colourful epilogue to the strange fantastic fairy tale
> atmosphere which has come over Parliament*'.

Fears of possible chaos during the coming months led
shopkeepers to fix shutters firmly over their shop windows.
In Bolton on the 7th May a huge operation was set in motion to
restore Bolton-based evacuees to their homes.[2] About 550
people were involved, 400 of them unaccompanied children.
The first scheduled to leave were 150 adults with children and
the intention was that they would back in London within six
weeks. These evacuees had been separated from their
communities for a long time. The apparent urgency to rush
them back left little time to consider that they might find
readjustment difficult.

Streets deserted in the heavy rain, displayed signs of
victory to the damp May morning. A night worker plodded
home from work. He was struck by the sight of flags flying
from the surrounding houses. Later, crowds of people gathered outside Buckingham Palace shouting 'we want the king'. At
3pm, the Prime Minister declared that representatives of the
German Command in Europe had signed an act of uncon-
ditional surrender. Overwhelmed by the news, scores of people
broke down in tears. Crowds at Euston Station froze as the
news was broadcasted over the radio (Wicks, *op cit*). The
autobiography of Andrews (1977) wonderfully captures the
spirit of Westminster at the time:

> '*Never before, or since, had I been in a crowd of the
> magnitude of the one now swamping every inch of
> London discernible through the deepening darkening. In
> theory I would have expected to find a crowd that size
> terrifying. In fact I found it neither frightening nor even
> wildly claustrophobic. As with all the crowds, all
> evening, it was too good-natured, and above all, too*

2   *Bolton Evening News* report of the evacuees, 7th May, 1945.

relieved, even for minor intolerance. The chatter, the laughter, the snatches of songs from hundreds and thousands of throats, rolled to and over our heads, like the rolling, roaring waves of a great amiably growling sea. Suddenly, silence. Suddenly, unbelievably, the lights of London came on. For a second or more, the whole crowd around us stayed silent. It was as if none of us dared trust our eyes, or even risk breathing in case the mirage disappeared. When it did not, at first almost hesitantly, the cheering started again, and then the cheers rose and rose in crescendo after crescendo'.[3]

Suddenly, after many years of blackout, lights flooded towns and cities. They blinded people. Children who had never known anything other than the Blitz felt stunned, enchanted and overwhelmed by them. But despite the initial jubilation, mixed emotions were beginning to emerge. The world had been dangerous and unpredictable. But people had become accustomed to it. Victory meant change and people were afraid. Following 8th May, streets began to swell with an army of drifting people. They were bemused by peace. They wondered aimlessly, hearts filled with a confusing blend of joy, grief, optimism and fear.

In provincial areas, such as Bolton, confirmation of the news took a little longer. On 8th May, local papers reported that:

'Bolton did its little best yesterday to make something of the Victory Announcement, but it was an unequal struggle. Never have so many people known so little about a vital issue. Confusion in the town as to which would be VE Day with all its repercussions, was so great that even after the radio announcement that today would be a national holiday, workers were still trying to confirm whether they should report for duty or not this morning, and children were visiting teachers' houses to find out if they were expected at school. Perhaps the biggest anticlimax of the day came at 3pm when crowds of people

3   Andrews L (1977) Chapter 9, pages 201–2 *No Time for Romance* Courage Books, Channel Islands .

*gathered at Victoria Square fully expecting some
announcement from the Mayor. The crowd waited
around for a while, then, as it became clear that nothing
was going to happen, gradually dispersed'.*

A thanksgiving service was held on May 10th, to
commemorate the victory when at last it was established.[4]
Such confusion could have added to the sense of anticlimax.
Some (reportedly) met the news with disbelief, followed by
smiles of relief. A banner hung over one family's door read
'Cheer up. Its grand to be alive'. Scores of families, however,
were not smiling with relief because having lost fathers and
husbands, the words did not apply to them.[5] One respondent
recalls:

*'There was very little support given to families left
without fathers, that I knew, other than friends and close
family. Not as we now know this sort of thing. They just
had to pick up the pieces and get on with life. There were
so many left in this situation, many supported each
other'.[6]*

For the children of such families, it must have been very hard
to deal with the loss of a father, when other children were
cerebrating the return of their own. Disillusionment set in
before the celebrations got off the ground. However, in the
days following 8th May, the people of Bolton had their share
of street parties and celebrations. Some continued through to
mid August, by which time families were reportedly full of
'smiles, tears and happiness' at the news that the men were
coming home. On August 16th, the mood of the town was
reported to be 'infectious with giggles that developed into
unrestrained laughter.'[7] There were parades across the town,

4   Article published in the Bolton Evening News, May 10th, 1945 entitled
    Victory Thanksgiving Service.
5   This motto was noted by one of the reporters for the *Bolton Evening News*
    who interviewed the families of absent men at war. Reported in the *Bolton
    Evening News* on August 15th, 1945.
6   This respondent did not include details of identity on the questionnaire he
    or she completed.
7   The author found these reports of 'unrestrained laughter' rather
    worrying. This is because it appeared from the reports in the *Bolton
    Evening News*, that this behaviour may have been due to hysteria rather
    than joy.

dancing in the street, bonfires in back streets and parties in the front streets.

Japan had yet to surrender. The Japanese appeared absolutely committed to fighting to the end. At the southern end of Okinawa, hundreds of Japanese soldiers and civilians had thrown themselves over the cliffs rather then surrender. Kamikaze pilots continued their devastating attacks on Royal Naval shipping. Finally and reluctantly, President Truman agreed to the dropping of two, newly invented atom bombs. He believed that the refusal of the Japanese to surrender could cost far more lives in the long-term. At the dropping of the Hiroshima bomb in August 1945 the Japanese exclaimed ('quizzically', according to reports) 'must be a new kind of bomb!' A few days later, announcements of the bombing of Nagasaki reported 'surrender in a few days a good bet'.[8] This news sent families of Allied Japanese prisoners of war into panic. They feared that their loved ones might have fallen victims to the bomb (*Bolton Evening News*, August, 15th, 1945). For maximum impact, the bombs had been dropped in quick succession.[9] This action was successful in that it finally ended the war. But the force of the destruction caused by the atom bombs, shook the world. This must have triggered other emotions that were associated with grief and severe trauma.

Optimism clashed with grief. The bereaved, who had no cause for celebration, had to endure the epidemic of loud, noisy festivities. Even those who had not suffered a bereavement must have found the clamour and semi-hysterical celebrations very wearing. The situation was not helped by the apparent lack of appreciation that such feelings might prevail. There were emotionally charged undercurrents in many of these reports. On May 7th, the *Bolton Evening News* had reported that, 'nowhere will VE day be more welcome than in the schools, teachers say they are finding teaching almost

8   In this section, the author wishes in no way to cause offence by either judging or jesting about the dropping of the two atom bombs. The citations above are accurate, and are reproduced to demonstrate how the devastation caused by them was underplayed (to say the least) at the time they were reported.

9   Woman aged 77 years and interviewed in 1997, discussed a young man who came to talk to her women's group about the bombing of Nagasaki. Unfortunately, she could not remember the details.

impossible. Knowing that there is a victory holiday near, the children are too excited to work and too full of war news to give their minds to anything else.' But, the emotional impact of nearly six years of war — almost a decade — cannot be wiped out by a declaration of victory and a few days of celebration. The report continues 'a contributing factor in unsettling the children, teachers believe, are the horror films of Belsen and Buchenwald'.[10] Tying these fragmented reports together points to a suggestion of mass hysteria among the population.

Reading such reports many years after the events described took place, there is a feeling that people had disintegrated into what Slevin (1991) refers to as *automatic pilot*. The term describes the kind of emotional detachment, the almost 'zombie' like response associated with crisis. People were now faced with the opportunity to digest all that had happened. Swamped by so many conflicting emotions, people became detached. As peacetime progressed, personal loss shifted to a more global appreciation. One veteran recalled that:

> *'After (the war) when you saw the effects of the concentration camps, and then, when you got home and saw the mess, and the lads who had been killed, all this, it was a kind of stepping back, to see the effects. In some ways there was more anger against the enemy then, than when you were at war'.*

The first troops to arrive home were repatriated prisoners of war (POWs). Yellow, sickly and emaciated, these men brought home with dramatic effect, the human price of war. Several of the participants vividly remembered their first encounters with these survivors:

> *'The Germans, the ordinary Germans, they had no beef with us, they didn't want to kill us, we didn't want to kill them. Yet, on the other hand, they seemed like us. I mean, it was better to be a POW with the Germans any day than the Japanese, but after the war we got a shock. When we saw some of those who had survived the concentration camps, they were just skeletons covered with a thin layer*

10   *Bolton Evening News*, May 7th, 1945.

of skin. Then you thought, well you had thought they were like you, then the shock when you saw that! But were they like you? That was the frightening thing!'[11]

The participant recalls his struggle in coming to terms with the fact that 'people like us' could be capable of such atrocities. The anecdote suggests a relatively easy acceptance that such behaviour is possible in those who appear different (the reference to the Japanese). But such inhumanity is more incomprehensible if recognised in people perceived to be *like us*. Earlier, we argued that the myth of the hero was built on very racist principles. Concepts that supported the desirability of population control for 'undesirables' had been a strong theme in the Eugenics Movement. This was as strong and influential in England as it had been in Germany.

Even taking into account the passage of time, the sense of the shock in the account is compelling. There is a jarring subtext. Remembrance of an enemy who was, after all, just like *us*. Perhaps there had been a desire at the time, to minimise unnecessary anxieties. Reports did little to convey just how badly effected some POWs were. On Monday, 21st May, local papers announced a series of welcome home parties planned for repatriated POWs. Initial reports were a little vague about what had been observed so far, but gradually a sombre picture began to emerge. Witnesses to the evacuation of camps in Tokyo Bay noted that the men were in a better condition than might have been expected. But some were so weak, they had to be taken on stretchers aboard the US Navy vessel 'Benevolence'. The survivors were malnourished and suffering from conditions, such as beriberi and dysentery. There was evidence of severe cruelty and neglect.[12] The information in this account is organised more consistently than the actual fragmented presentation of these early reports.

People were shattered when confronted with the harsh reality for the first time. Slowly, these worn out, demoralised ghosts drifted home. Having anticipated the arrival of the handsome, impressive man they had seen in uniform (and/or

11   War veteran interviewed 1997, aged 78 years.
12   Bolton Evening News, August 31st, 1945, *Hospital Ship Evacuates Allied Soldiers*

in photographs) some children rejected their fathers outright. Some were afraid and overwhelmed by their fathers (comparatively) huge stature, loud, deep voice and rough, hairy appearance.

After the war, there was a perceived need to get the men back into employment as soon as possible. In this way family life could return to normal. Given the traumatised state of many of the men, this assumption may not have been in the family's best interest. In the years immediately following the war, normal family life was considered in traditional terms. That is, mother at home, father as breadwinner. This is a very functional view of how things are. The author has recently conducted research on children and young people's perceptions of life and death (Kenny, 1998c). When speaking of the meaning of life, participants recalled what being a parent meant to them. The young man cited below, discusses what to him are the most important meanings of fatherhood. As the reader will note, the role of breadwinner is not mentioned at all.

> *'A dad is definitely to help bring some one else into the world, and to do your utmost best to make sure that they succeed in life. To give them all the love and care that they need. The things I liked about being with my dad when I was a kid was definitely going out and doing things, when we have a laugh or go to Blackpool or something. I think just being with him really. I mean my dad definitely was a good dad. I mean, you can relate to him, he's a real friend. So definitely I think, being a good dad is someone you can depend on. All the ups and downs of growing up, knowing that I could turn to him. Its difficult to say really, just being with him, just having someone to turn to.*[13]

The most important themes above are *being with* and *depending on*, ie. in the emotional rather then financial sense. These themes were identified by all members of the younger group. World War II war veterans had already been separated from

---

[13] Young man aged 24 years at the time of the interview. This material was gathered for the book *A Thanatology of the Child* (1998) but it is used in this context because it seems appropriate.

their families for some considerable time. The author argues that such men may have benefited from part-time work during the initial period of readjustment. This might have allowed them time and space to establish a relationship with their children. This is not to deny that many did succeed in re-establishing family ties, but the author is concerned here, for the large numbers that did not.[14]

Other men came home to find another man's child lying in the cradle. Private stories became public knowledge because of the innocence and honesty of children, some blurting out remarks such as 'we've got a new baby, a special one, he's black and all the others are white'.[15]

> '*I was too young to understand the reality really, only snatches of conversation, like 'he's been away 5 years, he's like a stranger to her, he's a changed man. Then of course there was the other side when women working at the Loco works found men in friendships while their husbands had gone away. There was always tales and gossip going around'.* [16]

Another participant recalled:

> '*I had no problems, but I know of children who did. Some did not recognise their fathers out of uniform upon their return. This caused a problem for both parents.*'

Some men found the rejections intolerable. They were met by families who were so overwhelmed, they could not bring themselves to look their men in the face. Others recoiled at the sight of the wounds.[17] Only one war veteran discussed disability in any length. From his account of a comrade who had suffered burns, however, it seems that even colleagues found such wounds difficult to bear:

> '*A friend of mine was burned terribly in one of those tank*

---

14   For a more detailed discussion of marriages that did fail, see Turner and Rennell (*op cit*)
15   Cited in Wicks, 1990, page 17.
16   59-year-old women affiliated to the Spiritualist Church in Bolton.
17   Such responses were more typical, although by no means confined to cases of facial injury, or burns victims in particular. It is also important to note that disabilities, particularly in this latter category, were equally common in civilians during the Blitz.

fires, so bad that he was discharged from the Army. His burns were terrible, terrible, I mean, a fine, good looking lad like that, had his looks ruined, and that would be with him for the rest of his life. I mean, I can't imagine that any woman would want him, so there would be no hope of marriage, of a normal life, because he was so badly burned. Oh I know it seems a terrible thing to say, but you could not bear to look at him, you know, we were glad when he was sent back, when he was discharged. We were his mates, and even we just couldn't bear to look at him, he was so badly burned'.

The participant's response to such injuries may seem harsh. But it is not surprising when we consider research into the attitudes of the able towards the disabled (disability is discussed further in the next chapter). Hospitals catered for servicemen who were too ill and too badly injured to be sent home. Repatriated POWs (some with arms or legs blown off) cried with relief to be home. Some had been denied decent food for so long and were overwhelmed when given a bowl of porridge (Andrews, 1977). Unable to face large meals or rich food, some actually died because they ate too much, too soon. Their stomachs had become too sensitive to cope with a large meal (Wicks, 1991).

As the VE day celebrations died down, the sense of anticlimax and demoralisation gradually deepened. At a more global and social level, there was widespread disappointment. People felt that the mechanisms required for the new Welfare State had not been implemented quickly enough. The change envisaged by socialists, such as Bevin, had provided motivation for fighting and imprisoned members of the armed services. For months, the vision of a bright new future had been the Utopia to which they expected to return. They came back to bombed out communities and demoralised, exhausted peers. Such a letdown had a catastrophic psychological effect on some of these returning veterans. *Chapter 3* discussed the harrowing landscape of war. Many veterans saw home as a respite, an escape from such terror. Instead they came back to a situation that was almost as bad, if not worse.

The effects of slum environments on mental health, identity and self-esteem have been explored by Conant (1962), who concluded that the economics and environmental ugliness of slums do contribute to the prevalence of crime and delinquency. Feelings of powerlessness, of wanting to escape, a perceived helplessness and lack of choice, also make significant contributions to psychological ill health (Seligman, 1975; Gilbert, 1992). Taking such research into account, it is not surprising — although not inevitable, since individual differences are important — that crime rates increased slightly after the two wars (see *Chapter 10*). Absent service personnel had been aware of the Blitz. But once again, fragmented reports had ill prepared them for the reality. As one World War II veteran recalled:

'There was shock you see, because I don't think that any of us had really understood what our families had to endure, the Blitz and all that. And to come home to it, oh it was a shock, to see everything bombed out. And you realised, and this came as a bit of a shock, that in many ways they had had it worse than we had. I mean, back home, we had some idea like, we knew that they were being bombed. But it was very difficult to comprehend what they were going through, especially when you had concerns of your own. But when we got back and we saw the effects of the Blitz, and we were talking to people, then we knew. But it was different, you couldn't really equate their experience with ours. We'd both had it rough, but it was different'

World War II differed significantly from wars that had been fought before. It brought about a state of total war, in which the risk to civilians were as great as for those who fought in the frontline. Six thousand civilians lost their lives in the Blitz during the winter of 1941, a figure that outstripped by far, the number of military deaths over the same period (Costello, 1985). Dismay at the extent of the damage was intensified when the new commitment to housing and rebuilding did not appear to be happening quickly enough. Economically, there was a short, sharp boom followed by a collapse of the financial system and mass unemployment. The Welfare State was not fully in place until 1948, by which time hopelessness and demoralisation had already set in. Ironically, many of the

changes that had been intended to improve people's circumstances, only made them worse. Service men and women who
had increased their levels of skill and education while in the
forces, were disappointed to find only menial jobs available to
them on their return to civilian life.

> *'Some of the men who had inside jobs before the wars*
> *(first and second) could not settle to inside work again,*
> *having been used to the open air, for up to six years'.* [18]

> *'When I left the forces, like many of my generation, I knew*
> *that I had to settle down back into civilian life, find a*
> *suitable career and try to achieve suitable qualifications.*
> *Naturally I missed the companionship of young people*
> *and disliked the more limited area of civilian life. I can*
> *remember feelings of annoyance and impatience with*
> *some people who had not been in the forces.'* [19]

Men, who had grown tired of the regulations and restrictions
of life in the forces, found that family life could be as much, if
not even more limiting (Turner and Rennell, 1995).

> *'Some men had enjoyed a more or less bachelor existence,*
> *enjoyed freedom to go out with pals every night that they*
> *were off duty. Some even got a buzz from being in danger*
> *and couldn't settle down to a quite, humdrum way of*
> *life'.* [20]

Some had also suffered a another kind of loss; the loss of self,
of innocence. Many felt that they would never be the same
again. They felt unable to share their experiences with their
families or even with each other (Dryer, 1990). Each of the
veterans who participated in the in-depth interviews, repeated
more than once that they were not killers. It was 'someone
else' who had done the killing. As we have noted elsewhere,
the requirement to kill runs contrary to western principles
that place a high value on the sanctity of human life. To be
forced to violate this taboo can lead to a compulsion to
relinquish or exorcise the 'killer' within. It has been observed
that this need to establish a new, less damaging sense of self

18   63-year-old male, affiliated to the Spiritualist Church in Bolton.
19   Ex serviceman aged 75 years when interviewed in 1997.
20   Female Methodist participant, age 73 years when interviewed in 1997.

can lead to some very unsettled behavior. War veterans may constantly change their jobs. They may move from one place to another in endless pursuit of a new identity — an identity that they can live with (Goodwin, 1987). The participants in this study noted this restlessness in World War II veterans.

Others developed an overwhelming desire to 'make amends', enthusiastically involving themselves in charities or community projects. Goodwin writes that some veterans become obsessive blood donors. Altruism helps ease the guilt of having taken the life of another person. Some, such as those involved in the formation of the American organisation, Vietnam Veterans Against the War, become active pacifists (VVAW, 1997). Such change can be the source of further emotional trauma. It involves letting go of ideas formally held so dear that the individual has been willing to die for them. The film, *Born on the Fourth of July* gives an inspiring analysis of how one ex combatant begins to question his support for the Vietnam War.

Some participants reported that they had little motivation for keeping in touch with other ex servicemen after the war.

> *'Friendships in that kind of situation are important, but they are not the same as they are in civvy street. Like, take the war, I made some wonderful friends during the war, but I didn't stay in contact with any of them afterwards. It was all like, in the past, we put it behind us. And, I know it sounds awful, but there were some friendships with some of the men who, like a friend of mine who was badly burned, you know, I've no idea what happened to him. And the terrible thing is, I don't want to know . . . you, its not that you don't care, but you feel that it would be interfering if you got in touch and anyway, you would feel uncomfortable. You just wanted to forget . . . there were so many things that you wanted to forget'*

The experience of travel, of encounters with people from other cultures, broadened the mind and outlook of service personnel. This led to yet further problems:

> *'I had changed my outlook on life altogether, and to be honest, that did create problems. I found myself getting*

very impatient with people back home because they were so narrow-minded, so critical of anyone who was different. You see, being away and moving around, seeing how other people live and all this, it does change you. You learn to be more accepting of people, more likely to let people be, if you like, to be what they are and not get on a high horse sort of thing if they were doing things that you might not approve of. Well when we got home, and I think this was the same for many of the lads, we noticed how people hadn't moved on in that respect. And the things that they got upset about, or what offended them, well to be honest, it seemed very trivial to us. But of course it wasn't trivial to them'.

The participant continues by discussing how the experience of war affected his married and family life:

'Its been a good marriage, for all the worries that I had. We are still together, and she's been a wonderful wife in every sense. But we didn't have what you might call a stable, traditional kind of marriage and that was partly due to the war. I couldn't settle you see, I was impatient and didn't really feel that I fitted in. But it was lucky for me, because I was still in the Forces, so we enjoyed the life that we had in the Forces, but there was a lot of moving around'.

Families who had coped in the absence of men (often with great difficulty) found themselves reunited with strangers. This dilemma of living with someone who is effectively 'lost' is similar to the problems faced by families who care for suffers of Alzheimer's disease (a form of dementia). The Alzheimer's Disease Society refers to this phenomena as a 'Living Bereavement'. Kastenbaum writes of the emotional impact this can have:

'It is not unusual for the spouse or child of an Alzheimer victim to express their own sense of being tortured. How unnatural it is to see the face and frame of a person they have loved for so many years, but to come up against a mind that has gone blank'.   (Kastenbaum, 1988)

Living Bereavement has been explored by the author (Kenny,

1989) in a study involving informal carers who perceived a personality change in their partners or parents caused by a chronic illness. She found that the term 'Living Bereavement' conveys very well the state of affairs that exists when two people who no longer recognise each other have to endure being together. They experience a bereavement that is not a bereavement in the way we commonly understand the term. The situation may have been worse if one of the partners experienced additional difficulties caused by such things as a disability, or suffered from PTSD.

When servicemen went missing (missing, presumed dead), this exacerbated some of the problems. Most participants spoke of the fear of every family that the telegraph boy might call to inform them of a death. This state of affairs might have triggered a process of 'Anticipatory Grieving'. The declaration of peace did not immediately solve the problem. In May 1945, for example, a Bolton woman was informed by the Air Council that her husband, who had been declared missing the year before, had now been officially declared dead.[21] A report of another man, reunited with his family, stated that:

> *'Even when a shipmate told them that their son had been killed, his relatives clung to the hope that he might be safe. After he had been posted missing 10 months, they received a letter from him, written in the hospital in Holland where he was a prisoner of war. Now he has come home among the repatriated, almost three years to the day when his ship, the destroyer Valentine sank in the West Shield.'*

Another report concerned the death of a man who had served in the Lancashire Fusiliers, leaving a widow and two children. This man had died on July 26th of the previous year. The deceased had three brothers, all killed. So this family suffered four bereavements in the space of a year having *waited* a year to be notified. The death of a POW revealed that he to had died over a year before he had been declared dead.[22]

As a participant in Turner and Rennell's (*op cit*) study

---

21   Monday, May 21st, 1945, *Bolton Evening News.*
22   Saturday, June 1945, the *Bolton Evening News.*

put it, 'we lived in a world of uncertainty, wondering if we were going to survive from day to day'. In such circumstances it seems understandable for people to enter a process of anticipatory grieving.[23] People begin anticipatory grieving when there is a strong likelihood that death will occur. Theorists such as Mulkey (1993) argue that once activated, it is only a matter of time before the next stage in the process, social death begins. Social death happens when individuals become alienated from family or community. They may still live in the biological sense, but socially they are dead. The person disappears from the thoughts of others.

Conversely, a person can be dead in the biological sense, but socially alive. Mulkey notes that Victorian mourning rituals, such as wearing symbolic clothing and jewellery, kept alive the memory of a deceased long after biological death had occurred. Social death then, has a fluidity that allows its placement on either side (before or after) of the biological divide. Mulkey further argues that social death at the present time is a gradual process in the case of older people. It is hallmarked by significant milestones in the life-cycle, such as retirement in men and widowhood in women. Entrance to a residential or nursing home suggests to all involved, that the resident is unlikely to come out alive. So the families experience anticipatory grieving, followed by the social death of the older person. The concept of social death that has been applied in other contexts by writers, such as Finckelstein (1995) who comments on how exclusion of disabled people can lead to their social death. The situation could not have been helped by the apparent lack of communication.

The veterans who came back from World War II did not feel able to share their experiences with their families and peers at home. It is not only the more negative experiences of killing, death and destruction that lead to such alienation. The armed forces constitute what Goffman (1961) has referred to as 'total institutions'. Briefly, this means that such institutions absorb the whole life (and indeed, identity) of those who are associated with them. Such involvement could sharpen the perceived in/out group boundaries between

---

23   Cited on page 115 in Turner and Rennell, 1995.

servicemen and civilians. The everyday concerns of those who had stayed on the home front, seemed (as one participant admitted) trivial to war veterans. Lack of a common goal or interest reduces the amount of meaningful communication that goes on between families and friends. Differences in perception and information gaps may lead to stereotyping of the perceived 'out' group. This, in turn, erects further barriers to interpersonal communication (Huzynski and Buchman, 1991). Talking is important, because it helps to bind people together:

> *Stories need communities to be heard, but communities themselves are also built through story telling. Stories gather people around them: they have to attract audiences, and these audiences may then start to build a common perception, a common language, a common-ality.* (Plummer, 1995, cited by Shakespeare, 1996).

Plummer writes of the need to find a common language. But when people have been separated for a long time, and have had very different experiences during this separation, then finding a common language can be very difficult. Sometimes, the sheer, perceived hopelessness can lead people to separate themselves further. Tajfel (1978) notes that if the boundaries that divide groups appear too sharp, too 'uncrossable', then members of each group are more likely to encourage behaviours that maintain and even strengthen such boundaries. This can be due, in part, to a need to maintain some positive identity. Such behaviour is well illustrated in the film *Born on the Fourth of July*. At the start of the film, the main character, played by Tom Cruise, firmly, aggressively and compulsively makes very clear his difference (and indeed perceived supremacy) from those who have not served in Vietnam. 'You don't know what its like out there' (emphasising ignorance) 'I've served my country' (emphasising supremacy). Such rhetoric is repeated time and time again by a young man who, due to his involvement in Vietnam, is a paraplegic. The film portrays a tormented man, who has a strong, vested interest in emphasising his difference. This serves as a strategy to help him come to terms with his disability (a case of, 'I might be disabled, but I'm still a better man than you').

Relationships are complicated, dynamic and diverse. Their success depends on many factors, including the expectations of those involved in them. Duck (1994) identifies 'shared meaning' as one of the most significant contributing factors in making or breaking relationships. Following this, Miell and Dallos (1996) argue that, if we are to understand relationships, then we need to understand the meaning that people assign to them. On what principles are a relationship based? What deeds or functions does it fulfil, for example, mutual interests, admiration, loneliness?

Miell and Dallos further comment that much of the previous research on relationships has neglected three important characteristics. These are, the degree of interaction or joint activities involved, their development over time and the functions of the relationship, ie. is it a friendship or an intimate sexual relationship? When considering any relationship, one has to consider what needs it fulfils and the meaning those involved attach to it (Weiss, 1974). These points are important for our discussion and we will refer to them again, where appropriate.

It is established that many veterans came home to communities that had evolved networks of care and support without them, and from which they felt alienated. Pulling together threads of a shared life that had been constructed on principles and needs that had existed before the war was difficult. For some it proved impossible. Most couples appear to have made a commitment to trying. But they faced discouraging odds. Men, who had been the unquestioned head of the family, found their authority challenged by wives who had grown used to their independence. When asked if people had any specific and important memories of the war, one respondent relied:

> *'Some anger — a love of country. Yes — my memories of women. They worked in factories, in the forces etc. I think that women as a whole saw most things differently after the war. I think this was an important step in women's independence'.*[24]

Some children greatly resented their fathers after the war. They had grown used to having their mother all to themselves

24   76-year-old women affiliated to the Spiritualist Church in Bolton.

and feared that their father might steal her affections. Servicemen, who had dreamed of a peaceful marital bliss, were disappointed when they discovered that wives and children could be untidy, disagreeable and downright noisy. The archetypal post war woman was not prepared to put up with being treated as a second class citizen. She had no ambition to devote her whole life to her children and her spouse. She had become knowledgeable about other aspects of her personality, and she was keen to express these. Many were anxious to hang on to the independence they had enjoyed during the war. A survey conducted in 1943 showed that as many as three in four working women hoped to keep their jobs after the war (Wicks, 1991).

Life was difficult enough having to cope with reunion with a stranger. Some, having grieved the loss of a spouse they believed killed, discovered that the latter had survived after all. Although most families welcomed such news, for those who had resolved the grief, the sudden appearance of their spouse delivered a terrible blow. Such a response should not suggest that the former attachment was shallow or insincere. To understand the response, it is necessary to observe how relationships shape identity. Widows, who took part in a study by Parkes (1972), reported their experience of loss as rather like a hole inside, or the amputation of a bodily part. It seems that significant relationships can become incorporated into a person's sense of self to such an extent that they are experienced physically as well as emotionally. To resolve the grieving process, a bereaved person detaches themselves from the deceased. Only then are they able to move on, to develop a new sense of self. It would be very difficult for a person to go back emotionally once this process has been concluded.

'My only recollection of such a problem, concerned a colleague of mine in 'the world of freedom' who for many years was I believe, unable to communicate regularly with his young Oxford graduate wife. When he did eventually return 'home' at the end of the war — it must have been a terrible emotional shock, because she suffered mental stress for many, many years afterwards'. [25]

25   Women aged 80 years when interviewed in 1997; Church of England.

> *'I remember a clever woman (who thought her husband killed) who had such a terrible shock when he unexpectedly turned up fit and well, that she suffered mental instability afterwards and his life was completely changed. And there must have been many broken homes and hearts to find another man or woman in residence'.*[26]

What is interesting about these two accounts is that, in each case, the women had a good level of education. Thus, level of education and possibly social class may have had some impact on a person's ability to cope with such experiences. The second participant quoted concludes her story by making reference to spouses who had extra marital relationships (this happened in cases of those at home or away).

> *'I knew one acquaintance who married a handsome Norwegian who left her at the end of the war. There were probably many similar cases, but also many happy marriages. The war jolted many ex servicemen and women out of their background and many did something completely different. We all missed the companionship of the Forces and many of us emigrated to find excitement'.*[27]

The participant ends her story by referring to the positive aspects of life in the Forces. Although the author has devoted a great deal of space to discussing the negative aspects of the war(s), it is important to acknowledge that for many ex servicemen and women, especially during World War II, the experience was not entirely negative:

> *'For some, who had grown accustomed to travelling in various countries of the world, and often open spaces, the return to the cold and wet climate needed much adjustment. Responsibilities and the discipline of life at home needed re-learning. 'People must change' is an adage which applies to so many situations, in work or domesticity. What about marriage? Many adjustments were necessary to achieve success'.*[28]

Many of the ex servicemen and women who took part in the

26 77-year-old Church of England woman, interviewed in 1996.
27 75-year-old ex serviceman interviewed in 1997; Roman Catholic.
28 76-year-old, ex serviceman, interviewed in 1997: Anglican.

study had very positive memories of their time in the forces. One remarked 'for some, Army experience actually broadened their horizons, making it easier to settle and a more enriched civilian life'.[29] Another veteran wrote 'I had no problems and enjoyed keeping in touch with people I has met in this country, in Europe from June 44 to June 45, and then in India, Ceylon, Singapore till May 1946'. For ex servicemen and women such as these, army life had actually enriched their experience, long term.' Another remembered:[30]

> *'I was very fortunate, the war gave me the chance to escape from what I regarded as a dreary civilian job. I was able to undergo interesting technical training in the RAF (which was of value in later life). I was able to indulge my fondness for aircraft, I met some fine people and made lasting friendships, and I served in exciting theatres of war (Normandy landing and the 14th Army in Burma — RAF support). There were moments of danger and fear, but there were not as many as I expected. Before I was 'called up,' I had grown accustomed to Air Raids in Manchester (we got used to anti-aircraft gunfire).'*

Conflict could occur because of service men's altered status once they returned to civilian life. After World War I this problem was not confined to Britain alone. Indeed, it probably made its greatest impact in America where the issues became compounded by racial prejudices. Black service men during World War I and World War II had enjoyed, at least during the war years, a limited equality in the forces. In France and England, Yanks were considered 'cool' and sophisticated, regardless of their social or cultural origins. Archer (1996) writes of black servicemen who, after World War I, discovered that although they had fought 'to make the world safe for democracy,' this democracy did not apply to them or their families. They were less tolerant of racial inequalities after their experience of war.

Such grievances led to an increase in the racial tensions that swept the United States. The Klu Klux Klan, determined to regain control of the situation, retaliated with violence. Within a

---

29   This respondent to the questionnaire did not leave any details of his /her identity or age.

30   Ex serviceman aged 75 years at the time of interview.

year of the war ending, hundreds of black people had been kidnapped, beaten, flogged, mutilated, murdered and lynched. No member of the Klan suffered retribution from the law for these crimes, so that disillusionment and despair became widespread among black Americans. Little wonder that, after World War I, so many flocked to the meetings of Marcus Garvey, the evangelical Jamaican, who preached black pride, that 'black is beautiful', and who advocated separatism and black power (Garvey's ideas, formed the basis of the philosophy of the Black Panthers). Having suffered similar disappointments following World War II and Vietnam, another generation of black Americans in the 1960s, flocked to hear the speeches of Malcolm X, to join his black Moslem group, the Black Power Movement, or the Black Panthers.

Overall, the experiences of reunited couples were varied; some adjusting well, some not so well and others not at all. Problems stemmed not only from changes that had taken place in the couples concerned due to separation, although the very different experience of those who went away and those who stayed was clearly significant. On July 16th, 1945, it was announced that the Marriage Guidance Counsel hoped to establish a centre in every town. It also aimed to become as professional as possible, drawing on the expertise of the clergy, doctors, psychologists and lawyers for advice. The counsel did not confine its work solely to families of ex serviceman and women. It was generally recognised that many couples; 'have been separated, and due to this, subjected to distractions that they would not otherwise face.[31] The next chapter will consider the effects that disability had on a reunited couple's relationship.

---

31   This announcement was reported in the *Bolton Evening News* on July
      16th, 1945. The announcement marked what must probably be, one of the
      first working examples of a multi disciplinary team.

Chapter 8
Disability, war and family life

This chapter discusses the extent to which disability may have had an impact on resettlement and marriage. Only one participant in this study discussed disability at any length, and the chapter, therefore, draws on mainly secondary sources. The author has tried to offer a balanced view that resists the influence of dominant, and mainly negative, social science theories of disability. It may be useful to consider these theories and, if they are relevant, they will be acknowledged. However, given that negative assumptions appear to dominate social science, the author has, instead, based some of her discussion on reasoned argument and speculation in order to achieve the desired balance. Of course, reasoned argument also needs evidence to support it. Throughout this book, the aim has been to set the war/post war experience mainly in the context of the north west of the United Kingdom and the author feels justified in drawing on her previous research. She relates the discussion to her previous research on older women's experiences of working in the textile industry (Kenny, 1994)[1].

1   In this study, the author was interested in finding out what criteria these older women had set when considering a marital partner. She outlines her findings below because she feels that important inferences can be drawn from them in relation to the discussion. The women emphasised the harshness of life and its unpredictability, before making responses. Their answers can be summarised as follows. When seeking a husband (and make no mistake about it, these women **chose** their men) they asked the following questions (arranged in order of priority). Will he be my friend? Will he be there for me and be willing to support me during the difficult times? Will he be a good father; will he take interest in the kids and give me a break from time to time? Will he be kind? Will he be a good provider? Non-acceptable expressions of masculinity included: men who spent all their money on drink or gambling, men who left their wives and children short of money, (these women expected and received, their husbands' *unopened* wage packet every week) and those who gave priority to time with 'mates' rather than family. Finally, those who could be violent. Indeed, although physical disability was hardly mentioned at all, during this and the current study, the effects of PTSD (most notably in relation to domestic violence) were frequently referred to. There was *no* mention (literally) of physical fitness, perceived attractiveness or of sexual prowess. On the basis of this earlier study, the author speculates with confidence

The women in this study (and their spouses) had led very harsh lives compared to contemporary experiences. As a result, they placed a high value on companionship and the sharing of goals in marriage. In sexual relationships, there were less (apparent) anxiety about attaining an orgasm and a greater emphasis on touching, holding and stroking. In other words, a 'good' relationship, from the perspective of these women, was about friendship, companionship and compassionate sexual relationships. This convinced the author that dominant ideas about what constitutes a good relationship change over time and across location. It would be wrong to assume that disability, in those partnerships where it did exist after the war, necessarily had a major and negative impact on a reunited couple. On the contrary, given all the other problems discussed, it may have helped bind them together. However, the literature suggests a more negative view. Cannandine (1981) writes that the risk of disfigurement in war is considered worse than being killed. After World War I, 1.5 million people were registered as disabled and the numbers were even higher after World War II because of the Blitz.

It is not just the disability that is important, but also the situation and conditions that caused it. War injury shatters the myth of the hero and reveals his or her vulnerability. The range and severity of injuries that are sustained in war are horrendous enough, but so, too, are the conditions in which they have to be dealt with. During World War I, ambulances staffed by a driver and one nurse (both usually women) patrolled the trenches for casualities. Braving shells and bullets from enemy fire, these teams gathered up as many of the wounded as they could carry. The Royal Army Medical Corps administered first aid in makeshift stations scattered on the outskirts of the trenches.

The most common types of wounds were those caused by shrapnel and bullets. These were often very deep, requiring

that, if the relationship had the potential to fulfill all the needs outlined above, then the effects of war injuries and/or disability were probably (relatively) negligible (that is, compared to say PTSD). Indeed, one of the women had been married to a disabled man for many years (although he was not a war veteran). She spoke movingly during her interview, of a very happy and satisfying relationship. This was because the couple had been such 'chums'.

surgery. Operations were performed in rooms that had been hurriedly prepared and were ill suited for this purpose. Surgical procedures had to be rushed because of the numbers of casualties coming through. During World War I, this could amount to as many as 10 000 a day during periods of heavy fighting. It is not always possible in war, to anaesthetise the patient. For example, Andrews (1977) nursed convalescent amputees in World War II whose limbs had been literally chopped or sawn off (using the sharpest and most suitable instrument to hand). The patient had been fully conscious throughout. Maggots were used to eat away gangrenous flesh, thus promoting healing. However, given the discussion in *Chapter 3* of the effects that the presence of rotting corpses had on the men, the author feels some concern about the psychological effects such a practice may have had. Maggots are associated with death and decay and as many of the men were so close to death, this practice engendered considerable revulsion. Many limbs were so shattered, they had to be amputated. In addition to the pain and shock from physical wounds, many of the men were confused and agitated from the effects of gas attacks. Others were mentally crushed because of what was then known as 'shell shock'. Many of the women who nursed during World War I came from middle-class, relatively protected backgrounds. Nevertheless, these women demonstrated extreme courage and strength of character. In addition to providing excellent practical nursing care, they drew on their rich social skills to calm and pacify terrified, confused men. They adopted a relaxed approach that departed from the more regimented doctrine which had existed previously (Channel 4, 1997).

The disabilities caused by such wounds are terrible, and are the type most commonly associated with war. However, the combat experience can cause other forms of chronic illness and/or disability later in life.[2] In such cases, it can be hard to establish the cause. Blindness, deafness and mental health

2   Relationships between illness and disability are complex, as are related discussions. There is insufficient scope in this chapter to do justice to the topic, but for readers who have an interest in this area, the author refers to Barnes and Mercer (eds.) (1996) text, for a more detailed (and indeed, better informed) introduction.

problems can develop over time. As modern warfare becomes more and more sophisticated, so too does the diversity of potential health problems and the related debates. Financially, such uncertainty can have serious consequences for a veteran and his or her family. If no clear connection can be made between ill health or disability and a veteran's combat service, then this can make it very difficult for them to claim related compensation and benefits (War Heroes, 1997; Airmen Memorial Foundation, 1997). Gulf War Syndrome is the most recent cause of debate. Troops who went to the Gulf were exposed to a variety of hazards, such as nerve gas and depleted uranium. They were given vaccinations, inoculations and anti-nerve agent pills without, some argue, sufficient regard for what the long-term effects could be. What such effects are long-term has been difficult to establish, as has the existence of 'Gulf War Syndrome' (Disabled American Veterans, 1997).

If we consider war disabilities generally after World War II, the situation was slightly better than it had been after World War I, when many disabled ex servicemen had been forced to beg on the streets (Wicks, 1991). Some provision and legislation had been implemented after World War II to protect the rights and standards of living for the disabled and their families.[3] Large numbers of ex serviceman also organised themselves into pressure and support groups, such as the British Limbless Ex Serviceman's Association. Risk of injuries caused by bombings and other trauma was not confined to war veterans during World War II, because of the Blitz. Since the two great wars, there has been a rapid growth of organisations devoted to supporting (disabled) war veterans. The largest in this country is the Royal British Legion. Founded in 1921, the Legion remains true to its initial aims which are; to promote the health and well-being of ex servicemen and women and their families, to raise and distribute money to support various incentives and to relieve hardship where it exists. Over the years, the Legion has diversified to meet the changing needs of younger and older service personnel.

3   This includes, for example, the passing of the Disability Act after World
     War II (Oliver, 1995).

'Housing 21' is one of the most recent incentives. This project provides small, reasonably-priced, warden-assisted accommodation for older, frail veterans (Royal British Legion, 1998).

The Star and Garter Hotel in Richmond, Surrey, opened in January, 1916. Its founding father was Sir Frederick Treves, then sergeant surgeon to King George V. His aim when he campaigned to have the hotel opened was to provide a 'permanent haven' for those ex serviceman who 'in the very flower of their youth, bedridden for life and by reason of their wounds, were paralysed and utterly helpless' (Star and Garter, 1997). Sir Frederick appeared pessimistic about the quality of life that could be expected for such ex servicemen. So the initial aims of the home appear to have rested on the principle of 'tender loving care'. However, the organisation has clearly benefited from the efforts of some very committed people over the years. At the present time, the hotel has an excellent reputation for care, rehabilitation and retraining. This gradual shift from care to rehabilitation and retraining, has influenced national and international incentives.

In Canada, for example, 'The Amputees Association of the Great War' (War Amps) was founded in 1920, by Lieutenant Colonel Sidney Lambert. Lambert was shocked by the lack of rehabilitation and retraining available to war amputees. From the very start, he was committed to founding an organisation that would fulfil such aims. The rationale was that such an incentive would provide every possible opportunity to live a full and independent life to war amputees (War Amps, 1996). Paralysed Veterans of America (PVA), founded just after World War II, commits to the same principles. In addition to rehabilitation, however, PVA also raises and contributes money to support research and education into the medical, social and psychological effects of paraplegia and spinal cord injuries (PVA, 1997). Despite the expansion of such organisations, many war veterans the world over, feel betrayed, neglected and discriminated against by successive governments and their local communities. At the time this book is written, Sheffield's 'War Heroes' are involved in a dispute with the local council, over protecting the value of war pensions (War Heroes, 1997). Disputes are common about whether the receipt of war pensions should or should not exclude a person from eligibility for other disability benefits. These decisions are usually left to the discretion of local councils, and considerable variations in practice and policy exist. Even resolving such arguments can lead to further disagreements about issues, such as defining disability and/or chronic illness and how disabling these are considered to be. Other arguments are put forward with respect to what constitutes essential needs (Lewis, 1997). At a practical and policy level, there has been an increase in the commitment to support disabled war veterans, although many would argue that such incentives have not gone far enough. But what about the effects war disability can have at a more personal level? Having completed this research, the author considers that the implications might not be as damaging as dominant social science theories on disability might lead us to suppose.

One participant in the study suffered a stroke many years after the war. His account makes a very interesting point. He argued that the stroke gave him permission to cry.[4] The man was quite certain that this had been a tremendous source of comfort to him. It allowed him the opportunity to mourn friends who had been lost in war many years before. This suggests a positive view of disability; that it can bring bonuses. Given that the theme of physical disability came up so infrequently in the data, the reader may feel inclined to ask why the author considers it a relevant aspect for discussion. First, she would argue that this gap in the data needs filling. The reader may consider, in contrast, the frequency with which PTSD **did** come up. The question posed is; Was disability a major issue for the partners involved, ie. would it have the kind of negative impact on a marriage that current notions about disability suggest? Much of the work in health psychology is negative about disability. Similar criticisms have been made of medical sociology by Barnes and Mercer (1996).

Psychology, sociology and anthropology reflect dominant, middle-class assumptions, regardless of how applied their approaches try to be. These assumptions have been challenged in recent years, from *within* academia by academic

---

4   The reader might note, the sense of 'agency' given to the stroke.

people with disabilities. The author would like to make the point that there are alternative voices, perspectives and interpretations. What can be interpreted from nothing?[5] Well everything actually! There are occasions when what is *not* said can be more important than what *is* said. Many older, working-class people in areas, such as Bolton, place different values and meanings on relationships. We need to question the degree to which dominant theories that explain the 'way things are' can be related to the experiences of reunited post war couples in areas, such as Bolton.

A second rationale for discussing disability is that, for some individuals, disability can be a legacy of war. This book looks at some of the practical implications. It is assumed that a substantial percentage of readers will be health professionals who support victims of traumatic experiences, which include those of conflict or war. On the basis of these concerns, it seems relevant to include such discussions. In psychology, the bereavement model has dominated discussions of responses to disability and this does appear to accurately describe the experiences of many people. Burns injuries and amputations are addressed most frequently in the war literature. Thus, our discussion starts by considering the application of the bereavement model to altered body image and research on physical attractiveness.

Berchild *et al* (1972) presented evidence in the 1970s, to suggest that physically attractive people are perceived to be nicer and more intelligent. He found that attractive people are more successful professionally and socially, and tend to achieve higher status jobs and promotions. This has been supported by more recent work (Adler *et al*, 1995). Thus, war injuries may have had an impact on some veterans' experiences of employment and/or opportunities after the war. It is also necessary to consider the dominance of the working-classes in towns, such as Bolton. In largely working-class areas, issues such as those discussed above would be irrelevant. Most working-class people in the town went into the local, traditional industries,[6] and issues such as promotion and professional status had no meaning. Physical strength and

---

5   The author refers here to the lack of information in the data on disability.

dexterity was more important in the heavier industries. There were, however, a variety of tasks that were performed mainly by disabled people in most areas, for example, cone cleaning in the textile industry. Even if a husband was unable to find employment, this might not have been detrimental to the family's finances. In Bolton, due to the patterns of labour that have traditionally existed, women were often more successful gaining paid employment than men. Historically, reverse role marriages have been very common in Bolton (Kenny, 1994). An unemployed male partner, who suffered a disability or impairment could even be a bonus to a working wife, especially if there were children.[7] Thus, in terms of career prospects and employment, injuries that influenced attractiveness probably had relatively little impact on a working-class family in a town such as Bolton.

Adopting a more personal view, however, any blemish or change in body image, whether it be moral or physical, can cause feelings of self-staining or tarnishing (Goffmen, 1963; Donovan and Pierce, 1976; Emerson, 1983). In cases of severe deformity, especially burns, some victims never resolve the grief they feel, although they may be capable of re-entering society to live ordinary lives (Bernstein, 1976). Society values normality on the one hand, while on the other, there is an expectation that traumatised individuals should do everything possible to rejoin mainstream society, despite any problems they may encounter when trying to pass as 'normal' Edgerton (1963).

Altered body image, caused by trauma, has a greater emotional impact than anticipated changes in physical appearance due, for example, to the effects of ageing. Rapid, unpredicted changes in physical appearance, do not allow the individual time to adapt. The established perception of self is somehow 'left behind' when the alteration is instantaneous, and the present reality is difficult to comprehend, let alone accept (Salter, 1988). Some individuals may experience a loss

---

6   The author acknowledges that working-class people in Bolton benefited as they did everywhere else from the World War II post war incentives in education and training that did lead to more upward social mobility.

7   This assumes that the impairment would not be so great as to prevent the male partner from helping out in the home.

of self (Emerson, 1983). People need time and support if they are to develop an acceptance of the alterations in their physical appearance.

In 1962, Richardson (cited by May, 1988) found that disabilities could be ranked according to a hierarchy of acceptance, with facial injuries occupying the bottom rank. Some of the facial injuries suffered by victims in London during the Blitz were so horrifying, the nursing and medical staff would not allow the victims to have mirrors. Surgical basins were kept out of sight until at least some of the damage had healed. In all cases of disfigurement, but particularly with facial disfigurement, patients had to be psychologically prepared before they saw their image in the mirror for the first time after the injury. Given that responses to altered body image can be quite intense, these precautions by the nursing staff were probably very wise.

Any condition affecting the skin can be very demoralising, diminishing self-confidence, self-steem and the person's ability to develop a positive body image (Hitchens and Creevy, 1988).[8] May (1988) considers burns injuries to be the most catastrophic of all. The prognosis for burns cases is still relatively poor compared to that of other injuries.[9] War veterans who suffered burns injuries will have suffered particular problems, and not just because of the cosmetic implications. The skin is the largest organ of the body and damage to it often leads to other forms of dysfunction. The depth of the wound plays an important role. Partial thickness burns may leave unsightly scars and restrict the elasticity of the skin in the effected part, but they rarely cause the same degree of skin contraction as that caused by a full thickness burn. The latter can lead to skin shrinkage, severe deformity and loss of function in the affected limbs. Burns can also lead to loss of sensation. This can be particularly tragic given that many people desire physical contact and touch (Lindsay, 1988).

8   One of the major sources of stress can be that skin disorders prevent
     sufferers taking part in social activities such as swimming.
9   This is because advances in modern drugs and treatments, have caused
     more and more people to recover (or nearly recover).

So often when we think of war, we associate it with the loss of life. As the author has argued, loss associated with biological death is only one form of bereavement that can be experienced. Responses such as denial, anger and hopelessness, are common in people whose body image becomes altered due to illness or trauma. Hull (1990) writes in 'Touching the Rock' of how he grieved for nearly five years when he lost his sight. Other writers question the application of bereavement models' to all cases of disability (Dobbs, 1993). Nevertheless, there is much to suggest that altered body image can trigger emotions associated with loss, trauma or a person's knowledge of their own impending death.[10] People who have reflected on their experience of coming to terms with disability, describe similar progresses. The course of the sequences or steps are not absolute or universal. Some people miss a stage entirely, while others may become 'stuck' at a specific stage and remain there for years, sometimes for the rest for their lives.

The most commonly reported response to a prognosis that devastates the person, is that of denial. The person may vow to themselves that they will prove the experts wrong. They may convince themselves that there has been a mistake, a misdiagnosis. Denial is a very effective coping mechanism. It disrupts the process of emotional break- down that might otherwise cause a person to 'snap'. Denial indicates that a person is unable to cope with reality. Fantasy often follows denial. Again, this is an entirely functional defence mechanism, providing hope at a time when the person lacks the emotional resources to cope with hopelessness. The person spends many hours daydreaming of a miracle cure, or of some unexpected act of fate that will change the situation. Fantasy provides a psychological 'safe base' to which the person can retreat once in a while, as he or she shifts towards an acceptance of reality.

This has to be a gradual process. The person needs strong emotional reserves upon which to draw if they are to cope with the stages that follow. These include depression,

---

10   Kubler Ross (1969) identified grief reactions in terminal patients, such as
        denial, anger, depression, bargaining (eg. I might get a second chance if I
        stop smoking now) before they are capable of accepting their fate.

hopelessness, anger and bitterness. These are painful and emotionally wearing. But some people cannot proceed to cultivate a different self-image, or do not have the level of rationality to set new goals for themselves, until they have worked through the earlier stages. Some people never resolve their grief, or they may resolve it in some areas of their lives but not others.

The psychological effects of a disability will be influenced by the extent and nature of that disability. Lovering (personal correspondence, 1998) notes that loss of a body part provokes deep grieving. Having a body that is 'whole' (even if parts are impaired) can provide some consolation. He notes a conversation he once had with a colleague, an amputee. Lovering had suggested that the two of them were more or less in the same boat (Lovering is a paraplegic). The colleague responded 'but your legs are there! You and others can see them and touch them. Mine are gone forever'.

Lack of adequate rehabilitation was one of the biggest problems facing World War II amputees. Some were discharged home within minutes of having shown that they could just about walk with the new prosthesis provided (Wicks, *op cit*). Such individuals were not given sufficient time to adjust and, therefore, experienced unnecessary mobility problems. These difficulties could be misinterpreted as evidence of malingering. When out and about and dressed in long trousers, an amputee might present with little more then a slight limp. Phantom limb pain was present in about 90% of amputees at this time (Critchley, 1950). Things have not improved much over the intervening years. The proportion of amputees who complain of phantom limb pain at the present time is still very high. How long it persists following the amputation varies from between two to seven years. Treatment therapies to ease the pain are depressingly ineffective. In 1988, Melzak and Wall wrote of phantom limb pain:

> *This pathetically low success rate (that is in pain management) reflects the extent of our ignorance about the mechanisms that underlie phantom limb pain.*

So some amputees, and this is still the case, may have suffered pain that was neglected, ignored, or treated by doctors who had little understanding of it. However, not all phantom limbs cause pain. Indeed, the existence of pain-free phantoms is reported by a large number of amputees immediately after surgery. The limbs are experienced as a tingling sensation. They seem identical, in terms of weight, etc, to the limb that has been amputated. The experience of this type of phantom limb usually fades over time. But in the few weeks after surgery, its presence can be put to good use. According to Melzak (1992), the process of helping an amputee become accustomed to a prosthesis can be greatly improved by encouraging the patient to think of the latter as a sock or glove that they are using to clothe the phantom limb.

Lovering (1998) suggests that military personnel may be more inclined to develop a poor self-image if they become disabled. Physical fitness tends to be revered more in a military context than in any other. Conversely, if the disabilities are the result of an act of bravery, the person can take great pride in them. Here again the question of meaning is important. Given that the experience of pain is very subjective and shaped by meaning, we can make inferences from studies of pain perception. Beecher (1959) was dumbfounded by the lack of pain in the affected area reported by many severely wounded World War II soldiers. Only one soldier complained of pain so severe that it required morphine. The soldiers were not suffering from shock, nor were they totally immune to pain, since they complained of it in other areas of the body. Beecher concluded that the lack of pain in these men was probably due to relief that they had escaped the combat situation with their lives. Another study with wounded Israeli soldiers conducted by Carlen *et al* (1978) reported similar results. These men were more concerned with guilt (because they felt they had let their comrades down) than with pain from the injury. Thus, things like 'survival guilt' or, conversely, relief at being alive, or the belief that the injury is a visible 'proof' of an act of bravery; all of these will have an influence on how the person perceives and adapts to his injuries. Finally, the degree of commitment a soldier has to a military career, and/or to what extent he may have been influenced by the military culture will also be influential.

In his discussion of how attitudes towards the disabled have evolved over time, Barnes (1996) begins with Ancient Greece. This was a society based on a military culture that placed great value on physical fitness. There was harsh intolerance towards any degree of imperfection and this carries a legacy into the military services and to athletes of today. Athletes also, in Lovering's experience, tend to be more severely effected by disability, because who they are is reflected in what they do. He notes that 'if a person's self-image was developed around what he or she is rather than who he/she is, then when that 'what' is destroyed or altered, the self-image collapses'.

Responses to war injury may differ between volunteers and those who base their life on a career in the military. We now turn our discussion to a consideration of the effects injury or disability may have on a war veteran's sexual relationships. Vietnam nursing veterans interviewed by Norman (1990) were very sensitive to the impact disfigurement could have on the young men for whom they cared. A nurse described the case of a young combatant who had lost an eye. The young man appeared well-adapted and in good spirits. One night he had difficulty getting off to sleep. So he asked his nurse to play cards with him. The two played for a while then, quite out of the blue, the soldier asked the nurse to give an opinion. Did she think, he asked, that he would be more attractive (to women) if he had an artificial eye? Or did she think he should wear an eye patch? He was to be discharged very soon. Once home, this young man wanted to do all the things that his peers did, including, of course, dating. This young man desperately wanted to be handsome again.

Owen's poem 'Disabled' powerfully conveys the impact war injuries can have on a veteran's sexual identity. For the solider depicted by Owen, the sight of a beautiful, desirable women is the source of remorse and intense frustration. This image is, for him, little more than a cruel reminder of what he can no longer ever hope to have. The author was struck by the themes of failure and punishment prevalent in this poem. She feels that it highlights how much the poet had been seduced by the myth of the hero. Did Owen privately despise this man, this *failed* military hero? Lovering (*op cit*) writes:

> '*most of us with any degree of sex drive want to be desired by the opposite sex, but it seems that men in particular are less able to see beyond the bodily flaws to the person beneath. My disability was not a factor in my after-polio courting. However, it could have been if my woman had looked at the mess of a body that I now live with and had not seen the person inside. A woman can crush a man and a man can crush a woman with his or her rejection on the basis of the body beautiful.*' He continues '*I have little exciting in a man's eyes to offer a woman, but I want to believe that I'm sexually attractive because I want to offer the woman I love that part of me that is sexual and desirable*'.

It could be said that, to a point, there now exists a greater sensitivity and acceptance of disabled people's sexuality, although negative attitudes and prejudices still abound (Shakespeare, 1998). There are still strong assumptions in some sectors that people with disabilities are asexual. Galler (1993) writes of a disabled woman who was admitted to hospital complaining of abdominal pain. An emergency appendectomy was performed, but the pain continued after the surgery. Further investigations revealed that the women was suffering from a sexually transmitted disease. This possibility had not occurred to the nursing and medical staff. They assumed that because of her disability she probably did not have a sex life. In recent years, there has been an increased commitment to the development of knowledge on sexuality and disability. This has led to some interesting challenges to dominant assumptions about sexuality. People who have lost parts of the genitalia, for example, may experience orgasm in the phantom limb (for example, a phantom penis (Melzak, 1992). Paraplegics and quadriplegics report experiences of orgasm in a variety of bodily parts (Wendall, 1992).

Although such work may be interesting and important, the author feels concerned by the dominant interest in the orgasm. She recognises that this is important, but challenges the, apparently dominant, view that this is all that sexuality is about. In a comparative study of texts on sexuality, Kenny examined the discourses in those written *for* 'normal' people versus those written *about* the sexuality of people with learning disabilities. She came to the conclusion that the discourses in both texts were not concerned with sexuality at all but rather, the management of orgasm.[11] To attain this, the sex act was recommend for 'normal' people, masturbation for 'abnormal' people (Kenny, 1992).

If we go back to a consideration of what impact disability might have had on families in Bolton, here again the author's 1994 study is useful. Everything, especially sexuality, has to be understood within the social and historical context in which it occurs. Working-class families in Bolton, well after the post World War II years, tended to have fairly large families. They lived mainly in tiny, two up, two down, overcrowded cottages. They also worked long hours, coming home sometimes so tired that they were unable to eat. Thus the opportunities and the energy for a couple to enjoy sex did not occur frequently. There was also a lack of knowledge about sexual technique compared to contemporary standards. Indeed, two of the older women told the author informally that they had spent most of their adult lives unaware of the fact that a woman could, or indeed should expect an orgasm.[12] When these women discussed intimate relationships with their partners, they talked of kissing, holding and stroking. Accounts of the tin bath placed in front of the fire were particularly moving. The women reported immense satisfaction at having their backs rubbed by a partner and of returning this courtesy. The author is not advocating a return to such social conditions, or to a lack of knowledge about sex. The question she poses is, did injury or disability affect the sexual relationship? It is always hard to make assumptions, especially without specific data to support them. When making such assumptions, it is always necessary to consider differences within groups. On the basis of the discussion above, the author takes the position that injury or

11   That is, as the author understands sexuality in its broadest sense.
12   The author notes that there were differences between the younger and older women's discussions on sexuality. This knowledge was disclosed by two women in their early eighties, interviewed between 1989 and 1991.

disability probably did not have a major effect on sexual relationships.

How might disability have had a broader impact on a reunited couple? The reader may recall the important characteristics of relationships discussed earlier. These included, interaction, development over time, the nature of the relationship and the needs it fulfils. Lovering (1998) writes that 'the institution of marriage suffers from the buffeting of the waves in the 'sea of life'. It is a fragile frigate whose strength depends on what materials were used in its construction, the quality of the construction, the size and frequency of the waves and the swells it must withstand'. This assumes that partnerships based on flexibility, strength of commitment and compromise have greater potential to last. But what happens when the stress becomes too great? Or if it develops along a lifespan course that runs contradictory to what both the partners involved anticipated?

Many couples might be prepared for gradual impairment and disability, considering these inevitable in the course of ageing. Such changes may be less acceptable for a young couple? What happens when the presence of a disability reduces the degree of social interaction for both parties? Or when the nature of a relationship changes from one of partnership, to that of dependence? And all this at a stage in life when neither partner had been prepared for it, and when pressures, such as young children, establishing a home etc, pose problems for most couples? Again, we must be careful not to be influenced by common-sense assumptions. In a study of psychological adjustment following disability brought about by polio, Halstead (1988) found that the younger the person when affected, the more able they were to make positive adjustments. Campell (1996) has noted that there is a general dearth of knowledge in the social sciences on the impact of disability at different stages in the life course.

Problems can emerge even if a disability is present at the start of a relationship. Ivie (1991) identifies the 'Florence Nightingale Syndrome' (that is, the assumption that the able bodied partner should take sole responsibility for care) as one of the most lethal stresses which can damage the success of a relationship. Of her experience of caring for her disabled husband, she writes 'I found myself becoming more and more resentful of his disability and misplaced my anger on to him as if it were his fault that he couldn't move. We were both frustrated and angry with one another most of the time'. She continues 'After five years of sleepless nights and endless demands on my time, I became so burned out that I ran away and I never came back'.

Of her caring experience, Blackmun (1991) also writes 'those caregivers who sacrifice everything for the needs of their husbands or wives, often end up in a cocoon of despair'. The 'Social Model of Disability' proposed by many disability theorists, challenges the assumption that disability inevitably leads to problems such as those discussed above. From this perspective, social isolation, for example, results less from the presence of disability (for both partners in the case of marriage) than it does to the presence of variety of social barriers. Much of the work in psychology has focused on the limitations that can be a consequence of disability.

But when we consider what adjustment must have been like for disabled veterans after the two wars, in the context of traditional working-class life in a town such as Bolton, none of the dominant social science, negative approaches seem relevant. Disability need not necessarily have influenced the family financially, even if the veteran was unable to work. His wife may well have sought and indeed successfully found, paid employment. In such cases the presence of a full-time father (as opposed to a full-time mother) may have been positively welcomed by the wife.[13] Unless the wounds had been very severe, it seems unlikely that perceived attractiveness would not have been an such an issue. When informal full-time care was necessary, extended families (until very recent times) would help lighten the responsibility (Kenny, 1998a).

13   Having been brought up in an extended family in Bolton, one of the things that astonished the author most when she came into academic life, was the assumption; first, that children had a single mother figure to relate to. The author grew up relating to multiple mother figures. Second, the assumption that mothering is always and could only be provided by a woman. One of the author's most significant 'mothers' was her maternal grandfather. This reflected a general pattern in the town. Unemployed and retired men frequently provided 'mothering' in the author's childhood community.

Considering all of the points made, it appears that the picture for many disabled servicemen and their families in Bolton might not have been as bleak as dominant psychological theories might lead us to suppose. Indeed, this might be the case for couples in other areas. Some participants in Wick's study reported that the husband's disability led to a closer relationship developing.[14] Learning to adjust may have presented greater challenges. But it also led to greater satisfaction and, indeed, increased the degree of shared activity. Some couples felt that this helped to bind them together. In such cases the relationship become more, rather than less secure. Sometimes, conditions that would normally lead to a restricted life, low self-esteem, and feelings of inferiority, have the reverse effect.

The presence of a disability may lead to, what Adler (1966) referred to as, a *will power*. This can lead to the development of charismatic personalities, such as Simon Weston (1985) who was severely burned during the Falklands War. Such individuals are successful in terms of their own achievements, and also help to inspire others. But their presence can also cause even greater feelings of inferiority and indeed, greater discrimination against those who fail to 'make it against all odds'. Disability, therefore, can bring mixed blessings to families.

To conclude the two chapters on resettlement, reunion could be difficult for many families after the war, but it would be wrong to assume that this was always the case. Difficulties arose because people needed time to get to know each other again. Children could feel resentful towards their fathers; past infidelities if discovered could lead to rejection. It appears that disability did not necessarily lead to problems. Ex servicemen and women sometimes missed their time in the forces and sometimes felt let down, demoralised or restless once they came home. Indeed, according to some post war reports, there were those who felt a little envious about missing out on the action. Few cases could be as tragic as the seventeen-year-old Bolton youth who was so upset because his parents prevented

14   Wick's study focused mainly on the experience of couples reunited in
      London.

him from joining the Army that he shot them, then took a hammer to smash in their heads.[15] This happened in July, 1945, by which time many war veterans may have been discussing their positive as well as negative experiences. It appears from this study that the positive aspects of service life were remembered and enjoyed by men and women. As one ex service woman below recalls:[16]

> *'The war was a hard time for families who lost relatives. I did not lose anyone very close and I found the war years interesting and exciting, in spite of living through the Manchester Air raids. My years in the Forces were full of incident and I was sent abroad, thus fulfilling an ambition. I would also say that in the Forces, we met all kinds of people, some of who are friends to this day'.*

Although such experiences could make it hard for some to settle into civilian life, for the majority the skills, knowledge, friends and contacts abroad (acquired while in the forces) continued to enriched the remainder of their lives.

15   *Bolton Evening News*, Monday, 9th July, 1945.
16   Ex service woman aged 75 years at the time of interview.

Chapter 9
Good mothers and bad mothers: The birth of mumtology following World War II

Regardless of marital status, women were encouraged to work outside the home during the two world wars. Indeed, refusal to take up employment from September 1941, for single women without children meant the risk of imprisonment. Following 1945 there was a change in philosophy and women were expected to return to their 'natural place in the home'. Responses to this attitude were mixed and, of course, there were regional differences. In the north of England, for example, paid employment was still fairly abundant. Labour shortages in some sectors, dampened the enthusiasm which encouraged working-class women to adopt a more middle-class lifestyle and become full-time mothers.[1] Social class was important. For many working-class families, the idea of having 'mum' at home full-time may have seemed like a dream come true. The Labour Unions (and this included men and women) had, for years, fought for a living wage that would make this possible (Segal, 1990).

Full-time paid employment is much less attractive, when it takes place in a dusty mill, or a filthy pit. However, the greater emphasis placed on mothering did carry bonuses. Most significant, in the opinion of the author, it led to the genesis of a voice and identity for women that had a powerful impact on the pacifist movement. Collectively, this reached a peak in United States in the 1960s, with the Women's Strike for Peace Movement (Thompson, 1983; Stoltenberg, 1990; Swerdlow, 1993).

This chapter considers, briefly, the impact that the growth of the new child care professionals had on the lives of women and their children. First, it considers the work of writers, such as Bowlby (1965) and the influence this had on policy and practice in health and social services. This is

1   Working-class women were encouraged to adopt middle-class attitudes,
     regardless of whether or not this fitted in with the ordinary, everyday
     practicalities of their lives.

followed by an appraisal of how the 'invention' of motherhood as a valid knowledge catagory (note, not just practice) could be quite empowering for women.[2]

Taken together, the two wars had increased the possibilities for a more equitable relationship between the sexes. Women learned that they were capable of performing traditionally male tasks. And they were able to compete in the masculine world of work, in addition to running a home (Costello, 1985). More relaxed attitudes towards sexuality also developed, although there were peaks and troughs in its celebration. Sexual liberation went out of fashion somewhat in the 1950s, replaced by the desire for a more traditional family life.[3] It would be wrong to assume that a conspiracy theory inspired by a return to the traditionalism came from government, or economic concerns. A broad swathe of opinion widely supported popular assumptions that the sexual divisions in marriage reflected attainment of the 'good life.' Tradition appears to offer a sense of security. The author has observed that the move towards traditionalism appears strongest during periods of relative instability. After World War I, for example, traditional values were considered beneficial during (and perhaps because of) the Depression.[4] Following World War II the gradually shift back to traditionalism was due to more diverse factors, including the invention of an idealised concept of motherhood, and the professional development and expansion of the child care experts who supported it.

Following World War II and putting regional differences aside, there were women in all areas who were reluctant to give up their jobs. Authorities, such as the Salvation Army told them not to be jealous of their husband's careers. Motherhood

---

2   The author acknowledges throughout that the emphasis on being a 'good' mother could be very disempowering and put tremendous pressure on mothers to conform to a more traditional feminine role. However, she also feels it necessary to offer an alternative view, which stresses that good can come from almost anything (even war, regrettably). The women's peace movement is one such good and we explore this here.
3   This extended after World War I into the 1920s, and after World War II for a short period in the late 1940s. There was another peak in the 1960s.
4   The writer refers to general changes after the war, but it is important to remember that the stay-at-home housewife has always been predominantly idealised, and a reality achieved by only a tiny minority, in the case of the northern working-classes.

became an institution. This was no long about attending to the practical needs of children, it was a whole way of life, a new persona. It was middle-class, educated and refined. Enormous effort went into cultivating it. Classes opened throughout the country to retrain women in the arts of housewifery. In August, 1945, Bolton colleges of adult education advertised classes on cookery, nutrition and family health. Working-class women needed to learn 'finer qualities', so classes in etiquette, elocution and flower arranging were also available. For some women, mainly the educated, the post war years presented a golden opportunity to make an art and a science of home-making and motherhood. Such women were mainly university graduates who chose to devote the benefits they had gained from education to the work of nurturing their husbands and children. Influential child psychologists, such as Bowlby, and Spoke and Frank, argued that 'no matter how proficient hired help may be, they cannot replace the mother in a child's life' (Cited in Swerdlow, 1993), Bringing up a family became the ultimate way for women to reach their full potential. The philosophy underpinning this specific cultivation of motherhood is summarised by Malcolm X, 'If you educate a man you educate an individual. But if you educate a woman, you educate a nation.' The rhetoric that drove this new science of motherhood was very persuasive and very influential in England and the United States of America.

In the States, by the mid fifties, the average woman could expect to work a year or two after leaving school. She would normally marry around the age of 20 years and she would withdraw from the labour force after the birth of her first child.[5] The US Bureau suggested that 'she will be likely to devote ten to fifteen years exclusively to the important functions of child rearing and child care' (cited in Swerdlow, 1993). The science of motherhood became so persuasive that it became an all encompassing persona, indeed, the only valid one for women. 'Experts' such as Frank and Frank (1955) published books instructing women on how to be women, how to get a man, how to select a husband. And all this had to be done secretly of course. More contradictions. A (normal)

5   US statistics compiled by the Women's Bureau in 1958.

woman had to want a man, plot to get a man, and appear all along, as if she *did not* want a man. The 1950s saw what appeared to be the 'good life' for people of all social classes[6]. In Britain, the Welfare State was up and running. There was a period of economic growth. Health education and the availablity of contraceptives offered people more choice about family size. Participants in the author's 1994 study, spoke enthusiastically of how much they welcomed the new baby clinics. These provided cheap vitamins, baby milk and child care advice. They were community centres where mothers gathered to weigh their baby and chat to other mothers. Health visitors and the advice they gave mothers on child care and child health were very much valued.[7]

Fathers were spending more time in the home and with their families. Gone were the pre-war, tough, red-blooded heroes. The fifties hero was tender, sensitive and a bit of a baby. He needed looking after, poor darling. And for this of course, he needed a sweet, tolerant and (ironically) more adult wife. The family holiday offered a new and exciting dimension to family life. The birth of holiday camps such as Butlins and Pontins were a strong reflection of what constituted ideas about the 'good life' at this time; health, wealth and togetherness.

The sociologists Willmott and Brown (cited by Segal, 1990) proposed the evolution of a symmetrical arrangement in family life. Men and women were equal but different, the two complemented each other perfectly. Such assumptions have been heavily criticised by feminists who point out that it ignores the rigid sexual division of labour that existed within such families. Men were spending more time in the home, but this did not necessarily imply that they were devoting more time to their wives or children.[8] However, no matter how inaccurate, the ideal did at least promote the idea that wives and children can be pleasurable and rewarding company to a man.

The incentive to promote traditional motherhood in

6   That is in British and American society.
7   See Kenny (1994).
8   See for example, Segal (1990)

places like Bolton was probably less of a priority. The north of England was one of the few places in England where working mothers still enjoyed the benefit of state nurseries, because in the north these did not close after the war.[9] The textile industry still needed workers and textile employers sought to improve recruitment to the mills by increasing wages, raising the status of the work and improving conditions.[10] The post war housing incentive brought further employment for women. In Bolton, the production line of Townsons (manufacturers of prefabricated homes) provided employment for many women.

Post war, Bolton women were in a better position to continue working than their contemporaries in other areas. But this should not lead to the assumption that they were more liberated. The increasing influence of the discipline of child psychology, and its accompanying band of experts, promoted the image of the perfect housewife and mother more strongly than ever. Their advice must have caused endless confusion for mothers because it constantly changed. In the war years mothers had been told not to spoil their children. They were informed that it was good for children to go to nurseries because it encouraged the development of social skills.[11] After the war they were advised to give their children 'quality time,' preferably full-time. 'Children need a family life' the experts said and, overnight, this scientifically proven fact (that most people had worked out for themselves long before it was 'scientifically proven') provided firm foundations for the new science of motherhood. It lit a torch of knowledge,

9   In other parts of the country, nurseries had been closed and married women were encouraged to stay at home.

10   Report on the recruitment of Cotton Workers, *Bolton Evening News*, 8th August, 1945.

11   This information was given to the author by her maternal grandmother when the former was in her twenties. Then a nurse, and the mother of her first child, the author (very much a 'text book mum' at this time) could not decide whether or not she should go back to work part-time. Her grandmother told her that she had heard 'umpteen' child care experts give different advice throughout the years, and that this advice had always complied with whatever had been the policies of government at the time. Thus she believed that child care experts work in collusion with governments. Heavily into the conspiracy theory and keen to outwit, by whatever means, 'them' the grandmother told the author 'do whatever you think is best and take no notice of the experts'.

liberating mothers from the darkness of ignorance. Never before had they understood that children need to be cuddled and talked to. And, cutting through the fog of ignorance that might have suggested otherwise, the experts announced 'children need to play.' To put it in a nutshell, the experts 'stole' mothering from mothers, and passed it off as their own invention.

In the author's view, it was not so much mothers who needed educating, but the professionals. Professionals in health and social services had been separating children from 'unfit' mothers for years. Often this was because of trivialities, such as an untidy house. The evacuee experience, particularly in Bolton, is important to this discussion because it illustrates the consequences of thrusting together, without adequate preparation, groups of differing subcultures. The author considers that, in this case, it was mainly cultural conflict which underpinned the problems encountered. Atti- tudes towards mothers have been governed by the assump- tions of the more dominant groups in society. The author argues that, historically, the context of working-class mothers' lives has not been sufficiently understood or appreciated by professional groups. Thus, theories such as those proposed by Bowlby had mixed blessings. On the one hand, his ideas did curtail the practice of removing children from 'unsuitable' homes.[12] But on the other, the necessity of having to work, made it difficult if not impossible for working-class women to live up to the ideal of full-time motherhood.[13]

Indeed, many women still find the image difficult to live up to. The ideal of full-time, devoted motherhood remains strong. Only recently for example, Angela Lambert of the Daily Mail moaned:

12   Indeed, it could be argued that this went too far. That is, there was a reluctance to remove children from homes that actually were neglectful and even abusive.

13   The author acknowledges the valuable contribution made by professionals. As she has pointed out elsewhere in this discussion, her research (Kenny, 1994) found that most working-class women, at least in Bolton, greatly appreciated the help and advice they received from health professionals in relation to family health and child care. The aim of her discussion is, not to invalidate the contribution of professional groups, but to emphasise the importance of education, particularly in relation to anti-oppressive practices.

'What can have transformed the granddaughter of all those decent, domesticated post war housewives, neat and modest in their pinnies and head scarves, into squalling, brawling viragos, capable of behaving as repellently as any yobs?'[14]

Overall, the article was well written and interesting. What a pity it was spoiled by Lambert's reliance on popular myth. The postwar housewives to whom Lambert refers had great difficulty adjusting to the idea that they should be the 'neat and modest' paragons of virtue that she imagined them to be. The perpetuation of such myths creates many problems for families. It can cause problems for women (and especially mothers) because, increasingly since the war years, many have felt inadequate if they cannot be superwomen. Nowadays, if women lack the stamina to do a brilliant job (and nothing less) in all areas; ie. paid employment, motherhood, sex partner, housewife, they can feel inadequate. It can cause problems for men and the parental relationship, encouraging men as it does to *expect* their wives to be superwomen.

To conclude this section of our discussion, women's contribution to the war effort created greater possibilities for equality of the sexes. But this was short lived. Having grown accustomed to the independence paid employment gave them, women were expected to relinquish this independence after the wars to make space for the men. If we take a simplistic look at what people are like, and view the whole affair from a functionalist perspective, the arrangement makes sense. But people are more complex than this. Thus purely functionalist approaches provide little insight into the struggles of the post war years. Motherhood aspired to the status of 'science'. As the sixties progressed, an army of new professionals made contributions to our understanding of children's emotional and intellectual development. This was a mixed blessing; in some ways empowering, in other ways less so. However, there was another aspect to this 'career' of motherhood (which will be discussed in the concluding section) that gave women a

14   Daily Mail, Saturday August 2nd 1997, Saturday essay by Angela Lambert entitled *What do these women tell us about our society?'* Publication accompanied by pictures of topical woman of the previous week.

sense of identity, power and assertiveness. This was their increasing involvement in the pacifist and human rights movements of the 1960s.

In the late sixties, thousands of American housewives went on strike for a day in the name of world peace. As mothers, they claimed to have a privileged say and one that should be listened to in the higher echelons of government. It was women, not men they argued, who gave birth, nursed and devoted their lives to raising children. As mothers, therefore, they asserted their right to insist on controls in the production of nuclear weapons, and to insist that their sons should not be sacrificed to those who would wage war (Swerdlow, 1993). Their arguments were essentialist and reflected a lack of regard for fathers, or for the many men who had contributed to the pacifist movement. But the women involved in the movement were middle-class, educated and well-organised. They made quite an impact at the time, although their arguments were by no means new. In *Chapter 3* we acknowledged that women can be as aggressive as men, while expressing this in different ways. However, women throughout history have spoken out quite passionately in favour of non-violence. The Greek Empire, for example, valued military force. Sappho was one of the most influential, learned Greek women of her time. She abhorred violence and military might. Her poems were eloquent, succinct and to the point. They reflected the stubborn assertiveness of her view that it was the simple things in life that matter, not the grandiose, elite or impressive. One of her verses (cited in Burn, 1974) wrote:

> *Some call a host of cavalry*
> *And some of foot the finest sight*
> *of all: and some a fleet at sea.*
> *But I would say, the hearts delight!*

Sappho was highly respected and people were not inclined to dismiss her views. One of her intellectual admirers, Plato, called her the tenth Muse. He said of her words; 'Few — but roses!' For many of those involved, the early suffragist movement was based on an acceptance that there were fundamental differences between the sexes. The assumption of these women was that the world would be a better, more peaceful place if a 'woman's touch' could infiltrate the higher levels of society. Indeed, many suffragists were also actively involved in the pacifist movement (Oldfield, 1989).

More recently, work by writers such as Gilligan (1982) and Ruddick (1989) have proposed the existence of a specially feminine 'voice', one that has a different moral code, a different form of rationality than that of the (presumed) dominant masculine voice. This kind of 'women power' advocates that a 'better' world can be achieved, if society adopts this feminine philosophy on life. There are several arguments that challenge this view. It is deterministic. It ignores the actuality of violence in some women and, by the same token, the lack of it in some men. It makes fathers redundant.[15] It assumes that the establishment of a matriarchy would be less oppressive than a patriarchy. This is simply not so. Matriarchies oppress *differently*.[16]

Indeed, the insidious nature of this kind of control is implicit in the fact that those involved in the *Women Strike for Peace* movement had a tendency to speak as if their children had no say, whatsoever, in whether or not they chose to enlist in a war. It is fair to challenge the view that the role of women is to produce sons for the sole purpose of ensuring national defence. But to make such a decision on *behalf* of a young adult! Children are not products. We do not own them. No matter how committed to pacifism, do parents have the right to prevent their offspring from taking part in, what the son or daughter may consider, a just and necessary war? Parents have the right to object of course, and to object strongly. But the author has difficulty accepting that parents have the right to deny their offspring responsibility for making important decisions such as this. Finally, the author objects to the cult value of the whole approach. This, she would argue, is not so much a philosophy of peace, as a consumer image. There is nothing wrong with having an image; this is how we express our individuality. There is something wrong with promoting

15 I am writing here of the father's potential to nurture and care for a child, and not necessarily to his 'wage packet' potential.
16 The author assumes the right to speak in the voice of authority here. She grew up in a subculture that was mainly matriarchal. She is glad to have had this experience **but** notes that oppressive structures do exist in this kind of social arrangement.

the view (intentionally or otherwise) that a person is more sensitive, more morally just, a better parent and person, simply by virtue of the fact that the person concerned happens to be a woman.

It could be argued that this amounts to yet another version of middle-class feminity to which working-class women are expected to aspire. It has led to some positive changes; for example, a challenge to the male dominance of the social sciences and a forum for alternative voices. But, the author argues, the fight for peace should begin in the heart. Having started here, it should reach out to encompass all aspects of ordinary life. A politics of peace should include all who are committed to it, women *and* men, not just those privileged with the time and finances to attend feminist conferences.

A politics of peace is not a product or an image that can be bought (or talked). It is a state of Being and a blueprint for living. Finally, despite the author's abhorrence of violence, she accepts (with considerable reluctance) that there are times when one literally *has* to fight for peace (and indeed, in order to survive). And she believes that a realistic politics of peace, must allow for this.

Chapter 10
Lacking in moral fibre: Crime, mental health and post traumatic stress disorder

In this chapter, we conclude with a discussion of post traumatic stress disorder (PTSD). The chapter begins with a brief history of the condition. We then consider how and to what extent PTSD may have contributed to accidents, suicides and homicides after the two wars, how milder forms may have affected families coping with reunion after World War II and damaged the self-concept of war veterans. The author relates contemporary research on PTSD to the data collected for this study. Much of the secondary sources used draws on the experiences of Vietnam veterans, who have clinically presented evidence of having suffered differing degrees of the disorder.

Important acknowledgements need to be made before embarking on further discussion. First, the combat and post combat experiences of Vietnam veterans differed significantly from that of World War I and World War II veterans. This does not invalidate the conclusions drawn in this chapter. The term PTSD describes an established, clinically-validated, traumatic stress response. In addition to war veterans, it has been recognised in victims of other forms of trauma, such as rape, disasters, torture and child abuse. It has been established that variables such as the nature of the trauma, social class, gender and so forth, lead to individual differences in the symptoms presented, and in their severity. There are no universals or absolutes. Symptoms are best understood along a series of continuums, around which a basic common cluster exists.

Second, there is no clear, clinical evidence from this study, to confirm the presence of the condition in any of the participants, but there is much to suggest it. The author found many themes in the data that were given meaning when placed within the context of certain theoretical frameworks, and the information provided by secondary sources. We must remember that many victims of trauma recover without professional support.[1] PTSD is not a mental illness but rather, a dramatic stress response.[2] The professional support and the clinical measures used in treating and identifying PTSD have been developed only recently, and there is much need for further development. Does this mean that the disorder is a recent phenomena, a product of the post modern world? If so, does its classification imply discovery or invention? Drawing on the past to make sense of the present can only lead to assumptions. But the author argues that such assumptions are valid. If the past can be used to increase our understanding of the present in qualitative as well as quantifiable ways, historical research will always make a useful contribution. In conclusion, the chapter briefly outlines some of the support now available for victims of trauma.

Historical background

The term PTSD refers to a condition commonly observed in victims of trauma. Various references to the disorder can be found throughout history. Samuel Pepys, observed symptoms in survivors that suggests a prevalence of PTSD following the Great Fire of London (Norman, 1990). Having read extensively about PTSD, Kenny points out that many works of art depict scenes in which the figures may well be suffering from this disorder. The validity of this theory increases, when related to auto/biographies. 'The Scream' painted by Edward Munch in 1895, presents a very graphic image of what could easily be termed PTSD. Munch was one of the founding fathers of an art movement called Expressionism. As his artistic talent matured, Munch's style became increasingly abstract, emotional and violently expressive. The public were shocked by the uninhibited style of his work and an exhibition of his was closed in 1892 because it caused an outcry.

Munch suffered progressively serious mental health problems for most of his life. He spent his last years in total

---

1   Although the author has little doubt that such support can make recovery less painful, and more complete than it might otherwise be.

2   The author hates dichotomies, but for the sake of making the point clear, PTSD is a *normal* rather than *abnormal* response to stress. This is not to deny that, in extreme cases, it can lead to abnormal and even dangerous behaviour.

isolation, having become increasingly socially isolated.
(Salmaggi and Pallavisini, 1977). 'The Scream' suggests many
of the symptoms of PTSD, including: disorientation, rage,
guilt, hopelessness and despair (see the expression on the face
of the screamer). The surrounding landscape is unstable,
incomprehensible, buoyant and filled with strong, colourful
contrasts.[3] What trauma (if any) does 'The Scream' represent?
Did Munch himself know or understand? The style and
composition of the work, suggests a kind of 'implicit' and/or
'flashbulb' memory of the type discussed later in this chapter.
Memories such as this are most common in young victims of
trauma (although they can present in adults as well). The
more severe the trauma and the younger the victim, the
greater is the potential for disassociation or suppression
(implicit) of memories (Briere and Conte, 1993). This 'traumatic amnesia' was first noted and investigated by Pierre
Janet in 1889 (Beall, 1997).

During World War I, a large number of soldiers presented
with a dramatic and, what appeared to be, hysterical response.
Exhibition of symptoms could be quite horrific. Some had
uncontrollable 'twitches', others would go into convulsions.
The men lost the power to comprehend, to remember, to
speak, even to control their saliva (Channel 4, 1997). This
'shell shock' as it came to be known was classified as a new
form of hysteria. Freud concluded that the condition
suggested a form of 'traumatic hysteria'. This presented a
challenge to earlier theories. Formerly, hysteria had been
regarded a 'women's problem' that had a biological base
(Showalter, 1987).

Following World War I over twenty hospitals opened in
Britain for victims of shell shock. The care and support
available to victims of PTSD is important. Many of the nurses
who cared for shell shocked victims adopted a compassionate
and caring approach. They did this despite medical opinion at
the time, which advocated a 'hard line' approach. In the
lunatic asylums conditions were very poor. The plight of the
victims was not helped by the stigma associated with PTSD.

3   The author considers that these sharp contrasts are the most disturbing
     aspects of the painting.

There were advocates who were willing to speak on behalf of those who suffered from the disorder. In 1920 at the unveiling of the Cenotaph in Bolton, a spokesman appealed:

> 'We further request your Royal Highness to take up the cause of our shell shocked and mentally unbalanced comrades, who are at present herded together with, in many cases, lifelong lunatics in our pauper asylums. The reports that leak out of the suffering and indignities imposed on our battlefield brethren in these institutions would, if they became public property, cause a revolution of feeling throughout the land. We are in possession of documents to prove many cases of unwarranted detention and ill treatment in these institutions. Is it just Sir, that those who have suffered for their country's sake should now be put indiscriminately into pauper lunatic asylums?'[4]

Not all of those effected by PTDS ended their lives in lunatic asylums. Some were cared for by their families. But without professional support this must have been very difficult. The torment sometimes proved too much, as the case below suggests:

> 'A discharged soldier who had been twice wounded in the head (whilst serving in the RASC) of 8 Bangor Street had been very depressed and frequently complained of pains in the head. When his sister — a widow with whom he lived, took a cup of tea to him at 5.30 on Friday, he then appeared to be his usual self. On going up to his bedroom 3 hours later, she found him lying on the bed, undressed, with his throat cut. The policemen who visited the house found a razor clasped in the deceased's right hand and stained with blood'. [5]

The family's general practitioner reported that the deceased had suffered from depression for some time, due to his bronchitis. On the basis of this information a verdict of suicide was recorded. Little account was taken of the head wounds that had caused so much distress. The deceased presented

4   *Bolton Journal and Guardian*, Friday, July 30th, 1920, page 10.
5   *Bolton Journal and Guardian*, November 12th, 1920.

symptoms of PTSD prior to his death, eg. irritability, depression, fatigue. There was no reference to the term 'shell shock'.[6]

Charles S Myers was one of the first physicians to conduct systematic research on PTSD. He believed, initially, that it had some organic basis but failed to establish this. Myers noticed that symptoms came on gradually, and that they often followed multiple rather than singular exposures to traumas. He thus argued the that the term 'shell shock' was inappropriate. PTSD is not caused by shells and shock is an acute response to trauma, rather than the chronic condition Myers had observed in his subjects. In the Second World War, the term 'combat fatigue' was adopted (Showalter, 1987; Norman, 1990).

Lieutenant Colonel T F Mann expressed grave concern for the mental health of World War II veterans.[7] He predicted, that following the celebrations reunited families would lapse into a mood of post war anticlimax. Mann's predictions were amazingly accurate. But his plea for greater support for trauma-damaged veterans fell on deaf ears (Turner and Rennell, 1995). One of the participants commented very bitterly on the lack of sympathy or support for victims of PTSD:

> *It was terrible during the First World War, because they didn't recognise it, so they just lined them up against a post and shot them (victims of PTSD). But during World War II, well they didn't shoot them, but they didn't support then either. They would get 'lacking in moral fibre' written on their file, and I'm talking now of men who had been out time and time again before they finally lost it. Lacking moral fibre! You cannot credit it can you?*

In 1945, Grinker and Spiegal identified nineteen common symptoms associated with severe stress reactions, including, fatigue, irritability and restlessness. [8] PTSD was listed under 'stress response syndrome' in the **first** edition of the *American*

---

6   This was the medically approved term for PTSD at this time.
7   Mann was psychiatric advisor to the Director of Military Training.
8   This followed case study observations of World War II airmen.

Diagnostic and Statistical Manual in 1952 and in the **second** under 'situational disorders'.

Subsequent to clinical observations on Vietnam War veterans, Horowitiz and Solomon (1975) noted responses such as denial, outcry (anger) and avoidance.[9] They also commented on the frequency with which intrusive trauma-related imagery and repetitive dreams were reported, and we explore this further. They concluded that the term, Post Traumatic Stress Disorder (PTSD), most appropriately described the symptoms noted. It is under this category that the condition now appears in the 1980, third edition of DSM–111. By this time, the work of other researchers, most notably Figley (1978a) had drawn attention to the diversity and complexity of the condition, so that in the DSM–111 it has been entered under three subheadings to include, **acute**, **chronic**, and/or **delayed**. However, as knowledge of the condition becomes more sophisticated, disagreements about definitions and categories increase. There is intense debate at the present time, for example, as to whether PTSD is best understood as an 'anxiety disorder' or a 'disassociation disorder' (Beall, 1997). *Table 1* presents some of the symptoms associated with PTSD.[10] The reader may note that these are all encompassing, involving physiological, emotional, cognitive and social domains, and that there is a large degree of overlap in the categories.

9   The author notes that many of these were identical to those associated with bereavement, although they were more extreme in the way they were expressed.
10   The author acknowledges the reductionism implicit in *Tables 1* and *2*. However she feels that it is helpful, for the sake of simplicity and ease of comprehension to present the symptoms in this way.

Table 1: Symptoms of PTSD (adapted by Kenny from Levin, 1989; Balwin, 1997)

Psychomotor domains	Affective domain	Cognitive domain	Social domains
Low energy	Shock and disbelief	Disorientation	Feeling and/or becoming very protective of significant others
Aches and pains, such as headaches, backache, stomach pains	Fear and/or anxiety	Flashbulb memories	
	Grief	Recurring, intrusive thoughts or nightmares about the event	A need for social withdrawal and isolation
Sudden sweating and/or heart palpitations	Denial		
	Irritability and/or restlessness	Amnesia of events and/or avoidance of having to think about them	Outbursts of rage or anger towards significant others (particularly if the sufferer feels betrayed)
Changes in sleep patterns	Emotional swings, ie. crying, quickly followed by laughing		
Constipation of diarrhoea		Difficulty concentrating or remembering	Difficulties in feeling compassion or empathy for others
Hyper-vigilance and	Survivor guilt		
	Detachment		
Hypersensitivity, ie. easily startled by noises and unexpected touch	Emotional numbing	Having difficulty making decisions	
	Same and feelings of self-blame	Feeling 'shattered' and unable to focus concentration on daily activities	An intense need to control and/or protect significant others
Greater susceptibility to colds and illness	Being on edge, easily startled and becoming overly alert		Lack of trust and suspicious of others
	Depression		

Since World War II, there has been a marked increase in research on PTSD leading to the publication of some notable works. Healy's (1993) contribution offers an excellent introductory source. In addition to a comprehensive history, Healy delivers a thought-provoking critique of workers such as Freud and Janet, who made some of the earliest contributions to the field. Krystal's (1987) research with concentration camp survivors is also very important. This provides a detailed analysis of the progress of PTSD. A large American study that began in the 1980s is significant because it identifies other variables that can affect the condition, such as group identity, gender and social class. Minority group members, for example, were found to be more susceptible than non-minority groups (Kulka, 1990). These findings draw attention to the fact that social structure is as important as individual differences. They also support the value of a multi-disciplinary, eclectic approach.

As acknowledged, most contemporary work on PTSD has been informed by work with Vietnam veterans. Norman and Deerden concluded from their work, that effects in less extreme cases, included feelings of social isolation, irrational fears and problems establishing and maintaining relationships (Norman, 1990). Cases of PTSD have been detected in victims of torture and kidnapping (Kinzie, 1993), physical and sexual abuse (Briere and Conte, 1993), people who have committed murder (Schacter, 1987), and in a multitude of other traumas. The nature of the trauma has an influence on the severity of symptoms, some predominating over others, depending on the case. Victims of disasters most frequently report severe attacks of survival guilt (Wright, 1989; Worden, 1982). The trauma of a near death experience can lead to feelings of irrational fear and vulnerability, as well as the commonly reported euphoria (Weinberg, 1994).

Research in Northern Ireland identifies PTSD in victims of explosions and terrorist attacks (Wilson and Cairns, 1992). Their work notes the influence of social discrimination and deprivation and McWhirther (1992) argues that:

'There is probably more evidence now from Northern Ireland on the psychological effects of civil strife than from anywhere else. It is hoped that continuing analysis and synthesis of available data and further research will help to define and develop theory. It is also imperative that such research has a humanitarian utility. Research findings must be communicated more effectively, especially to those in the caring professions'.

Professional people who support victims, or who administer aid in the event of a disaster, also risk developing PTSD. Unfortunately, it can also be present in the relatives and partners of sufferers (Goodwin, 1987). The catastrophic impact that two people, both suffering from this condition, can have on each other is powerfully conveyed in the 1993 film 'Heaven and Earth'. This is a heartbreaking portrayal of a relationship breaking down. Each partner, imprisoned by a private cocoon of grief and rage, is an inadequate source of support for the other. Instead, each has a savage compulsion to wage destruction on the other.[11]

PTSD as an experience: implications for mental health

We can infer that many civilians will have suffered from PTSD during the Blitz. Examination of the diary kept by Ryle's mother (1979) indicates many of the symptoms. The mother records in the diary, her experiences over the three months that her husband was reported missing in action. She makes frequent references to minor physical ailments; headaches, aches and pains, tiredness and fatigue. Hypersensitivity to minor irritations is evident. A relative visits. The woman's voice is too loud, her perfume overpowers. Her hat appears huge and ridiculous. The narrative fragments and loses its coherence. The overall 'flow' suggests a woman overwhelmed with stress, shock and grief. Yet Ryle notes, her mother never betrayed any emotion during this period of time.

Social isolation, denial and learned helplessness are other delayed symptoms that can hit the person unexpectedly. The intensity of such feelings can lead people to 'lash out' in an attempt to seize some control. From an official perspective, what appears to be little more than an irritating act of civil disobedience is, for the agent, a profound statement. It authenticates his or her human integrity. Consider the story below:

> '*It was when I came back on my third leave, I was all right the first two times. But about the time I was due to go back, I thought, 'I'm not going back', really sort of matter of fact like that. I don't know why I thought like that, it was crazy really, but on just before my last leave, seven of my mates had been killed all in one go. I didn't*

11   A colleague of mine, Jeremy Weinstein pointed out the value of the film in raising awareness and promoting some understanding of the grieving process. This advice initiated endless trips to the video shop and hours devoted to watching war films. This was valuable and something I would recommend to anyone conducting research into the type of human experiences covered in this book. For readers who have an interest in reading Jeremy's fascinating (1997) paper on the topic, the reference is provided in the list.

feel at the time that it happened that, well you just got used to that sort of thing, I mean I didn't come home feeling particularly upset, I'd just shut it out. But all the time I was on leave I put it out of my mind, then it hit me when I was due to go back. I just couldn't take it any more really, it was just too much. I do remember thinking 'I wonder what they'd do if I just didn't go back?' Well (laughs) I found out! They stuck me in jail. But I can't remember much about it. I do know that when I got out, everyone was celebrating, and I just kind of drifted through that. It was all like a dream. I have bits and pieces of memories of being in a cell, but not very clear. I remember everyone celebrating, and me thinking, matter of fact like, just the same, 'oh how boring, how irritating' — I had nothing to celebrate! It all happened a long time ago, I got out, so maybe cos the war was over, I never really served much time. You'd have thought I would, I mean, just stubborn I was. Didn't know I had it in me to be so stubborn.'

The participant above was quite difficult to interview because he was so ambivalent about telling of his experiences. The interview was very short (about 15 minutes) and the gentleman changed his mind and asked to terminate the interview halfway through.[12] During the interview, the man remained (or at least appeared to remain) totally detached from the experiences recalled. Yet despite this, the interview ended rather abruptly. His rationale; too bored to talk any more. A distance over twenty years separates this man from his war experiences. Yet they still appear to haunt him. A need to suppress the memory conflicts with an almost macabre compulsion to explore the details. The man admitted to having had a drink problem for many years. What can we make of his account? What motivated his stubborn refusal to return to the war? Was this man a coward? Such an explanation would be difficult to support since the man had fought quite bravely for the greater part of the war. Was he malingering? There is no evidence to support this. The man had initially chosen to enlist

---

12   The participant did agree to let me use the small amount of data I did
       gather for this book.

and this was the first time that he had ever resisted going back.

Although this interview was very short, the extract provides a concise but detailed framework of classic PTSD symptoms. First, the interview is abruptly terminated. When asked to discuss their feelings, many veterans respond in this blunt manner. This typical, almost manic abruptness, in its extreme form is represented by the main character (played by Kevin Bacon) in the film, *Murder in the First*. We discussed in *Chapter 3*, how devastating the experience of combat can be. The nature of modern warfare is that combatants have no knowledge of who is responsible for the death of a friend. One cannot predict in which direction the missiles will fly. Witnessing the sudden, unexpected death of a comrade forces an acute identification with one's own mortality. Combatants feel like time bombs, ready to extinguish any second. Death is everywhere and it is dealt with as quickly and efficiently as possible, or ignored. The very nature of the combat situation allows no freedom to grieve. The persons can be plagued by a powerful sense of survival guilt, particularly if they have had to compromise the safety of others to preserve their own life (Goodwin, 1987). A profound sense of hopelessness begins to emerge. The person can do nothing to change the situation. If it continues, the person responds by making the most potent statement possible. They retreat into themselves and go into denial (Howard, 1976). Of extreme cases of denial such as this, Lovering (1998) writes:

> '*When our emotions are so devastated that we are on the verge of a total breakdown and other defence mechanisms have failed to disrupt the shattering process, the weapon of last resort is denial. Persons who are in denial are simply telling the world that they have reached the last straw, and that they cannot, at this moment tolerate reality.*'

This kind of emotional retreat is a widely recognised response. The diverse ways it presents have been portrayed in some very commendable films, such as *Birdie* (1984) *Taxi Driver* (1976) and *Murder in the First* (1995). The sense of hopelessness, its accompanying need to 'remain at peace', to be isolated and left alone, continues for years after the initial denial response. The man's admission that he has a drink problem is another typical response. In the combat situation, veterans have to commit acts that their peers consider obscene. This makes it very difficult for them to talk about their experiences. Indeed, Kenny's recollection of conducting interviews with the war veterans in this study, gave her cause to consider the paper written by Kelly (1996) on 'Identity, self-concept and the post operative stoma patient'.[13]

Kelly writes of the anxiety caused by the stoma patient's 'secret', particularly in situations when its existence may need to be disclosed (for example, in the event of an anticipated sexual encounter). Kelly notes that, before making such disclosures, the person has to consider and prepare for negative reactions. The veterans in this study appeared to have similar concerns about disclosure. But their 'stigma' was of a very different kind. Whereas the participants in Kelly's study had to contend with prejudices based on desirable (clean) bodies, veterans' testimonies include an admission that they have broken a taboo that states 'Thou Shalt Not Kill'. They have a personality that (from some people's point of view) has become spiritually and/or morally soiled. Disclosures about the act of killing were, the author noted, 'tested out' and delivered bit by bit. This must have been very painful for the men. Shakespeare (1996) notes that the 'coming out' process (for gays, for example) can be a very painful, traumatic process. These men were 'coming out' about something very significant indeed. They were effectively 'coming out' as **non** killers, while at the same time having to admit that they had killed.[14] In other words, they appeared to be using the telling of their stories to map out a

13   Illiostomy is a radical surgical intervention conducted for treatment of sever ulcerative colitis (inflammation of the gut lining). The surgery can involve complete removal of the large bowel, while the small bowel is redirected to open through the abdominal wall. This causes permanent, faecal incontinence. The person must wear a bag permanently, but this is not usually visible when the person is fully clothed (Kelly, 1996).

14   Of course the men were quite right, they were (are) not killers. To kill in order to survive is not the same as being a killer, Kenny argues. However, she still feels concerned that the men may not have trusted her view of this, although she did her best to reassure them at the time.

space for themselves. This was a space that secured respite for a more likeable self who would be given the freedom to grow. Continuing his discussion, Shakespeare (*op cit*) draws on the work of Plummer (1995) who suggests that the varieties of narrative in modern stories can be divided into five categories. These include stories of a journey, enduring suffering, engaging in contest, pursuing consumerism and establishing a home (or identity). The stories that emerged in this study appear to have fulfilled many of the above criteria.

The ambivalence evident during the interviews caused the author a great deal of concern, but she found that the men appeared grateful to have been given the opportunity to talk. Indeed they thanked her several times for having created the time for such an opportunity. The emotional relief that can arise from participating in interviews has been noted by other workers (eg, Hutchinson *et al*, 1994). However, throughout the interviews Kenny had the feeling that, for the men, the act of killing had served as a very negative form of initiation. As they told their stories, they did so in a manner that suggested (Kenny's interpretation) that the act of killing had left them permanently changed, permanently aged before their time. This is common. Goodwin (1987) writes that many war veterans report feeling like old men in young bodies. A vicious circle can start. Social skills are lost. The person becomes more and more isolated and inadequate. They are unable to 'fit in'. Substance abuse helps numb a deep, enduring anguish born from loneliness, fear and regret (Howard, 1976).

Counsellors and therapists who work with victims of PTSD are anxious to point out that it should not, in itself, be regarded as a mental illness. Rather, it is best considered in terms of a delayed reaction to stress. Neither do they wish to minimise the seriousness of the consequences that can arise from stressful experiences. There are normal and abnormal responses to stress that include physical symptoms, such as aches and pains, sweating and heart palpitations, and emotional responses, such as those associated with bereavement. More distressing responses also occur, such as flashbulb memories (Brown and Kulik, 1977) hyper-awareness and hyper-vigilance (Levin, 1989).

When considering the characteristics of people who indicate a high suicide risk and the symptoms of PTSD, the similarities are alarming. People who express suicidal thoughts, for example, (and many victims of trauma do) typically experience strong feelings of worthlessness, insomnia and restlessness. They can view their bodies as being in a state of putrescence (Crook, 1992). Behavioural high risk indicators include social isolation, aggressive or disruptive behaviours and alcohol or other forms of substance abuse (Blumenthall and Kupfer, 1990). Unresolved responses to stress situations, and a predisposition towards suicidal thoughts can, if chronic, lead to associated physiological changes. However, there are differences in victims of trauma and those who attempt suicide for other reasons. In relation to PTSD, for example, the neurotransmitter, catecholamine, features most frequently in the literature (Murburg, 1994). Whereas people who have attempted suicide frequently, often have reduced levels of the chemical serotonin (American Psychiatric Association, 1996).

We now consider some of the crimes and accidents that occurred following the two wars. Kenny does not infer that PTSD caused these events. She does, however, consider that extreme stress might give some people a greater predisposition towards the kind of behaviour that leads to such events.

Crime rates and juvenile delinquency increased following each of the two wars. A large percentage of the more violent crimes were committed by ex servicemen. Assumptions are always difficult when we draw on historical accounts, whether primary or secondary. Insanity pleas in the case of homicides were common, and understandable given that this offered an escape from execution. However, 19 of the 30 murders recorded during the years 1918 and 1921 (that is, the first three years after the war) were committed by soldiers or ex servicemen. Most of the victims were wives or sweethearts, killed because of real or imagined infidelities. Other murders were financially motivated. These were committed by Absent without Leave, however, who were probably desperate and perhaps felt they had nothing to lose. Desertion carried the death penalty.[15] Two murders had been committed by servicemen who had a crime record prior to joining the Forces.

Some were committed by men who could not endure military service. Such was the case of Thomas Clinton. Clinton was drafted to the Royal Welsh Fusiliers in 1916. There was an immediate clash of personalities between Clinton and a Sergeant Lynches. Clinton managed to control his resentment for three months. Then he snapped and shot Lynches in the head. Clinton was instantly repentant. The crime did not appear premeditated in any way. He was, nevertheless, hanged, on March 21st, 1917. A week later followed the execution of Leo O'Donnell aged 22 years, for the murder of Lieutenant William Watterton. Theft was the alleged motive. Each of these men claimed insanity but, as we have noted this was a plea common at the time.

However, in many cases involving service men, insanity pleas were often supported by evidence of war trauma. Within a few weeks of his discharge home, Henry Perry murdered an entire family. His insanity plea was not treated very sympathetically. He had seventeen previous criminal convictions, most of them involving violence. Perry had suffered severe beatings and torture while imprisoned by the Turks.

James Ellor convicted of murdering his wife Ada in 1920, also pleaded insanity. Ellor was greatly distressed when Ada left him to stay with a friend. One night when Ada was alone, Ellor visited hoping for a reconciliation. She refused at which Ellor flew into a fit of rage. He beat her to death with a hammer. His trial revealed that Ellor had suffered frequent bouts of insanity before the attack. These had been caused by exposure to gas and pain from severe wounds. Fielding's account of the case is concise, but provides some support for Ellor's plea. Ellor had become desperately dependent on his wife. Ellor had lost control and appears to have 'blacked out' during the attack. He made no attempt leave the murder scene, or to remove evidence. He waited for Ada's friend to come home, then meekly confessed.

Rage is another useful survival mechanism in the context of war. It replaces fear at a time when responding to it, threatens survival (Middleton, 1992). It provides a dramatic energy force that can be directed for the purpose of killing

15   Steve Fielding (1995) *The Hangman's Record.*

(rather than risk being killed). This is a strategy that can be very difficult to unlearn. Goodwin (1987) notes that some veterans are very dangerous. Many are very much aware of the danger and fear that they may harm their loved ones. It is this fear (often prompted by incidents of domestic violence) that persuades them to seek help. Many are literally terrified of their potential for violence. The person is unexpectedly consumed with intense rage, often for no apparent reason. Some, recognising the danger, take steps to avoid hurting others. They may discipline themselves, instead, to hit out at objects, furniture, anything rather than another human being. Some withdraw abruptly if they feel ready to snap. Sometimes they vent their rage upon themselves. Self-harm is very common among war veterans.

Brown and Kulik (*op cit*) suggest that spontaneous violent responses can be provoked by 'flashbulb' memories of the combat situation. Veterans so effected can be provoked by the most ordinary, everyday occurrences. The sound of popcorn popping (a reminder of the sound of gun fire), the smell of diesel oil (used to burn excrement from overflowing latrines). The stench of stale urine provokes memories of the spectacle of death (the bladder empties at the point of death). Death, in itself, was not the issue that came up time and time again in these interviews. The greatest cause of distress was the sight of rotting corpses, of dismembered corpses, of witnessing people (often within brief moment of time) *becoming* corpses:

> '*Why it was terrible in the concentration camps. Anyone who's been a POW will tell you. The Japanese, they wasn't content with just beheading them (the POW) why they put their heads up on stakes, just one after another in a line. They used ordinary prisoners for bayonet practice. I didn't see that for myself, but I know of many who did, and I've seen pictures of it. Can you imagine living like that. Seeing someone alive one minute and then dead the next, especially if that person's head ended up on a stake. I mean, how could you ignore it? How would you deal with the fear, all the time that it might happen to you?*[16]

16   75-year-old World War II war veteran, interviewed 1997.

The sight of men in uniform can prompt a protective response (for themselves and others) in some cases of PTSD. One Vietnam veteran was so intimidated by a group of policemen advancing along the street that he fled, grabbing a nearby pedestrian as he went. Dragging his 'casualty' along with him, the veteran concealed the pair of them in a (perceived) place of safety.[17] Any of these occurrences and, indeed, many others are sufficient to provoke an obsessive episode in which vivid recollections of the filth, carnage and decay of the battle field are dramatically replayed (Brown and Kulik, *op cit*).

Most veterans do not develop serious mental illness. Nor do they become violent criminals or murderers. But the trauma of war, may have been a strong contributing factor in at least some post war crimes. Crime and juvenile delinquency rose once again following World War II. This time it was attributed to the absence of fathers and to mothers working. Yet many of these crimes had been committed, not by juveniles but rather by adult ex serviceman. Again, jealousy because of real or imagined infidelities was the motive for many of the crimes. There was also a spate of accidental killings in Bolton. This suggests that some men may have had an unbalanced state of mind when they arrived home. Accidental killings occurred when ex service men chose to show off. One such case involved two paratroopers. The friends had gone out on a pub crawl. They carried with them souvenirs, loaded pistols that they had brought back from Germany. At each public house visited, the paratroopers pulled out the pistols and started firing, first at safe targets. They boasted to their friends of how they had killed Germans. They were drinking and soon lost count of the number of cartridges they had used. In the last public house they visited, one of the men, believing his pistol to be empty, pointed it at his friend's head and pulled the trigger, killing his friend outright.[18] At his trial, he described the incident:

'I pulled the trigger, not realising there was a cartridge in the breech and saw my friend fall. Surprise made me

17   This case is reported in Goodwin (*op cit*).
18   Bolton Evening News, July 11th, 1945, *Killed Friend: Paratrooper Didn't Know Pistol Was Loaded*.

stagger back and drop the pistol. I rushed back to pick up the pistol to shoot myself and everyone jumped on me. I had no intention of shooting him and I would sooner have died than done it.'

Another man's girlfriend, playfully asked him to 'shoot me'. He shot her dead. This man knew his rifle was loaded. But he believed he had the skill to block the passage of the bullet as it propelled towards the barrel.[19] The macabre suicide pact of an absentee and his sweetheart (both in their early twenties) was reported in June, 1945. The women had been strangled and then suffocated. Her body had been found in the bedroom of her home. The body of the absentee (who had shot himself) was found two days later in Alnwick. He left a suicide note confessing to the murder of his (assumed) partner. It read 'she could not stand the razor blade, so she asked me to strangle her. It was terrible for me, but she passed away with her lips to mine. She kissed me all the time.'[20] These three tragedies occurred between June and July, 1945. This was just over a month after peace had been declared.

The long-term effects of trauma, particularly in war, cannot be understated. The experience of having to 'kill or be killed' has a profound impact on a person's self-concept. Most combatants tend to be quite young, often at the stage of psychological development when they are trying to build a positive sense of self and a clear identity (Erikson,1968; Lifton, 1976). Erikson's theory offers a lifespan perspective, that takes into account interactions between the individual and the environment. Various milestones in the lifecycle, can lead to outcomes that are positive or negative. Adolescents and young adults struggle to avoid a state of confusion, in which their identity may become vague, unclear. Adolescence is characterised by a person having a number of beliefs, which they 'test out' before making commitments (Fatchett, 1995). 'Testing out' in safe situations allows space for retreat. Many young veterans enlist in a war to fight for principles to which they may not be fully committed. But there is no space for retreat in war. A perceived helplessness to change the

19 Bolton Evening News, July 6th, 1945, *Tragic End to 'Shoot Me' Joke.*
20 Bolton Evening News, June 9th, 1945, *Strangled While She Kissed.*

situation adds further to a negative self-concept. Many delinquents with low self-esteem lack a belief in themselves, lack
faith that they can ever do anything of value (Erikson, *op cit*;
Burt, 1969).

   Knowledge that one is capable of taking life, plants seeds
for the growth of a perceived ugliness inside. This inner
'dirtiness' can make a person predisposed to episodes of deep
depression. Kenny is reminded of one of the dark sonnets
written by Hopkins *'Carrion Comfort'*. [21] In this work, written
during one of the poet's depressive phases, he expresses his
perception that he is rotten. He experiences his body as filthy,
putrid, rotting meat. His surroundings are heavy, dark and
oppressive. Thus, the sight and stench of death and decay all
around (real or imagined) can be incorporated into the self. At
the same time it can be projected outside, so that others and/
or the environment is perceived as corrupt and dirty. De Niro
in *Taxi Driver* graphically portrays this phenomenon. The city
is perceived as a progressively filthy and corrupt place, as the
main character retreats more and more into a private world of
fantasy. It is common for such sufferers to deal with the
complexities of their emotions by dividing the world into
simplistic dichotomies, good and bad. In *Taxi Driver* De Niro
projects all his perceived **good** onto a twelve-year-old
prostitute, played by Jodie Foster. Evil, and, indeed, full
responsibility and blame for her situation is projected onto her
pimps. The film reaches its climax when De Diro wipes out the
evil (ie, kills all the pimps) in order to preserve the perceived
goodness in 'innocent' Iris. Even those who appear to have
adapted well, may be plagued by recurrent nightmares, in
which they are pursued by something or someone. They often
wake with a start as the dream reaches it climax. The dreamer
collapses, unable to run any longer. If cornered, they turn to
retaliate, only to find that their weapon is empty (Bessel *et al*,
1998).

---

21   Hopkins was a nineteenth century English poet. He suffered from manic
      depression for most of his life and his works reflect the extreme mood
      swings characteristic of this condition. Hopkins sought spiritual sanitary
      in the church by becoming a Jesuit priest. But his work suggests that in
      life, he never found the relief that he so desperately needed anywhere, not
      even in religion.

The more an individual becomes obsessed with thoughts and obsessions of impending death, the more he or she struggles to assert the validity of his/her existence. Yet paradoxically, this same obsessive fear of death can become a wish for it. This, too, endures long after the combat experience (Goodwin, 1987). The theme of death and decay was mentioned by all three of the veterans who took part in the in-depth interviews:

'Do you know the first dead German I ever saw, he must have been about 19 or 20, no more than that. He was propped up against a wall, his head was tilted to one side, like this, and his mouth was half open like this (mimics). In an odd sort of way, he looked really comical, staring into space, with this ridiculous, blank look on his face. His body was dried like a prune, and he was as black as coal with the decay. The stench that was coming from him, it sickened you . . . he looked and he smelt ridiculous. Do you know what I did? I had a cigarette in my hand, and I put it in his mouth. The sight was even more ridiculous, this dead, smelly black corpse, with this blank expression, with this smoking fag in his mouth. We were hilarious, my friends and I. We fell about laughing at him, he was such a grotesque, such an ugly and ridiculous figure, all we could do was fall about laughing and laughing at what a ridiculous figure he made. Love do you think I was terrible?'

We may feel disgust for the extreme detachment suggested above. But in dangerous situations it serves as dynamic defense mechanism that ensures survival. Detachment such as this follows a process of objectification. The process severs emotion from the cognitive aspects of experience. Awareness of the surrounding death and destruction is muted so that the individual is prevented from becoming too overwhelmed by it. Lifton (1973) refers to extreme states such as this as emotional deadness.

Lifton goes on to explain that the process which propels a person towards emotional deadness, starts within a few days of a combatant's experience of war. It is facilitated by the use of pseudonyms that blunt the anguish and reality of combat.

Thus, during the Vietnam War, the Vietnamese were 'gooks' 'dicks' 'slants' — anything but human beings. Forests and villages were wiped out by 'Puff the Magic Dragon' (an AC-47 gunship with rapid firing mini Gatling guns). The dead, enemy or no, were 'zapped' but never killed (Lifton, 1973).

Despite its immediate survival value, research shows that if maintained for too long, the person becomes alienated from their own sense of humanity. It is not unusual for a veteran to describe himself as emotionally dead many years after his experience of combat. This extreme lack of concern or even awareness of one's human significance is conveyed by Kevin Bacon in *Murder in the First*. When threatened with the possibility of the gas chamber, he replies without concern or emotion, 'I'm dead already.' The effects can be so profound that the sufferer questions the truth of his very existence; 'Am I real or just a dream'? Emotionally castrated, they have no measure of empathy or tenderness. They strenuously avoid learning to feel again. They fear that if they ever do, then they might lose control completely (Shatan, 1973). For the veteran cited here, this does not (thankfully) appear to have happened. He continues and responds to my observation that:

Interviewer: *Well it doesn't sound very nice, but then, I wasn't there.*

Interviewee: *That's it, that's it. I mean that's what war does, I mean, after the event, even only hours after, I thought about what I had done, and I was appalled. I mean, that corpse had been someone's husband, son, someone's brother. Seriously, how would they have felt if they'd have seen us showing such little respect. Oh, I hated myself, but most of all, I couldn't understand myself. I mean, the need to laugh, the real need to fall about laughing. I'd never seen a dead soldier, I mean, the indignity of it, to rot, to have to rot publicly like that. And the image he presented, as much as I hate myself for doing it, I can still find myself sort of tittering to myself at how he looked. A comic figure, too bizarre and too horrible and grotesque to be taken seriously.*

As we acknowledged, such pervasiveness of death can cause a person to wish for it. A war veteran in 'The Deer Hunter', secures employment by positioning himself up as the 'bet' in a game of Russian Roulette. Ironically, this was the fate he had escaped in combat. He makes a great deal of money, but he keeps none of it. Instead he sends generous wads of cash to a disabled ex comrade. Risk behaviours are common. Some war veterans have been involved in numerous car accidents. Indeed, this might be what prompts them to seek help. After a number of accidents, they begin to realise that they might be trying to kill themselves (Goodwin, *op cit*). The participant continues by explaining that the sight of death could give rise to hysterical responses.

'And knowing that it could be me! I don't understand why, when you see such horror there is this terrible, overwhelming urge to laugh'.

Here, as in *Chapter 3*, stress is placed on the sight and presence of death on the battlefield. The emotionally dead (or living dead) fear death constantly. Research illustrates that fear of imminent death, the superstition that it lurks just around the corner, influences a diversity of paranoid anxieties, obsessions and stress responses. Many war veterans are very vigilant people. The experience of combat has so 'fine tuned' their automatic responses that they respond to anything that reminds them, even remotely, of the combat experience. They may feel uncomfortable when someone walks too closely behind them. They may avoid open spaces. They feel most relaxed when sitting in the corner of a room, with a wall surrounding them (De Fazio, 1978).

Fear of imminent death causes insomnia. Veterans fear sleep in case they never wake up. Nightmares can put their partners lives at risk. Partners of Vietnam veterans have reported waking up choking because their spouse, who is still asleep, is throttling them. This, too, is another symptom of the hyper-vigilance discussed previously. The disabling effects of this condition should not be underestimated. The person, literally, becomes a nervous wreck. They habitually start in response to a loud noise. Some can be so severely affected that they fall to their knees. All of these behaviours are learned techniques that ensure survival. But if an individual has to adapt to them for too long, then they are powerless to abandon them when the combat situation is left behind. Appreciation for the enemy's humanity is another source of frantic remorse. Many veterans break down when they remember having killed someone (Goodwin, *op cit*).

'I knew that these corpse had people back home who loved them. I knew it was wrong, I knew how terribly, terribly hurt those people would be to know that people like me were laughing, really love, I did think about it. But that is war. This terrible urge to laugh at the dead apart from other things, you did things then that you would never have dreamt of doing in civvy street.'

The author recalls having been very moved by this story. The storyteller seemed such a mild and sensitive man. He recognised (and remains tormented) by the humanity of the dead. Yet at the same time, he knew there was a need to detach himself, to dehumanise and objectify the dead. He notes his disgust at himself for laughing. Yet the understanding that this could be his fate strips him of any power to control his behaviour. He was laughing. But his heart was breaking.

Klien's 'Object Relations Theory' provides insights to account for such behaviour (Kahane, 1992). The abridged version stated here suggests that, when overwhelmed by the recognition of a perceived ugliness in ourselves, we have the capacity to 'shut it off'. Disturbing aspects of the self are assigned to the unconscious. On the one hand the participant demonstrates a willingness to confront and explore a part of himself that was familiar with in war. But he is equally anxious to disassociate from it. Later he asserts:

'Like I said, on the one hand there was this urge to laugh, but at other times you would want to grieve, not just for the Allied dead, but for the enemy. I mean, they were just like us, just ordinary lads. They didn't want to kill us any more than we wanted to kill them. And for all that, I mean I'm talking about genuine respect, there was a lot about the Germans that you could genuinely respect, but

the next thing you would be hating them. You forgot, it was amazing how quickly you forgot that they were human, and it was back to kill or be killed again. The whole thing I felt, was totally confusing. I mean, is it any wonder that so many came back totally ruined mentally. It did affect you, it really did. When I came back, I was determined to live a good life, I like to make people happy. I really like to give presents. I like the look on people's faces when you give. I just love that happiness that you see on their faces, not so much at what you have bought, but the happiness because you have remembered them. It's like, for a moment, there's a kind of connection, that's the lovely thing about human beings, that a little thing like giving a gift, even a small one, can bring you together, make you both remember that you are both human. You see love, I do respect human life, I do respect . . . I love that human thing. And that is why giving is so important to me, it's also a way of letting people know that we have remembered them.'

This man's ability to cut off his emotions is not confined to the enemy; he transfers it to friends. He asserts that his comrades were more than friends, brothers. He then insists it was possible to 'cut them out!

'That was the funny thing also, that you could feel such deep friendship for a man, and then forget about him completely, within a couple of hours really, of being dead.'

This assertion suggests a degree of denial. Survival guilt is another cause of distress and PTSD. Seeing a friend killed, to be helpless to change the situation, must surely be one of the worst profound sources of trauma one could ever imagine. Yet people are amazingly resilient, and often draw on their inner resources to cope with such experiences. Other cautious pauses in this study prior to making disclosures, were caused by the need to 'test out' whether or not the author was sympathetic to a belief in ghosts. We live in a society that considers such beliefs a little strange or 'quirky'. This is despite observation by the author that many people actually do hold such beliefs.[22] This could explain why there was a short period of 'testing' before the veteran below gave an account of the following event. It was because Kenny had admitted that she believes in ghosts:

'You know, in the Forces there are lots of people who believe in ghosts. Yes, I would say that is very much the case. Many people have had experiences, or know people who have had experiences, of their dead comrades coming back. Usually it is to help, or to guide. Like there are stories of dead comrades who guide the living safely through fog, or mines fields or whatever, yes those are very common. And its believable you see. If you understood the kind of loyalty, I mean duty. There is a strong sense of duty to take care of each other in the Forces. I don't believe myself that when someone dies, that they go straight away, especially if there is unfinished business. I know of one pilot who was injured so badly he couldn't control his plane. He thought he was about to die, that the plane would crash. Then all at once, he felt this arm reaching out and taking control of the plane. It was his brother (also a pilot) who had died a few months before. He couldn't see him (the brother) but he knew it was him. He could sense his presence you see. Yes, there is a very strong belief in an afterlife, especially in combat. I think people find it comforting to be honest. And then some events in war are so spectacular and so shocking that they leave a trace behind. I mean, if you think of it in terms of energy. I mean I've heard loads of stories of planes being heard overhead, or of planes blowing up, when there wasn't a plane there at all.'

22   Christine Kenny firmly believes that the dead (and sometimes the living) leave 'presences' but as to whether these constitute spirits with consciousness or awareness, she is not sure. She also feels that disclosing this information to her participant was quite justified in this context. There are times when disclosure can help to promote trust. Disclosure should always be offered with caution, however, and with a clear rationale for having chosen this option (Kenny and Wibberley, 1994). She further justifies her disclosure on the basis that she was not attempting to deceive when she shared it (for the purpose of say, extracting additional information). It was an honest response to a question. The participant asked outright if she believed in ghosts and she answered in the affirmative.

The participant's observation is supported by numerous anecdotes, but unfortunately, no empirical evidence. Halfpenny (1986) writes of similar phenomena, noting that ghostly music has been heard by many people on several disused airfields. In *Chapter 7* we discussed the concept of social death, that is, the process when living people become effectively dead, due to their absence. We also noted that the living can extend the social life of a person, for example, by acts of remembrance. Weinstein (1998) writes of the need for the bereaved to maintain a continuing relationship with the dead.

A belief in ghosts is one way that a person might maintain such a relationship. Whatever rationale can be offered to explain such beliefs, Kenny argues that these should never be dismissed out of hand. A belief in ghosts appears to have sound psychological functions. It offers hope. It is comforting and it allows the bereaved to maintain a relationship with the deceased. In the context of war, it may provide a source of protection against survival guilt. The man concluded his interview by stating his belief that, on the battlefield, the dead stay around sometimes to comfort the living, to let the living know that they are all right. A belief in ghosts might also help to distract from the harrowing psychological effects that the constant presence of corpses can have.

A spirtual faith can have a psychologically purifying effect and, based on this and the other concepts discussed above, Kenny argues that a person who confesses to a belief in ghosts, or in other forms of paranormal phenomena, should never be ridiculed or contemptuously dismissed.[23] No has the right to take away another person's hope.

In relation to the veterans self-concept (long-term as well as short-term) this could be very important. Another participant continues the death narrative:

'Being at war is terrible. The smell of death is everywhere, it's in your skin, the stench of it is in your nostrils all the time, even in your urine, you know, you

---

23 An exception to this rule of course, would be in cases where the existence of such beliefs suggests that they are in some way potentially damaging to the person or others.

are soaked with it, this terrible, kind of sweet smell of death.'

The man tries hard to distance himself from the part that is tarnished and stained (Goffman, 1963), and which is linked to the carnage and decay. He likens it to a *malignancy*, infiltrating his body and, as the surgeon operates on a patient to 'cut out' deseased tissue, so the man would 'cut out' this malignancy of the mind. Running parallel is an expressed desire to do good, to reach out and to make a connection with other human beings. As noted in *Chapter 7*, many war veterans express a need to make amends, to do some good. They may become obsessive blood donors. When the author considers this in relation to the story above, she is reminded of the symbolism attached to blood mixing or sharing in many cultures. The man cited above stresses his need to make connections. Donating blood may be one way in which some veterans make such connections. Giving blood could offer a means to establish a sense of brotherhood.

Others become conscientious objectors. For such veterans, the most effective means to make amends, is to protect others from the same fate. The American Veterans Antiwar Association make this aim very clear in their 1998 fact sheet:

'We believe that service to our country did not end when we were discharged. We remain committed to the struggle for peace and for social and economic justice for all people. We will continue to oppose senseless military adventures and the real lessons of the Vietnam war'.

At the conclusion of the interview, the man stated a preference for cremation when he dies. His rationale was that 'he does not want to rot'. This participant is just one of the many ex servicemen who returned from the war, apparently stable, both mentally and physically. After his discharge from the services, he lived an ordinary, uneventful life but during those years he remained tormented by memories of carnage and death. Despite the pain that such memories cause, because it exists, it is evidence of the survival of his humanity. This man, and many like him, has been fortunate. Indifference to the dead can lead to the kind of macabre situation explored in

'Apocalypse Now' (1979). In this scenario, the characters become indifferent to the landscape of death that shrouds them. Isolated from the rest of the war, they act out personal, relatively insignificant, dramas, among the 'props' of rotting, dismembered carcasses. Their behaviour typifies what Aries (1974) refers to as a 'promiscuity between the living and the dead'.

Self-help and professional support

The participant cited at the end of the last section revealed that he suffered a stroke in later life. This brought an unforeseen bonus. It granted him permission to cry. Considering this interview, it is surprising that so many veterans fail to develop mental health problems. Some must have developed highly effective coping strategies. Indeed, there is evidence in the data to suggest that this was the case. One man spoke of the many soldiers who kept dairies and wrote poetry.

Writing poetry to dispel powerful emotions was probably very therapeutic and may have protected the men from developing PTSD at a later date. Delay in the expression of PTSD can be due to repression of painful memories. Repression has important survival qualities, but if painful memories are pushed too far into the unconscious (the semiotic), they become inaccessible to symbolic representation in language. The semiotic is purely sensual. It consists of mental imprints of the sensory and effective elements of experience; that is, visual, olfactory, affective, auditory and kinetic experiences (Bessel *et al*, 1998). This can lead to the formation of implicit or non-declarative memories (Squire, 1994; Schacter, 1987).

Evidence suggests the paradoxical nature of implicit memory. It appears to represent a form of repression that is somehow incomplete. Hovering on boundaries between conscious and unconscious thoughts, such memories wait to 'pounce' unexpectedly. Typically, the victims have no conscious recollections of the traumatic event, but they are subject to sudden, unpredictable 'flashbulb' recollections.

The individual who stores such memories can be unaware that they exist. Many years after the traumatic event, a quite ordinary experience could trigger strong emotional responses which include: panic attacks, paranoias, phobias or nightmares. Alternatively, the experience may be replayed over and over again in replicated, fragmented nightmares (van r Kolk *et al*, 1984) and counselling or therapy may be necessary. A therapist can facilitate the process that allows the sufferer to make explicit the implicit. Transformation of such memories into a narrative form provides a structure and problems can be revealed and mapped out. This process may transform memories from implicit to declarative or explicit.

Declarative memory refers to a conscious awareness of facts or events that have happened to the individual. The ability to confront the trauma and express its meaning is one of the most significant steps to recovery. This is why the stories of survivors should always be taken seriously. The listener should never dismiss or contradict them. Victims need the freedom to construct their own meaning from their experiences. Meaning must evolve to accommodate the victims personal frame of reference. Victims need to appreciate that that their interpretations have validity (Squire and Zola Morgan, 1991).

In recent years there has been an explosion of interest and research into PTSD. This has led to greater public awareness and the development of various forms of support. These include the formation of victim support groups (Goodwin, 1987) psychoanalysis, counselling and cognitive behavioural therapy. The work of many neo-Freudians, such as Jung and Klien, Lacan and Kristava, have provided invaluable theoretical bases for therapy (Connell, 1987). With regard to support specifically designed for men, Jungian approaches have provided the foundations for support groups that adopt a spiritual, holistic approach. Founded by workers, such as John Rowan (1983), these draw on the Jungian notion of the archetypal, collective unconscious.

Therapy aims to explore how a man loses contact with the more authentic, spiritual aspects of his inmost self. Its rationale is that male socialisation and traumatic experiences, such as war, can cause a man to become divorced from his feminine 'shadow', ie. the feminine part of himself. This leaves a space that is open to invasion by harmful, violent archetypal forces. Rowen refers to this process as 'spiritual wounding'.

The therapeutic approach adopted to counter this, involves encouraging men to make a connection with the sensitive, feminine aspects of their personality.

Jungian theory and, indeed, all psychoanalytic theory lacks scientific validity and many of the assumptions underpinning it can be very naïve. It is an expensive approach to implement. So far, research into its effectiveness has been limited to a somewhat elitist group of middle-class men, mainly from a counselling background. However, given that this is a new approach, it would seem premature to dismiss it.

Early (1993) has completed extensive investigations into Jungian approaches and has shown how these can be applied to practice. Following Rowen (*op cit*), she draws on the archetype, arguing that this provides a route for the expression of trauma experiences. The struggles and anxieties of trauma victims are traditionally portrayed in fairy tales, folk songs and in popular culture. These representations express the collective, timeless struggle that human beings wage against the forces of injustice and evil.

Another therapeutic approach that has drawn on Jungian theory is that of art therapy. The effects of traumatic experiences may prove so catastrophic that memories of them are relocated so deep in the unconscious, they rest outside the language boundary. However, the victim may access them using other mediums, such as colour and/or other expressions of sensuality. Cohen's contribution to the field of art therapy illustrates how art can be utilised to help survivors understand, manage and transform the trauma experience (Cohen, 1995). He adopts a holistic approach and is concerned not only with enabling the person towards self-growth, but also with improving their relationships. Thus, literature, art, drama, music and other creative activities, present useful vehicles for the expression and dispersal of painful emotions. Jungian approaches, despite their scientific naivety, do offer a rich theoretical base from which to develop practice.

Cognitive behaviour therapy provides a means for victims to reorganise and restructure their perceptions. In this way, clients can develop different, more effective ways of coping with their fears, for example, fear management rather than fear response. Techniques include breathing exercises, cognitive restructuring and distraction techniques. (Foy, 1992; Saigh, 1992).

Professional support is very important, but we should not forget the various self-help techniques that exist (see *Table 2*; adapted from Balwin, 1997). Briefly, these can be divided into three categories. 'Inner resources', referring to practices that draw on personal, inner resources, for which the person may need little material or social help. 'Other resources' refer to others, ie. friends, colleagues, lovers. 'Material/structural resources' can be more difficult to realise because they are dependent on access, finances and policy. All three categories of techniques should be encouraged as individual, family and community responses to support victims of trauma. Any caring society, claiming a commitment to helping victims of trauma, will ensure that they are available.

Table 2: Helpful coping strategies (adapted by Kenny from Levin, 1989; Balwin, 1997)

Inner resources	Outer resources	Material/structural resources
Cry Hard exercise such as jogging, aerobics, walking Prayer and/or meditation Commitment to something personally meaningful and important every day Write about your experiences — for yourself or to share with others	Reach out and connect with others, especially those who have experienced similar events Talk about the traumatic experience Humour — share a joke with others Hug those who you love and/or care about — close physical contact stimulates the secretion of opioids. These are the bodies natural pain killers. They also make you feel good Proactive response — be socially involved, make a contribution to your community support groups	Hot baths Music and art Avoid using stimulants such as coffee, tea, sugar and nicotine. Try to ensure that you get a good, balanced diet. Eat warm foods such as turkey, boiled onions, baked potatoes, cream based soups (these help you to feel relaxed). Take up a hobby or enrol to study a subject that you have always been interested in. Seek professional help that seems most helpful and appropriate to your needs.

This chapter has discussed the extreme effects of war, ie. the development of PTSD, related mental health problems and crime. It has centred mainly on extreme manifestations of the condition and it should not be assumed that all men who serve in a war, suffer these problems. It is also clear that however well or badly people adjust following a war, its effects remain with them for the rest of their lives. These discussion highlight the resilience of the many who survive and cope well. Levin (*op cit*) notes:

> *The Chinese character for crisis is a combination of two words — danger and opportunity. Hardly anyone would choose to be traumatised as a vehicle for growth. Yet our experience shows that people are incredibly resilient, and the worst traumas and crisis can become enabling, empowering transformations.*

Finally, the author comments on her experiences during the interviews and when reading the questionnaire responses. Conducting the research for this book has been a very moving experience for several reasons. First, the veterans interviewed disclosed much more about their experiences of war, and in far more graphic detail, than was anticipated. This was not done to shock, or to be offensive but rather from a genuine desire to talk openly about their experiences. Initially, Kenny was concerned because she was unsure what the impact of such forthright story telling might be on her participants.[24] But after the interviews, the men were so obviously grateful to have been given the opportunity to talk, that this concern was quickly dispelled.

Reflecting on the interview process, Kenny considers that, during these interactions, much more than simple story-telling was taking place, ie. giving factual accounts of events. Rather, it seemed that the participants were taking the opportunity to redefine themselves. The repetition, for example, of the phrase 'kill or be killed'. The repeated affirmation that they were not killers, together with a recognition that they had once been killers. There was a need to tell not only their own stories, but also those of comrades lost during war. This was seen as an act of loyalty. Indeed, stories of the war dead

---

24   And, indeed, writing for the questionnaire responses were just as emotionally loaded.

were accompanied by an obstinate declaration that we should not forget.

Conclusion

Shakespeare (*op cit*) argues that 'identity is an aspect of the stories we tell to ourselves and to others'. The stories told by these men reflected an intersubjectivity that was unexpected, especially from military personnel. There was a need to establish, not just a positive identity for themselves, but also for the friends and comrades they had lost. The cathartic possibilities of talk have long been recognised in counselling and psychoanalysis. But, in this context, talking seemed to have a spiritually purging effect.[25] Part of the gratitude for having been allowed to talk was that such talk appeared to wash away the stains, if not permanently, then certainly temporarily.

Finally, Kenny was astonished by the 'feminine characteristics' expressed in these stories. When she began her research, she expected, erroneously, her participants to glorify war. Instead, she found men who spoke of the horrors and indignities of war; they spoke of their fear and vulnerability in the face of death, and of the ongoing dread that they, too, might become one of the hundreds of rotting corpses that littered the surrounding landscape. They spoke openly, passionately and unashamedly of their love for their comrades and of their perceived inadequacy in coping with grief.

They told of a need to cry and of the difficulties and resentment that stemmed from being denied this right. This denial was because of a strict, implicit code that stated 'men do not cry'. Interviews always throw up the unexpected and, significantly, this research has done much to shatter many of Kenny's earlier assumptions about men, masculinity, war, violence, and their presumed association. The research also modified assumptions that the decision to go to war is taken too lightly.[26] She is reminded of something Albert Bryan, a

25   Given the psychological soiling effect, that the act of killing, plus the
     constant presence of the dead appears to have had on the men.
26   Although this assumption has not been dispelled completely, for Kenny
     believes that there are occasions when this can happen, eg, World War I,

Bolton historian, once said to her mother, 'When you read history, and of the deeds of men through the ages, you learn of human nature, and it doesn't change that much' (Miller, work in progress). Given that the men still maintain the importance of remembrance, the final chapter considers this and the functions of war memorials.

ie. insufficient thought is given to non-violent alternatives.

Chapter 11
War memorials

During Kenny's research, the importance of remembering was a recurring topic. It is a major concern for those who experience a war and the author argues that even those who have not experienced war should still know of and 'remember' the people who gave their lives. Passionate opposition to war is an even better reason to remember. It is argued that war memorials are a source of comfort to the bereaved, but they remind the rest of us of the price paid by communities for our own peace. Memorials demand a commitment to building a better, more harmonious world. Kenny does not advocate cultural relativism. She believes that some principles **are** worth standing by, that some things **are** worth fighting for. War memorials are important because they remind us that **some** things are important.

Critics have argued that war memorials can be counterproductive to the promotion of peace. This is because they serve as propaganda to reinforce action and conformity during times when these are most needed. Memorials built in the United States of America to commemorate the Vietnam war have been the source of much conflict. Families of those who died in Vietnam have campaigned for some formal, tangible recognition of the sacrifice made by those who were lost. Pacifists, who opposed USA involvement in Vietnam, challenge the value of what they see as glorifying it (Wass and Niemeyer, 1995). Others argue that, in addition to roman-ticising war, memorials promote 'appropriate' gender roles. War memorials nearly always feature men in action and encourage the kind of masculine qualities that are valued most during a war, ie. a strong sense of duty and glorification of the 'supreme sacrifice'. When women are represented in war memorials, their role is one of passive waiting and eternal mourning for lost men. The stress on honour and duty was recognised with cynicism by one of the women in this study. In response to the question of what war memorials signified to ordinary people, she replied, 'that of bravery of the highest order. That men and women should give their lives for what they believed in. For our so called 'freedom".[1]

Reports published of war memorials in the Bolton area following World War I, suggest that they can have propaganda effects. Post war dissatisfaction was gathering momentum by the early 1920s. This is suggested in the following comment-ary on the memorial service held in Bolton and delivered by the Reverend R W Thompson:

> *'The occasion was not one of mourning but of gratitude that we were delivered from the hands of the enemy, through the sacrifice of those who died. There is, he added, a general mood of disillusionment and reaction and he appealed to everyone to be loyal to those who had given their all that we might be saved. We must be loyal to the motive in which they went, loyal to the task they achieved and to the underlying purpose of their sacrifice. It is easy in the aftermath of war to be cynical. We are carrying heavy burdens and the high mood has failed for a time. The nation chose the right course and nothing that has happened since can alter the fact that these men were determined to be true to the obligations of honour and to the cause of the weak against the cruel and to right against might. Their impulses were noble and we should be loyal to that spirit. They call us who survive to live in the same spirit and to see that they did not die in vain, so that the world may grow old in peace and not in strife'.*[2]

The account above appears to have a propaganda function, but this might not have been intentional. The Reverend Thompson was trying to ease grief and help members of the congregation to assign some meaning to the loss of life. Find-ing some meaning for loss can be very comforting. Horton (1981) asserts that it is not so much death that we fear, as meaningless death. But that such justifications for the war were considered necessary, suggests that some people were questioning the sacrifice, the spirit and the motives, not just of

---

1   This woman was aged 62 years when she completed the questionnaire in 1997; religious affiliation, Christian Spiritualist.

2   Memorial service delivered by the Rev R W Thompson, reported in the *Bolton Journal and Guardian*, Friday 12th November 1920.

the young men who went to war, but also the decision of government to declare war in the first place. Many did consider that their loved ones had died in vain.

Despite this, war memorials can still be a great source of comfort to the bereaved. A 76-year-old male participant wrote that war memorials were:

'Something to catch the eye, as may well a picture which, unless brought to mind would not be 'seen' by most people. War memorials are observed on Armistice day, by visitors to town or village.'

This participant places the word 'seen' in quotation marks, emphasising the importance of finding a way to visualise the dead and their memory. War memorials symbolise and eternalise memories of those who died miles away from home. Those bereaved who had no body to view, no corpse to which they could pay their last respects, had no way of confirming and accepting that a death had occurred. The importance of providing some way for the bereaved to 'see' the loss, further suggests the significance of a corpse in helping the bereaved to acknowledge their loss.

Davis (1993) notes that after the two wars the demand for memorials came from ordinary people. Campaigns to erect memorials were generally organised by bereaved mothers who had lost sons. They felt particularly grieved because those who returned received medals, whereas those who died, had nothing to commemorate them:

'I think that people looked on them as an acknowledgement that their loved ones had given service and sacrificed their lives for freedom for the rest of us.'[3]

'Monuments were erected to remind us what amount of young and old lives were sacrificed for our freedom, and also as a permanent tribute to these men. I think that they looked on them as an acknowledgement that their loved ones had given service and sacrificed their lives for freedom for the rest of us.'[4]

3   59-year-old woman affiliated to the Spiritualist Church in Bolton.
4   See *Footnote 3*.

Pressure to erect war memorials may have been partly motivated by the fact that so many men who died, also went missing, and there was no body to confirm the loss. Others were buried so far away from home that it was difficult, indeed sometimes impossible, for the bereaved to visit the grave. The distress that people suffer in the absence of a body may stem from a frustrated desire bury the dead. The significance of war memorials differed. Their popularity depended on whether people had suffered a bereavement or not:

'They were more significant in areas where people suffered a great deal because of heavy regiment involvement or bombing. The significance (of memorials) depends entirely on the relationship and emotional feelings of the people seeing them, age was also significant.'[5]

Another respondent pointed out how important the memorials were to relatives who had no grave to visit:

'The monuments in many cases became the place to take flowers to when there wasn't a grave at all, or it was in some distant land, or at the bottom of the ocean. This was very hard to bear! A cousin of ours lost at El Alamein had no grave as there was no body left to bury. Through a medium I was told that the cousin's tank was on fire and that the crew were trapped.'[6]

The campaigns to have some of these war memorials erected may have been therapeutic in themselves. They may have helped the bereaved progress through the tasks of grief. For some people, this need to grieve and to remember the dead continued long after the war:

'War memorials — very significant! We still parade three times a year and pay homage to our lost comrades (VE/ VJ/Armistice, Nov 11th). Wherever I go I find myself looking at war memorials (you see them in the smallest villages) and I sit for a while with my memories.'[7]

5   Female respondent aged 73 years.
6   Female, Methodist respondent, aged 73 years at the time of her interview
     in 1997.
7   Male respondent aged 77 years when interviewed in 1997, Church of
     England.

In western society, there is an expectation that people return to normal after a limited period of mourning. But the quotation above suggests that grief cannot be resolved quite so easily. One of the strongest themes to emerge from this study, was a belief that those who died during the two wars, should not be forgotten. As an 83-year-old male participant put it 'I think that ordinary people realised the debt left owing to those serviceman who died, and felt that they should never be forgotten for the sacrifices they had made.' Another 59-year-old woman wrote that people considered war memorials as 'an acknowledgement that their loved ones had given service and sacrificed their lives for the freedom of the rest of us'. The bereaved often find it helps to take action, rather than waiting for something to happen (Littlewood, 1993). Campaigns to have memorials erected may have eased feelings of despair. Some of the participants expressed powerful indignation at the fact that, 'few new war memorials were erected after World War II'. Usually names were added to existing World War I monuments — consequently the significance of Remembrance Day faded.'[8]

There is much ritual and symbolism attached to a funeral. Some writers suggest this provides a psychological millstone to the grieving process (Hadenstein and Lamer, 1963), but there is widespread evidence for the view that funeral rituals offer valuable support to society in general, as well as to those who have been bereaved (Littlewood, *op cit*). The services that accompany the unveiling of a war memorial serve diverse functions. Davis (1993) describes war memorials as 'public expressions of private grief.' The rationale for the creation of the tomb of the Unknown Soldier was that any bereaved mother would have a place to mourn her son:

> *'The monuments in many cases became the place to take flowers to when there wasn't a grave at all, or if it was in some distant land or at the bottom of the ocean. This is very hard to bear. A cousin of ours, lost at El Alamein had no grave as there was no body left to bury.'*[9]

---

8   Male respondent age 75 years when interviewed in 1997, Roman Catholic.
9   Woman aged 73 years, brought up as a Methodist.

Without a body, it can be very difficult to find some way to pay tribute to the person (or persons) who have died. War brings individual and collective bereavements. Western society is very individualistic and family life is private. The language available to describe, or even understand, the scale of collective grief, such as that discussed in this book, is limited. Catastrophic grief responses, however, are evident in reports of the times, and in much of the data collected:

> *'I think that people thought of the awful loss of life in the war. Some felt a sense of shame. Most people felt that we **should** honour the memory of our men and women who had paid the final price of our freedom, and hoped that it **would** be beneficial'.*[10]

Catastrophic grief brings home identification of collective, as well as individual, moral responsibilities. This is often under-played in our individualistic western world. The western emphasis on individual responsibility too often leads to the assumption that important decisions are best left to the rulers; those elected to govern. The writer above refers to the sense of shame many people experienced after World War II. This collective shame was referred to by many who were interviewed. It found a powerful public assertion during the first 'two minute silence':

> *'Never has Bolton been so hushed up in the middle of a busy day, as in the two minutes following 11 o'clock on Tuesday forenoon. The town honoured the King's request for an Armistice Day tribute to the glorious dead in the spirit as well as the letter, and for the full space of two minutes a pall of silence that could almost be felt enveloped the town. Some hundreds of people assembled on Victoria Square and, as the Town Hall clock boomed out the first stroke of 11, two fireman discharged a maroon, the flags of the Town Hall and the public library were run down and the people stood with bowed heads and traffic came to a standstill. For two minutes there was neither sound nor movement except that a few*

---

10   A 76-year-old woman, affiliation — Spiritualist, responding to questions about the significance of war memorials.

women, overcome by the thoughts which the anniversary recalled, sobbed and wiped away tears.'

Bolton's first two minutes silence began with a meeting in Victoria Square. Its impact was so powerful that its boundaries could not be defined. Silence swept like a fog across the town. Machinery was switched off, shops, offices, mills, traffic, all activity even in the schools, came to a grinding halt. As the clock struck 11am, silence hit the town. People froze. The silence was deafening.

> *'At Eagley and Edgerton and in the parish of Walmsley, the Armistice hush was loyally observed alike. The great silence was remarkably impressive and was heralded promptly at 11am by the calls of the buzzers at Eagley Mills and Messrs Deans, Limited and the bell at Dunscar Bleach Works. The bell was tolled at Walmsly Church. From Dunscar and Edgerton, motor lorries were observed, stopped on Belmont road from the reservoirs to Sharples.'[11]*

After World War I, immense public pressure was exerted to erect war memorials in all areas of Bolton. In response, plans were underway by 1919. A few days before the two minutes silence, the Executive Committee of the Bolton Branch of the National Association of Discharged Sailors and Soldiers met to discuss their idea that:

> *'Bolton's War Memorial should be in the form of a large hall and institute to be utilised for recreative and business purposes and dedicated to those who had fallen and served in the war, the buildings to be in direct control of the public, who would be represented by persons appointed directly from each ward. They should be free from politics and neither should be used for furthering any party, but unitised entirely to discuss the mutual difficulties and share each others pleasures also, the grievances and injustices occasioned by indifferent or apathetic administration, can be dealt with by ex servicemen and their widows.[12]*

11   Bolton Journal and Guardian, November 14, 1919 *The Great Silence: How Bolton Observed It.*

The Committee recommend that the building should be self-supporting, that it should have photographs of all who had died in the war and that it should be open to men and women over the age of 18 years. The committee were determined to exclude political groups from all meetings scheduled for the proposed memorial building. This suggests a lack of confidence and perhaps a growing cynicism towards political organisations. The idea seemed a good one. But it never materialised. Had it done so, then the memorial building might have provided a base for working-class people to empower themselves; to work together to improve their lot. Many working-class ex servicemen and their families suffered terrible hardship following World War I. The proposed memorial building might, therefore, have provided a more useful and practical way to honour the dead.

A year after the proposal for the memorial building had been presented (and apparently failed) the Cenotaph in Nelson Square, Bolton, was unveiled. This occurred amid much pomp and ceremony, and a service attended by his Royal Highness, Prince Albert.[13] It was an impressive occasion that attracted huge crowds of people:

> '*A guard of honour of the R.F.A was drawn up on the pavement at the lower end of the enclosure, and the rest of the parade on the south side of the square, whilst along each side of Bradshawgate, were about 400 members of the Bolton Branch of the Discharged Soldiers and Soldiers Associations and 250 Girl Guides.*' The Prince expressed his, '*honour and privilege of unveiling the memorial in the memory of your comrades who fell in the great war. The hardship they underwent and the sacrifice they had can never be forgotten by us, and this splendid and fitting memorial will serve to perpetuate to generations to come, the imperishable and glorious memory of those men who fought and died to save their country.*'

12   Bolton Evening News, November 14, 1919, *Ex Servicemen's Suggestion.*
13   Bolton Journal and Guardian, July 30th, 1920, *Bolton's Sunny Welcome to Royal Visitor: Impressive Unveiling of the Cenotaph.*

The speech failed to impress. By this time a great many veterans and their families were suffering financial hardship. A speaker for the Discharged Sailors and Soldiers Association made an appeal to the Prince on behalf of those who were struggling, unemployed, disabled and suffering mental health problems (most of whom by this time, had been incarcerated in pauper lunatic asylums). The speaker making the appeal concluded:

> *'We suggest a Commission should be appointed to consist mainly of representatives of ex servicemen: if and when this is done, we have an admirable and workable scheme to lay before it, which, if adopted would be worthy of the best traditions of the British Empire.'*

This speech suggests a conflict of interests between those in power — the decision makers, and ordinary people. A large percentage of the war memorial speeches after World War I, referred to how just and how fair the British system was compared to Germany. The message conveyed had been that the British were not abusive, but rather protective of the helpless. But the speaker above makes an appeal to see such principles put into practice. There is little space for abstractions in this appeal. Such differences led to a conflict at the time about how the war dead could best be honoured. To the speaker cited above, a memorial to those who fought for a better world should (ideally) provide the means to bring about a better world. Honouring the dead from this perspective, would mean honouring the living as well. But to local and national government, the purpose of a war memorial, was to worship and glorify the 'ultimate sacrifice'.

The reports of the activities of the ex servicemen's committee in Bolton following World War I, suggests that many did not want to dwell on death. They wanted to get on with living. Nevertheless, plans for a grand and impressive concrete memorial continued. On the 8th of October, 1920 a reported announced: [14]

14   Bolton Journal and Guardian, November 14th, 1919, *The Great Silence: How Bolton Observed It.*

'The first contribution towards the beautiful Bolton of the future, which has existed in the minds of lovers of the town for some years, was introduced to the General Purpose Committee of the Town Council. Briefly, the scheme provides for the rearrangement to Queen's Park, which would become the town's principles show face, and the site of some of its fine buildings, as well as the centre for the town's pride in art and architecture.'[15]

This was a very splendid scheme indeed. It involved the construction of a causeway running from Deansgate to Spa Road designed to provide an outlet for traffic on the west side of town. For the memorial itself, the subcommittee recommended:

'A noble campanile, erected in a position that would enable it to be seen uninterruptedly, both from the new causeway and from Chorley New Road and containing the names of all Bolton Men who fought in the great war in the navel, military and air forces of the crown.' It was also proposed that *'when the scheme is completed, the campanile would be flanked on one side by an art gallery and on the other by a museum.'* The memorial was to be modelled on the famous campanile that had stood for many centuries in St Marks Square, Venice, until it had been destroyed by fire in 1911. In terms of the scheme's potential to liven up the dull, industrial landscape of Bolton, it had much to commend it.'

Objective reading of the plans many years later (alongside accounts of the Depression) make it hard not to conclude that the money invested in this might have been better spent improving living conditions for workers in the town. Most Bolton people at this time were working up to twelve hours a day in dirty unhygienic industrial conditions. They lived in crowded, two up, two down, back to back houses, with no bathrooms or indoor toilets. There was no NHS so, if a person was ill, the families had to pay for medical attention. Few Boltonians at this time enjoyed good health and infant

---

15   Bolton Journal and Guardian, 8th October, 1920, *Bolton War Memorial: Campanile as Part of Big Scheme.*

mortality was very high. Given the harsh struggle to survive, it is hard to imagine how people would have found time to browse around art galleries. But when people are in grief, they do not always think in terms of practicalities. Once the memorials had been erected, the people of the town were delighted with them. By the 15th October, 1920, the *Bolton Journal and Guardian* was reporting that:

> '*Almost every district parish and denomination in this part of Lancashire has either decided on its war memorial, or is presently debating the question. Principle differences of view arise as to whether memorials should be interior or exterior. Whenever funds flow, there can be little doubt that an exterior memorial lends itself to better treatment and wider appeal, as it is seen by members of all denominations as well as the general public.*'

Throughout 1919 and 1920, the local papers were packed with news of memorial services and the unveiling of war memorials. Many of these were quite modest honouring the dead from local parishes. The memorial at Deane and St George's Churches consisted of plain, dignified bronze tablets that carried inscriptions for all the war dead in the parish.[16] These memorial services attracted large crowds of people who were greatly comforted by them. For the bereaved, the services allowed a public acknowledgement of grief and an opportunity for collective mourning. The effects were long lasting, as the writer below suggests:

> '*In Whitehall stands the Cenotaph in memory of the men who gave their lives in the Great War, and in Westminster Abby is the Tomb of the Unknown Warrier, symbol of the Nation's debt to all who died in war service. In towns and villages throughout the country war memorials have at some odd moments, in spite of their familiar appearances, reminded us of Europe's four year orgy of destruction, the stupendous self-slaughter of humanity, in a period of prolific suffering. In the country which won 'victory' there was at first perhaps, something*

16   Bolton Journal and Guardian, 12th November 1920, *Church War Memorials.*

of the spirit of Roman triumph as well as the
thankfulness for peace in our celebrations, but that mood
was short. When we gathered on succeeding Armistice
days to observe the two minutes silence our minds dwelt
on the ugliness and stupidity, not on the glory of war, and
those who conducted the services, called on us to dedicate
ourselves to peace.'[17]

Here the meaning of the 'ultimate sacrifice' has changed. The
war memorial stands, not for glory but for remembrance of the
cruelty, waste and ugliness of war. The irony of the extract is
that it was published on September, 1st, 1939, just months
before the outbreak of World War II. War memorials do touch
us, as the speaker says, at the most unexpected times. For
those have never experienced war, their absolute meaning
dwells in a space that rests beyond the boundaries of any
experience. Those impressive men in uniform, cast like
Midas's daughter in bronze and stone, stand apart, divorced
from anything we can ever hope to understand. But to those
who have survived a war they appear sacred. In a letter
published in the *Bolton Evening News* in 1996, a writer
expressed concern for the littered, neglected appearance of the
war memorial in Victoria Square. The writer appeals for us to
remember 'it is there (the war memorial) for the people who
lost loved ones' and concludes, 'it must be upsetting for them
to see the memorial in such a poor state'.

Following World War I (and indeed World War II) many
of those who returned felt a sense of alienation from their
communities. There was also a feeling of hopelessness.[18] War
memorials and remembrance services provided an opportunity to acknowledge grief and regret. They may have served
to dissolve differences, open up dialogue and bind people
together. By the same token, they could increase feelings of
difference; of alienation (Fulton 1995). Writing of the 1918
Armistice, Brittain (*op cit*) observed:

'Already this was a different world from the one that I
had known during four lifelong years; a world in which

17   Bolton Evening News, September 1st, 1939, *Topic of the Week: We Do Not*
      Want War: Yet, Dangerous Powers of the Dictators.
18   Brittain V (1933) *Testament of Youth*, Chapter 10, page 460.

people could be lighthearted and forgetful, in which themselves and their careers and their amusements would blot out political ideals and great national issues. And in that dimly lit alien world I should have no part. All those with whom I had really been intimate were gone. Not one remained to share with me the heights and the depths of my memories. As the years went by and youth departed and remembrance grew dim, a deeper and ever deeper darkness would cover the young men who had once been my contemporaries.'[19]

Collective grief, guilt, moral questioning and responsibility prevailed strongly following the two wars. There was also an equally strong desire for normality, to put the pain behind. A 63-year-old male participant (who wrote that he was too young during the war to understand what was going on) when asked about the significance of war memorials wrote, 'the only Cenotaph I have any connection with is the one at Starcliff Methodist Church at Moses Gate. There are 15 names on it. Three of these have my family name.' Here lies the implicit expression of a different type of loss, a mourning for lost possibilities. The writer grieves for family members never known, of friendships and relationships never made. What were they like? What would it have been like to have known them? War memorials then, are significant to the whole community, not just the bereaved. As another respondent put it, they provided, 'a memorial to people whom you and others knew, and information regarding those whom you didn't see regularly, yet knew they had been through the war.'[20]

Despite the scale of loss during the two world wars, there was no revival of the elaborate Victorian mourning ritual. Instead, there was an increased interest in spiritualism (Littlewood, 1993). This appears to have been a very general thing shaped by perceptions of death that had changed because of the war. This effected almost everyone, regardless of whether they had experienced a bereavement or not. As one respondent put it:

---

19   Brittain, 1933, *op cit*, Chapter 10, page 496.
20   70-year-old woman affiliated to the Spiritualist Church.

*'Many people felt that the near possibility of death for
their loved ones or themselves was always with them.
They thought more seriously about what happened after
death. **Would they see their loved ones again**?'*[21]

This book has explored the very different experiences of
those who went to war and those who stayed at home. These
differences made it difficult, and sometimes impossible, for
families to reunite. This was a tragedy, and equally tragic
were the thousands of couples whose lives together were
destroyed. It is not just the loss of life (and ways of life) that
makes a war so terrible, but also, the loss of possibilities. War
memorials stand as a monument to those who died and as a
reminder to those who live. In a sense, books such as this
serve as war memorials. This in itself poses problems, most
notably (from the author's point of view) in relation to the
approach adopted and the audiences we academics hope to
reach. As academics, what is our role when we teach history?
When we research populations, who should have ownership
of the data we uncover and how accessible should it be?
Kenny is inclined to ask, 'Whose history is it anyway?'

If we draw on too much academic language and theory,
our work becomes inaccessible to those whose stories we have
used and who we might most wish to inform. Yet if we are too
descriptive, then we do not do justice to our data because we
present it in simplistic ways that can sometimes do more harm
than good. Social scientists have special problems. Given that
our experience shapes our perceptions and our selection of
'appropriate' theory, whose story are we telling? That of our
participants? Or, do we use other people's stories as vehicles to
tell our own? How useful are today's theories in helping
explain the events of the past? We must always remember that
we view yesterday through the lens of today. The way we
construct theoretically informed histories can add to the
doubts. No matter what sources we use, there are always gaps,
so we move to other sources, and other sources. We sew our
patchwork quilt together, a meaningful pattern made from
disparate yarn, fabric and cloth. But let someone come along,

21   This woman was aged 76 years at the time that she responded to the
      questionnaire in 1997. She is affiliated to the Spiritual Church in Bolton.

take it apart and put it back together, then we have a different pattern, a different story. But that is the nature of research. We can even question the very nature of history. What is it? Shakespeare (1996) contrasts the view of traditional historians, who see chronology and continuity, with post structuralists who challenge the very idea that such continuities exist. Kenny takes the middle ground, arguing that if we could take an aerial view of history, then we would see something that could be likened to roads on a map. There may be main roads running through, but their continuity is disrupted at various stages by interception of side roads. These side roads are important; they suggest alternative directions, new locations and other views. And when it comes to the construction of identities, this is important.

Wertsch (1997) notes that, 'Knowledge of the past is widely viewed as a crucial ingredient in the construction of identities' and he continues 'This perspective assumes that we don't know who we are if we don't know where we came from'. But Wertsch also continues by arguing that history can shape many different types of identities for many different purposes. He compares for example, the instruction of history in schools, with exploration of history of the type that takes place in Higher Education. The first dictates identities, the second creates them.

There are alternative histories, alternative identities and Kenny is keen to play her part in helping to create them. Different stories challenge dominant voices and help those excluded to find a space. Space is important because where there is space, there is room for growth. In relation to people with a disability, Shakespeare (*op cit*) argues that, 'Disability identity is about stories, having the space to tell them, and an audience that will listen' and that 'Theory has a part to play in this process. But (metaphorically, if not physiologically), it all starts with having a voice. Shakespeare concludes that, 'Our task is to speak the truth about ourselves'.

The author believes that the men and women who took part in this study did their very best to speak the truth about themselves. They told stories of loss that went beyond biological death, loss of community, loss of relationships, even to an extent, of themselves. Yet just as powerful in these stories were the themes of birth, growth and change. War it seems, brings gains as well as losses.

The men, especially, astonished Kenny by revealing different perceptions of masculinity, in particular, as expressed within a military context. The military context is one that has most powerfully promoted images of tough masculinity. Yet in these accounts, it was the military that challenged this view, as the theme of human vulnerability coloured the data like a fog 'blanketing out' the dominant view. It has been the author's task to present these stories and to illuminate their meaning within an appropriate theoretical framework. But having done this, whose story has she told?

Conclusion

What makes a good book?

In the end, Kenny put such concerns to one side and aimed, instead, to simply do her best to write a good book. So, what makes a good book? She has always had a passion for reading. It comes second only to writing as her most treasured pastime. What makes a good book? A good book is a good read. It is an experience. As such, a book should inform, educate, but most of all, it should pull on the emotions. It should **make** experience. A good book makes you laugh, it makes you cry, it makes you contemplate. In writing this book, she has often felt inadequate. Nevertheless, she hopes that she has achieved at least some of these aims.

Of the three thanatologies produced, she has found this the most difficult. Research is hard work. The production of this book has changed many of her earlier assumptions; about war, gender, men and violence. Listening to and reading the stories, examining a huge amount of material, watching war film after war film, has proved a very difficult (and painful) process. But from Kenny's own point of view, it has been worth the effort. Her main concern is that she has done justice to the data; that her interpretations have shown respect for the people who allowed her to share and to use their stories. Kenny's greatest change in ideology has been in relation to her ideas about war. When she began the research, she considered war from a very abstract, detached perspective. At its conclusion, she ends with a reiteration of the point, so powerfully made at the conclusion of the film 'Heaven and Earth'. The greatest battles in life are fought, not in this land or that, but in the heart.

References and bibliography

Adler G (1966) *Studies in Analytic Psychology.* Hodder and Stoughton, London

Adler RB, Rosenfield LB, Towne N (1995) *Interplay: The Process of Interpersonal Communication.* Harcourt Brace, Orlando

Airmen Memorial Foundation (1997) Help for Blind Veterans *Blinded Veterans Association* (BVA) (1-800-827-1000 TROA, LA) also available on internet — Disability home page, USA

Andrews L (1977) *No Time for Romance* Guernsey, Courage Books

Archer J (1996) *They Had A Dream: The Civil Rights Struggle from Frederick Douglass to Marcus Gravely to Martin Luther King Jar and Malcolm X.* Puffin Books, New York

Aries P (1974) *Western Attitudes Towards Death.* John Hopkins University Press, London

Balwin D (1997) Warning Signs of Trauma Related Stress *American Psychological Association*, Trauma Information pages, http://www.trauma-pages.com

Baldwinson D (1995) *Reading War* unpublished seminar paper presented at South Bank University, Combined Honours, Politics of Health Research Interest Group, South Bank University, London

Barnes C (1996) Introduction. In: Barton L, Oliver M, eds. *Disability Studies: Past, Present and Future.* The Disability Press, University of Leeds, Leeds

Barnes C, Mercer G, eds. (1996) Exploring the Divide Introduction to *Exploring the Divide: Illness and Disability.* The Disability Press, University of Leeds, Leeds

Beall LS (1997) Post traumatic stress disorder: A bibliographic essay. *CHOICE* **34**(6): 917–30

Beecher HK (1959) *Measurement of Subjective Responses to Pain.* Oxford University Press, New York

Berchild E, Walster E, Bohrensteddt G (1972) beauty and the beast. *Psychol Today* **5**(10): 46

Bernstein NR (1976) *Emotional Care of the Facially Burned and Disfigured.* Little, Brown & Co, Boston

Bessel A, Van der Kolk, Fistler R (1998) *Dislocations and the Fragmentary Nature of Traumatic Memories.* Harvard Medical School, Department of Psychology. David Balwins Trauma Information pages, Eugine, Oregon, USA, home page http://www.trauma-pages.com

Blackmun S (1991) For better for worse. *ACCENT for Living Magazine* Winter: 20

Blumenthal S, Kupfer D (1990) *Suicide Over the Life Cycle: Risk Factors, Assessment and Treatment of Suicide Patients.* American Academic Press, Washington

Bonta B (1993) *Peaceful Peoples: An Annotated Bibliography.* NT Scarecrow. Metchen

Bonta B (1996) Conflict resolution among peaceful societies: The culture of peacefulness. *J Peace Res* 33(4): 403–20

Bowlby J (1965) *Child Care and the Growth of Love.* Penguin Books, Harmondsworth

Bowlby J (1980) *Attachment and Loss: Vol. 3; Loss, Sadness and Depression.* Hogarth Press, London

Burt C (1969) *The Young Delinquent*. University of London Press, London

Burn AR (1974) *The Pelican History of Greece*. Penguin Books, Harmondsworth

Brown R, Kulik J (1977) Flashbulb memories. *Cognition* **5**: 73–99

Briere J, Conte J (1993) Self-reported amnesia for abuse in adults molested as
    children. *J Traum Stress* **6**(1): 21–31

Brittain V (1933) *Testament of Youth: An Autobiographical Study of the Years
    1900–1925*. Fontana Books, Glasgow

Cambell A (1981) *Girl Delinquents*. Basil Blackwell, Oxford

Campbell ML (1996) A life course perspective: Ageing with long term disability:
    maximising human potential. *Q News Lett Ageing Disabil Rehab Network
    Am Soc Ageing* **1**(3): 1–2

Cannandine D (1981) War and death, grief and mourning in modern Britain. In:
    Whaley J ed. *Mirrors of Mortality: Studies in the Social History of Death*.
    The Stanhope Press, London

Carlen PL, Wall PD, Nadvaorna H, Steinback T (1978) Phantom limbs and related
    phenomena in recent traumatic amputations. *Neurol* **28**: 211–17

Casey C (1997) Eugenic: The sinister subplot to the search for social Utopia. Daily
    Mail: Saturday Essay, August 20th

Cavalier R (1996) A dialogical perspective of feminism and pornography:
    Pornography as crime. *CMC Magazine,* (Internet publication— Rape home
    page)

Clatterborough K (1990) *Contemporary Perspectives on Masculinity: Men, Women
    and Politics in Modern Society*. Westview Press, Oxford

Cohen BM (1997) *Managing Traumatic Stress Through Art: Drawing from the
    Center*. Sidran Foundation, New York

Conant JB (1962) Social dynamite in our larger cities. *Crime Delinq* **8**: 102–15

Connell RW (1987) *Gender and Power*. Polity Press, Oxford

Costello J (1985) *Love, Sex and War: Changing Values, 1939–1945*. HarperCollins,
    London

Cruse Editorial (1992) When the body is missing. *Cruse Bull* **8**: 3

Critchley M (1950) The body image in neurology. *Lancet* **1**: 335–40

Crook M (1992) *Please Listen To Me: Your Guide to Understanding Teenagers and
    Suicide*. Facts on File, New York

Dale PN (1995) *Many Mansions: The Growth of Religion in 19th Century Bolton*.
    Kwikprint, Bolton

Davenport-Hines R (1990) *Sex, Death and Punishment: Attitudes to Sex and
    Sexuality in Britain Since the Renaissance*. HarperCollins, London

Davis J (1993) War memorials. In: Clark D, ed. *The Sociology of Death*. Blackwell
    Publishers, Oxford

De Bois EC, Ruiz VI (1990) *Unequal Sisters*. Routlege, London

De Fazio VJ (1978) Dynamic perspectives on the nature and effects of combat
    stress. In: Figley CR, ed. *Stress Disorders Among Vietnam Veterans: Theory,
    Research and Treatment*. Brunner/Hazel, New York

Disabled American Veterans (1997) *Gulf War Information Sheet* Washington, Autry
    D Contact (202) 554-3501 — Disability home page USA

Dobbs A (1993*) Rehabilitating Blind and Visually Impaired People: A Psychological
    Approach*. Chapman and Hall, London

Donovan M, Pierce S (1976) *Cancer Care Nursing*. Appleton-Century Crofts, East
    Norwalk CT

References

Duck S (1994) *Meaningful Relationships.* Sage, Thousand Oaks

Dryer G (1995) *The Missing of the Somme.* Penguin Books, Harmondsworth

Dworkin A, MacKinnon CA (1992) The anti-pornography civil rights ordinance. A brief description. *Judiciary Committee of the Commonwealth of Massachusetts* (internet publication)

Early E (1993) *The Raven's Return: The Influence of Psychological Trauma on Individuals and Culture.* Chiron Publications, New York

Edgerton E (1963) *The Clock of Competence: Stigma in the Lives of the Mentally Subnormal.* Routledge and Kegan Paul, London

Emerson J (1983) Living through grief. *Nurs Mirror* **157**: i–ii

Erikson E (1968) *Identity, Youth and Crisis.* W W Norton, New York

Fabbro D (1978) Peaceful societies: An introduction. *J Peace Res* **15**(1): 67–83

Fatchett A (1995) *Childhood to Adolescence: Caring for Health.* Bailliere Tindall, London

Fielding S (1995) *The Hangman's Record: Vol 2: 1900–1929.* Chancery House, Beckenham

Figley CR, ed (1978a) *Stress Disorders Among Vietnam Veterans: Theory, Research and Therapy.* Bruner/Mazel, New York

Fisher S, Cleveland SE (1968*) Body Image and Personality.* Dover Publications, New York,

Finckelstein V (1995) The commonality of disability. In: Swain J, Finckelstein V, Oliver M, eds. *Disabling Barriers — Enabling Environments.* Sage, London

Foy DW (1992) *Treating PTSD: Cognitive Behaviour Strategies.* Guildford Press, USA

Frank L, Frank M (1955) *How to be a Women.* Bobbs-Merrill, New York

Freud S (1917 — reprinted 1950) *Reflections on War and Death.* (Translated by AA Brill and Kutter AB). WW Norton, New York,

Friedman MJ (1998) *Post Traumatic Stress Disorder: An Overview.* National Center for Post Traumatic Stress Disorder, United States Department of Veteran's Affairs http://www.dartmouth.edu/dms/ptsd/

Fulton R (1995) The contemporary funeral: Functional or dysfunctional. In: Wass H, Niemeyer RA, eds. *Dying: Facing the Facts.* Taylor and Frances, London

Galler R (1993) The myth of the perfect body. In: Beattie A, Gott M, Jones L , Sidell M, eds. *Health and Wellbeing: A Reader* The Open University, Milton Keynes

Galtung J (1996) *Peace by Peaceful Means: Peace and Conflict, Development and Civilisation.* Sage, London

Gandi M (1951) *Non-Violent Resistance.* Schocken Books, New York

Gandi M (1955) *Gandi: An Autobiography or My Experiments with Truth.* Penguin Books, Harmondsworth

Gilbert P (1992) *The Evolution of Powerlessness.* Lawrence Erlhaum Associates, London

Gilligan C (1982*) In a Different Voice: Psychological Theory and Women's Development.* Cambridge University Press, Cambridge

Goffman E (1961) *Asylums.* Penguin Books, Harmondsworth

Goffman E (1963) *Stigma: Notes on the Management of a Soiled Identity.* Penguin Books, Harmondsworth

Goodman P (1993) Her Stories of the Second World War. Unpublished paper presented at Manchester University

Goodwin J (1987) *The Aetiology of Combat Related Post Traumatic Stress Disorders*. American Psychological Association. David Balwin's Trauma Information Page http://www.trauma-pages.com

Gordon L (1988) *Heroes of Their Own: The Politics and History of Family Violence*. Vicking, New York

Goror G (1965) *Death, Grieving and Mourning in Contemporary Modern Britain*. Cassell, London

Grinker RR, Spiegal JP (1945) *Men Under Stress*. Blackinson, Philadelphia

Hadenstein RW, Lamer WN (1963) *Funeral Customs the World Over*. Bufin Printers, Milwaukee

Halfpenny BB (1986) *Ghost Stations: True Ghost Stories*. Casdec , Co Durham

Hall LA (1991) *Hidden Anxieties: Male Sexuality: 1900–1950*. Polity Press, Oxford

Halstead LS (1988) Late complications of poliomyelitis. In: Goodgold J ed. *Rehabilitation Medicine*. Mosby CV and Stouis MO, New York

Healy D (1993) *Images of Trauma: from Hysteria to Post Traumatic Stress Disorder*. Faber and Faber, London/ Boston

Hersh RH, Miller JP, Fielding GD (1980) *Models of Moral Education: An Appraisal*. Longman Group, New York

Horton PC (1981) *Solace, the Missing Dimension in Psychiatry*. University of Chicago Press, Chicago

Holdsworth A (1988) *Out of the Doll's House: The Story of Women in the Twentieth Century*. BBC Books, London

Hooks B (1989) *Feminism and Militarism: A Comment on Hooks* — cited in Segal (1988) *Slow Motion; Changing Masculinity's, Changing Men*. Virago Press, London

Horowitz MJ, Solomon GF (1975) A prediction of delayed stress response syndrome in Vietnam Vets. *J Soc Iss* **31**(4): 67–80

Howard S (1976) The Vietnam warrior: His experience and implications for therapy. *Am J Psychother* **30**(1): 121–35

Howell S, Willis R , eds (1989a) *Societies at Peace: Anthropological Perspectives*. Routledge, New York

Hull J (1990) *Touching the Rock: An Experience of Blindness*. Arrow Books, London

Hutchinson SA, Wilson HS, Wilson HS (1994) The benefits of participating in research interviews. *J Nurs Scholar* **26**: 22

Huxley A (1937) An Encyclopaedia of Pacifism: 2nd edn. Reprinted in: Seegley R (1986) The Handbook of Non-Violence. The Peace Pledge Union of the United States

Huzyncski A, Buchman D (1991) *Organisational Behaviour*. Prentice Hall, Harmondsworth

Illich I (1977) *Limits to Medicine: Medical Nemesis and the Expropriation of Health*. Penguin, Harmondsworth

Ivie S (1991) Marriage to quad ends in divorce. *ACCENT for Living Magazine* Summer: 19–22

Kahane C (1992) Object relations theory. In: Wright E, ed. *Feminism and Psychoanalysis: A Critical Dictionary*. Basil Blackwell, Oxford

Kastenbaum R (1986) Death in the world of adolescence. In: Corr AC, Mc Neil MC, eds. *Adolescence and Death*. Singer Publishing, New York

Kastenbaum RJ (1988) Safe death in the post modern world. In: Gilmore A, Gilmore S, eds. *A Safer Death: Multi Disciplinary Aspects of Terminal Care*. Plenum Press, London

References

Kearl MC (1996) Death and politics: A psychosocial perspective. In: Wass H, Neimeyer RA, eds. *Dying: Facing the Facts*, 3 edn. Taylor and Frances, USA

Kelly MP (1996) Negative attributes of self: radical surgery and the inner and outer lifeworld. In: Barnes C, Mercer G, eds. *Exploring the Divide: Illness and Disability*. The Disability Press, University of Leeds, Leeds

Kemp CH (1968) *The Battered Child*. University of Chicago Press, Chicago

Kenny C (1989) Caring: A Living Bereavement. Unpublished project completed for the BSc (Hons) Psychology, Bolton Institute, Bolton

Kenny C (1992) Sexuality, Mental Handicap and the Management of Orgasm. Unpublished report completed for the MSc in Applied Psychology, Manchester University, Manchester

Kenny C (1994) *Cotton Everywhere: Recollections of Northern Women Textile Workers*. Aurora Press, Bolton

Kenny C, Wibberley C (1994) The case for interactive interviewing. *Nurse Researcher* **1**(3): 24–8

Kenny C (1998a) *A Northern Thanatology*. Quay Books, Dinton

Kenny C (1998c) *A Thanatology of the Child*. Quay Books, Dinton

Kinzie JD (1993) Post traumatic effects and their treatment among south east Asian refugees. In: Wilson JP, Raphael B, eds. *International Handbook of Traumatic Stress Syndromes*. Plenum, New York

Krystal JH (1987) *Integration and Self-Healing After Trauma, Alexithymia: Psychoanalytic Reformations*. Analytic Press, New York

Kubler-Ross L (1969) *On Death and Dying* New York, Macmillan

Kubler-Ross L (1983) *On Children and Death*. Macmillan, New York

Kulka RA (1990) *Trauma and the Vietnam War Generation*. Report on findings from the National Vietnam Veterans Readjustment Study. Bruner/Hazel, USA

Lakoff R (1975) Language and Woman's Place. Harper and Row, London

Lewis P (1997) Lords Boost for Disabled: Ruling will help the disabled live better lives Internet Publication — Disability home page, UK

Levin P (1989) *The Trauma Response*. American Psychological Society, Eugene, Oregon: David Balwin's Trauma Information Page http://www.trauma.pages.comm

Lifton RJ (1973) Home from the War. Simon and Schuster, New York: cited by Goodwin (1987) David Balwin's Trauma page — http://www.trauma.pages.com

Lifton R J (1997) *The Life of the Self*. Simon and Schuster, New York

Lindsay M (1988) Sensory impairment and body image. In: Salter M, ed. *Altered Body Image: The Nurses Role*. John Wiley, Chichester

Linn R (1986) Conscientious objection in Israel during the war in Lebanon. *Armed Forces Soc* **2**(4): 489–511

Linn R (1996) When the individual soldier says 'no' to war: A look at selective refusal during the Intafada. *J Peace Res* **33**(4): 421–31

Littlewood J (1993) *Aspects of Grief: Studies of Bereavement in Adult Life*. Routledge, London

Lorenz K (1966) *On Aggression*. Harcourt, Brace & Co, New York

Lovering P (1998) Sexuality and Disability. Personal communication. Email: arcsphx@primenet.com

Lovering P (1998) *Out of the Darkness* Internet publication Disability home page USA http://www.premenet.com./ aresphx

Manning H (1985) Sudden death. *Nurs Mirror* **160**(18): 19–21

Marshall B (1947) Men against fire. Washington DC, Department of the Army. Cited by: Costello J (1985) *Love, Sex and War: Changing Values 1939–1945*. Collins, London

Marshall JD (1974*) Lancashire*. Latimor, Plymouth

Martin MT (1993) Commentary on beliefs of preventability of death among the disaster bereaved. *Nurs Res* **14**(5): 576–94

May L (1988) Body image disturbance in burns. In: Salter M, ed. *Altered Body Image: The Nurses Role*. John Wiley, Chichester

McClelland A (1997) Effects of pornography on the rape myth. *Pornography and Free Speech Series*. Internet fact sheet publication

McWhirther L (1992) Trouble, stress and psychological disorder in Northern Ireland — A commentary. *Psychol Bull Bri Psychol Soc* **5**: 351–2

Melzak (1992) The Phantom Limb. Unpublished paper presented at the *British Psychological Society Annual Conference*, Scarborough

Middleton P (1992) *The Inwards Gaze: Masculinity and Subjectivity in Modern Culture*. Routledge, London

Miell D, Dallos R (1996) *Social Interaction and Personal Relationships* Sage, London

Miller J (Work in Progress) Mr Bryan. To be submitted when complete to, The Record: The Journal of the Lancashire Authors Association, Eccles

Miller JB (1976) *Toward a New Psychology of Women*. Penguin Books, London

Mulkey M (1993) Social death in Britain. In: Clark D, ed. *The Sociology of Death*. Blackwell Publishers, Oxford

Montagu A (1970) *The Direction of Human Development*. Hawthorn Books, New York

Montagu A (1978*) Learning Non-Aggression: The Experience of Non-Literate Societies*. Oxford University Press, London

Morgan R (1977) White men are most responsible. In: Morgan R, ed. *Goodbye To All That: The Personal Journal of a Feminist*. Random House, New York

Morris D (1967) *The Naked Ape*. McGraw Hill, New York

Murburg MM (1994) *Catecholamine Function in Post Traumatic Stress Disorder: Emerging Concepts*. American Psychiatric Press, Washington

Nance J (1975) *The Gentle Tasaday*. Harcourt Brace, New York

National Victim Centre (1998) Myths and Facts about Sexual Violence. Pornography and Free Speech Series, Internet fact sheet, USA

Norman E (1990*) Women at War: The Story of Fifty Military Nurses who Served in Vietnam*. University of Pennsylvania Press, Philadelphia

Oldfield S (1989) *Women Against the Iron Fist: Alternatives to Militarism*. Basil Blackwell, Oxford

Oliver M (1995) Redefining disability: a challenge to research. In: Swain J, Finckelstein V, French S, Oliver M, eds. *Disabling Barriers — Enabling Environments*. Sage, London

Paralyzed Veterans of America (1997) Factsheet — Internet, Disability home page, USA

Parkes CM (1972) *Bereavement: Studies of Grief in Adult Life*. Routledge, London

Parson ER (1986) Life after death: Vietnam veterans struggle for meaning and recovery. *Death Stud* **10**(1): 11–26

References

Parsons IM (1974) *Men Who Marched Away: Poems of the First World War.* Heineman Educational Books, London

Payne S (1991) Why are women poor? In: Payne S, ed. *Women, Health and Poverty.* Harvester Wheatsheaf, Hemel Hempstead

Pitt M, Philips M (1991) *The Psychology of Health: An Introduction.* Routledge, London

Plummer K (1995) *Telling Sexual Stories.* Routledge, London

Rape Fact Sheet (1998) Myths and facts about sexual violence (Internet publication, Rape Information home page)

Reader's Digest (1995a) *Life in the Twenties and Thirties.* Reader's Digest Press, London

Reader's Digest (1995b) *Life on the Home Front.* Readers Digest Press, London

Richardson N, Richardson S (1995) *Fallen in the Flight: Farnworth and Kearsley Men Who Died in the Great War: 1914–1918.* Neil Richardson, Radcliffe

Rose H (1994) *Love, Power and Knowledge: Towards a Feminism Transformation of the Sciences.* Polity Press, Oxford

Rowan J (1983) *The Reality Game: A Guide to Humanistic Counselling and Therapy.* Routledge, London

Ruddick S (1989) *Maternal Thinking: Towards a Politics of Peace.* The Women's Press, London

Ryle P (1979) *Missing in Action: May–Sept, 1944.* Howard A & Wyndham Co, London

Saigh PA (1992) *Post Traumatic Stress Disorder: A Behavioural Approach to Assessment and Treatment.* Pergamon Press, Oxford

Salmaggi C, Pallavisini A (1977) *2194 Days of War: An Illustrated Chronology of the 2nd World War.* Windward, London

Salter M, ed. (1988) *Altered Body Image: The Nurse's Role.* John Wiley, Chichester

Schacter DL (1987) Implicit memory: History and current status: Learning, memory and current status. *J Exp Psychol* **13**: 510–18

Seegley R (1986) *The Handbook of Non Violence.* The Peace Pledge Union of the United States of America

Segal L (1990) *Slow Motion: Changing Masculinities, Changing Men.* Virago Press, London

Seligman MEP (1975) *Helplessness: On Depression, Development and Death.* Freeman and Co, San Francisco

Shakespeare T (1996) Disability, identity and difference. In: Barnes C, Mercer G, eds. *Exploring the Divide: Illness and Disability.* The Disability Press, University of Leeds, Leeds

Shakepeare T (1998) Able minds incarcerated by traditional attitudes. *The Times Higher Education Supplement*, April 24: 20

Shaton CF (1973) Stress disorders among Vietnam combat veterans self-help movement. *Am J Ortopsych* **43**(4): 640–53

Showalter E (1987) *The Female Malady: Women, Madness and English Culture* London, Virago

Sibley D (1995) *Geography of Exclusion.* Routledge, London

Slevin M, Sir N (1991) *Challenging Cancer: From Chaos to Control.* Routledge, London

Squire LR (1994) Declarative and non-declarative memory: Supporting learning and memory. In: Schacter DL, Tuluing J, eds. *Memory Systems.* MIT Press, Cambridge MA

A thanatology of war

Squire LR, Zola Morgan S (1991) The medial temporal lobe memory system. *Science* **153**: 2380–6

Star and Garter (1997) *Caring for Those Who Served* (factsheet) Star and Garter Hotel, Richmond, Surrey

Stoltenberg J (1990) *Refusing to be a Man*. Fontana, London

Swanwick KK (1987) *I Have Been Young*. Gollancz, London

Swerdlow A (1993) *Women Strike for Peace: Traditional Motherhood and Radical Politics in the 1960s*. University of Chicago Press, Chichester

Tajfel H, ed. (1978) *Differentiation Between Social Groups: Studies in the Social Psychology of Intergroup Relations*. Academic Press, London

The Royal British Legion (1998) Information fact sheet http://www.britishlegion.org.uk//

Thompson D, ed. (1983) *Over Our Dead Bodies: Women Against the Bomb*. Virago, London

Turner B, Rennell T (1995) *When Daddy came Home: How Family Life Changed Forever in 1945*. Random House, London

Van r Kolk BA, Blitz R, Burr WA, Hartman E (1984) Nightmares and trauma: Lifelong and traumatic nightmares in Veterans. *Am J Psychiatry* **141**: 187–90

Vietnam Veterans Against the War Inc General Information Page Home page http://www.prairenet.org/vvaw : Email: jtmiller@uniuc.edu

Walton JK (1987) *Lancashire: A Social History: 1558–1939*. Manchester University Press, Manchester

Walzer M (1970) *Obligations: Essays on Disobedience and Citizenship*. Harvard University Press, Cambridge MA

War Amputees (1997) *History of the War Amps of Canada* Canada (War Amps)

War Heroes of World War 11 (1997) Email factsheet WAR HEROES@GEOCITIES

Wass H, Neimeyer RA (1995) *Dying: Facing the Facts*. Taylor and Frances, USA

Weinstein J (1997) A dramatic view of grieving. *Counselling* **8**(4): 256–7

Weinstein J (1998) The Need for the Bereaved to Maintain an Ongoing Relationship with the Dead. Unpublished paper, South Bank University, School of Health and Social Care, Erlang House, London

Weinberg N (1994) Self-blame, other blame and desire for revenge: factors in recovery. *Death Stud* **18**(6): 583–93

Weiss R (1974) The provision of social relationships. In: Rubin Z, ed. *Doing Unto Others*. Prentice Hall, New Jersey

Wendall S (1992) Towards a feminist theory of disability. In: Holmes HB, Purdy LM, eds. *Feminist Perspectives in Medical Ethics*. Indiana Press, New York

Wertsch JV (1997) Narrative tools of history and identity. *Cult Psychol* **3**(1): 5–20

Weston S (1985) *Walking Tall: An Autobiography*. Bloomsbury Publishing, London

Wicks B (1991) *Welcome Home: True Stories of Soldiers Returning from WW2*. Bloombury Publishing, London

Wilson R, Cairns E (1992) Trouble, stress and psychological disorder in Northern Ireland. *The Psychologist Leicester,* The British Psychological Society

Worden JW (1982) *Grief Counselling and Grief Therapy*. Springer, New York

Wright B (1988) Sudden death: Aspects which incapacitate the carer. *Nursing* **3**(31): 12–14

Wright S (1989) *Sudden Death*. Macmillan Press, London

Ziemke EF (1994) *WW1.1* (1993–96) Microsoft @ Encarta 97 Encyclopaedia, Microsoft Corporation

Films

Apocalypse Now (1979) Distributed by: United Artists
Born on the Fourth of July (1989) Distributed by: Universal Pictures
Birdie (1984) Distributed by: Trim Star
The Deer Hunter (1979) Distributed by: Universal Pictures
Heaven and Earth (1993) Distributed by: Warner Bros
Murder in the First (1995) Distributed by: Warner Bros
Taxi Driver (1976) Distributed by: Columbia Pictures

Television

Roses of No Man's Land: An Edited Transcript (1997) Channel 4 Television, 124 Horseferry Road, London, SW1P 2TX

Appendix I
Girls who want to work: Seeking new avenues:

Bolton possesses a class of girl for which anxiety is being felt. She is a new type — a war product, whose welfare depended on the ex agencies of the war, and whose future is at stake. This is no disparaging comment on the capabilities of our womanhood to declare that, as a town, Bolton never produced the trained domestic. Today there are positions vacant in town for at least a hundred of all grades of servant at wages ranging from between £35 and £50 a year, with food. As much as five shillings a day and the usual extras are offered for day servants, but they cannot be found. Always we have to rely on the girls from agricultural districts and, of course, as a busy industrial area, we are no exception to the rule in this respect. The textile industry provides a more important and more innumerable occupation. Some of our female operatives are stated to be paying income tax. They have liberty at nights and fixed hour of labour that the girl of today thinks much about. There is work for thousands of weavers if they could be obtained. And you know that in this district, the employers are very partial to female workers in the weaving shed, always has been, and always will be, because they look upon it as 'women's work.'

War time typists at a discount

Where are the hundreds of bright-eyed young damsel who adorned our commercial houses, banks and offices in the years of the war? You remember how gladly they embarked upon their professional careers when the Army drained the reservoir from which the males were drawn, how they entered special training in shorthand, type writing and the essentials of business. From families where it was never before necessary that the girls would turn out to work, they sallied forth — it was an adventure to them. They liked it. The work was agreeable, there was freedom and the consciousness that one was doing something in the great struggle to keep alive. It became evident that too many girls were being trained as typists. Gradually, we have marked the girls from the clerical staff, with the return of the lads from the Forces, we have been receiving into the commercial world the youths who were coming of age when the war was raging. What is to become of the modernity, educated, highly intelligent girl?

Many of the clerks and typists to whom demobilisation meant unemployment have taken up jobs as shop assistants. Textile work does not appeal to this type of girl; domestic work, the terms 'servant' 'skivvy' and 'maid' are equally taboo. The difficulty is that it is essential in view of the high cost of living that these girls who hitherto had no responsibility should now work to keep themselves. A large number received the dole but at present the majority of about 300 girls on the Unemployment Register in Bolton are clerks and short hand typists. What future do we have to offer this type?

Appendix Two
List of organisations concerned with the promotion of peace/care of war veterans

Amnesty International, 1 Easton St,
    London, WC1X: 0171 833 1771

Beauty Without Cruelty, 57 King Henry's Walk,
    London, N1: 0171 254 2929

British Red Cross, 100 Brook Green, Hammersmith,
    London, W6: 0171 602 1967

British Refugee Council, 3 Bondway, London, SW8: 0171 582 6922

Campaign for Nuclear Disarmament, 162 Hollway Road,
    London, N7: 0171 607 2302: 0171 700 2349

CAPA Civil Rights Support Group, 3rd Floor, St Hilda's Community Centre,
    18 Club Row, Bethnal Green, London, E2: 0171 729 2652

Centre for Conflict Studies, University of Ulster, Colraine, Co Londonderry,
    BT5 21SA: 0126544141

Greenpeace (London) 5 Caledonian Rd, London, N1: 0171 837 7557

Human Rights Watch, 33 Islington High Street,
    London, N1: 0171 714 1995

Living Green Trust, 28 Pancreas Road,
    London, NW1: 0171 258 1823

Medical Foundation for the Care of Victims of Torture,
    96–98 Grafton Road, London, NW5

National Conscience Party, UK Charter, 12 Eustance House,
    Old Paradise Street, London, SE11: 0171 207 2635

Peace Brigades International, 5 Caledonian Road,
    London N: 0171 713 0392

Rights and Humanity, 65a Swinton Street,
    London, WC1X: 0171 837 4133

Royal British Legion, Metropolitan Region,
    The Johnson Centre, Chester House, 1 Brixton Road, London, SW9:
    0171 735 4091

The Royal Star and Garter Home for Disabled Sailors, Soldiers and Airman,
    Richmond, Surrey TW10 6RR: 0181 940 3314

War Child, 7 Greenland St, London, NW1: 171 916 9276

War Resisters International, 5 Caledonian Rd,
    London, N1: 0171 278 4040

Index

Index